Ready® Classroom
Mathematics

Grade 7 • Volume 2

NOT FOR RESALE

978-1-7280-1301-5
©2021–Curriculum Associates, LLC
North Billerica, MA 01862
No part of this book may be reproduced
by any means without written permission
from the publisher.
All Rights Reserved. Printed in USA.
1 2 3 4 5 6 7 8 9 10 11 12 13 14 15   22 21 20

Curriculum Associates®

Contents

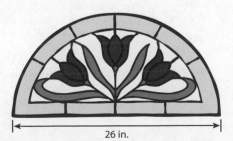

26 in.

UNIT 2

Numbers and Operations

Add and Subtract Rational Numbers

Contents (continued)

UNIT 3

Numbers and Operations

Multiply and Divide Rational Numbers

UNIT 4

Algebraic Thinking

Expressions, Equations, and Inequalities

Contents (continued)

Average Sleep **7.9%** of day

UNIT 6

Geometry

Solids, Triangles, and Angles

Contents (continued)

Unit 5

Proportional Reasoning

Percents and Statistical Samples

✓ **Self Check**

Before starting this unit, check off the skills you know below.
As you complete each lesson, see how many more skills you can check off!

I can . . .	Before	After
Calculate simple interest.	☐	☐
Solve percent problems involving markups, markdowns, tips, tax, and commission.	☐	☐
Solve percent problems involving percent change or percent error.	☐	☐
Identify random samples.	☐	☐
Make statistical inferences from random samples.	☐	☐
Compare data using measures of center and variability.	☐	☐
Agree or disagree with ideas in discussions about random samples and explain why.	☐	☐

Prepare for Percents and Statistical Samples

➤ **Look at the expressions and missing values in each box. Write a title for each box that represents what the expressions and missing values have in common. Then add at least two of your own examples to each box.**

_____

_____

_____

Box 1:

$\dfrac{250}{1,000}$

$\dfrac{1}{4}$

25 hundredths

0.2500

half of $\dfrac{1}{2}$

_____ of 80 is 20.

5 is _____ of 20.

Box 2:

25% of 400

1.00 × 100

50% of 200

$\dfrac{200}{2}$

1.00 is _____%.

4% of _____ is 4.

Box 3:

50% of 24

24 × $\dfrac{1}{2}$

150% of 8

24% of 50

$\dfrac{2}{3}$ of 18

$\dfrac{1}{3}$ of _____ is 4.

_____ is 15% of 80.

Pick one given example from each box and explain how it represents your title. Then meet with a partner and compare your titles and examples.

Dear Family,

This week your student is learning about solving problems with percents.

A percent is a rate per 100, and it can be expressed with the percent symbol (%), as a fraction, or as a decimal.

$$25\% = \frac{25}{100} = 0.25$$

Here are some common situations involving percents that you may recognize.

- A store advertises a 25%-off sale, or **markdown**, of the regular prices.
- A business owner sells an item for a **markup** of 10% more than she bought it for.
- There is a 5% sales **tax** on an appliance purchase.
- A server receives a 15% tip, or **gratuity**, on the amount of a restaurant bill.
- A salesperson earns a 14% **commission** on car sales.
- A bank offers a savings account that pays a **simple interest** rate of 2% on the principal, or amount deposited.

Your student will be solving problems like the one below.

> Rani buys a $35 desk with a 15%-off coupon. How much does Rani pay for the desk?

➤ **ONE WAY** to find a discounted price is to find the amount of the discount and subtract it from the original price.

$$15\% \text{ of } 35 = (0.15)(35)$$
$$= 5.25$$
$$35 - 5.25 = 29.75$$

➤ **ANOTHER WAY** is to find the percent of the original price that Rani pays.

Receiving a 15% discount is the same as paying 85% of the original price.

$$85\% \text{ of } 35 = (0.85)(35)$$
$$= 29.75$$

Both ways show that Rani pays $29.75.

 Use the next page to start a conversation about percents.

Activity Thinking About Percents Around You

➤ **Do this activity together to investigate percents in the real world.**

Do you have a pet that always seems to be sleeping? Different types of animals sleep for different amounts of time.

A brown bat sleeps for an average of 82.9% of a 24-hour day in order to conserve energy when it is cold or when food is limited. That is almost 20 hours of sleep!

Giraffes sleep standing up so they can more easily defend themselves from predators. A giraffe only sleeps for an average of 7.9% of the day, or less than 2 hours!

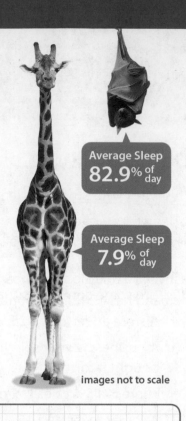

Average Sleep
82.9% of day

Average Sleep
7.9% of day

images not to scale

? Where else do you see percents in the world around you?

Explore Percents

Last Year's Middle School Band Students

 = 10 band students

Previously, you learned how to find the percent of a number. In this lesson, you will learn about solving problems that involve percents.

➤ **Use what you know to try to solve the problem below.**

Last year, a middle school band had 80 students. This year, the band has 120% of that number of students. How many students are in the band this year?

 TRY IT

Math Toolkit double number lines, grid paper, hundredths grids

DISCUSS IT

Ask: How did you get started finding the number of students?

Share: I got started by . . .

Learning Target SMP 1, SMP 2, SMP 3, SMP 4, SMP 5, SMP 6
Use proportional relationships to solve multistep ratio and percent problems.

CONNECT IT

1 **Look Back** How many students are in the band this year? How do you know?

2 **Look Ahead** You can think of 120% as 100% + 20%. Similarly, you can think of 80% as 100% − 20%. Percents are used in calculating **simple interest**. You can owe interest on a loan or earn interest on a bank account or investment.

Simple interest formula: $I = Prt$

The amount of interest, I, is based on the principal, P, the interest rate, r, and the time you borrow or invest the money for, t. The principal is the starting amount. The rate is written as a decimal. For simple interest, time is measured in years.

a. Suppose you borrow $300 at a yearly, or annual, simple interest rate of 3.4% for 3 years. What values would you use for P, r, and t?

b. Suppose you borrow $400 at a yearly simple interest rate of 3% for 3 months. What values would you use for P, r, and t?

c. A **markdown** decreases the cost of an item. A **markup** increases the cost. Suppose a store puts an item on sale for 25% off. Is that an example of a *markup* or a *markdown*?

d. Often when you buy something, you pay a percent of the price as a **tax**. Suppose you pay a 7% tax on an item. What percent of the price of the item will you pay?

e. Many people gives tips, or **gratuities**, for good service. Many salespeople earn **commission** on their sales. Jason earns a 9% commission on a $1,000 sale. How much is Jason's commission?

3 **Reflect** Is it possible for a single price change to be both a markup and a markdown? Explain your thinking.

Prepare for Solving Problems Involving Percents

1️⃣ Think about what you know about percents. Fill in each box. Use words, numbers, and pictures. Show as many ideas as you can.

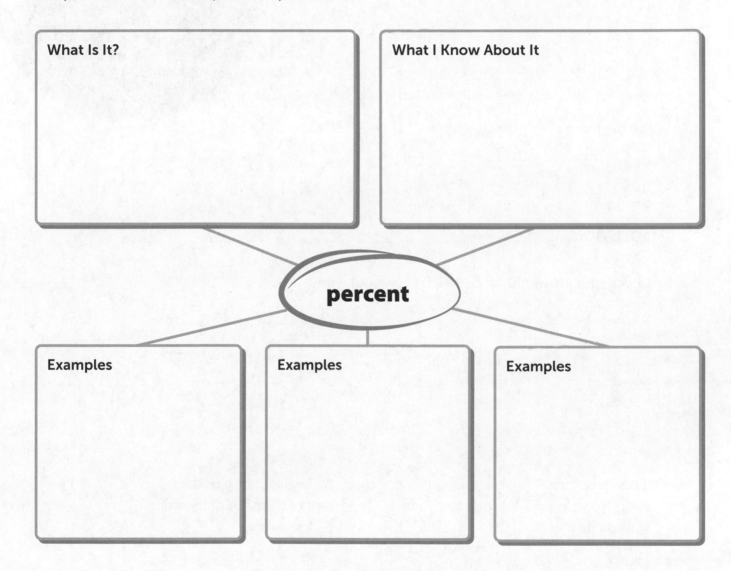

What Is It?	What I Know About It

percent

Examples	Examples	Examples

2️⃣ Isabel says that 0.02 can be expressed as 20%. Is she correct? Explain why or why not.

3 Last year, a rapper performed 40 times. This year, the rapper performs 125% of that number of times.

Last Year: 40 performances
This Year: 125% of last year

a. How many times does the rapper perform this year? Show your work.

SOLUTION _____

b. Check your answer to problem 3a. Show your work.

Develop Finding Simple Interest

NEW CAR LOAN

4.2%
annual simple interest rate

➤ **Read and try to solve the problem below.**

Dario borrows $12,000 to buy a car. He borrows the money at a yearly, or annual, simple interest rate of 4.2%. How much more interest will Dario owe if he borrows the money for 5 years instead of 1 year?

TRY IT

Math Toolkit double number lines, grid paper

➤ **Explore different ways to find simple interest.**

Dario borrows $12,000 to buy a car. He borrows the money at a yearly, or annual, simple interest rate of 4.2%. How much more interest will Dario owe if he borrows the money for 5 years instead of 1 year?

$12,000
LIKE NEW

Model It

You can use the relationship between time and interest.

After one year, Dario will owe 4.2% of $12,000 in interest.

0.042(12,000) = 504

Year	Total Interest
1	$504
2	$1,008
3	$1,512
4	$2,016
5	$2,520

Model It

You can use the simple interest formula to find the interest.

$I = Prt$

I = interest P = principal r = interest rate t = time (in years)

1 Year

$I = Prt$

$= (12{,}000)(0.042)(1)$

$= 504(1)$

$= 504$

5 Years

$I = Prt$

$= (12{,}000)(0.042)(5)$

$= 504(5)$

$= 2{,}520$

After 1 year, Dario will owe $504 in interest.

After 5 years, Dario will owe $2,520 in interest.

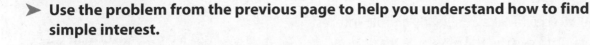
➤ **Use the problem from the previous page to help you understand how to find simple interest.**

1 Look at the table in the first **Model It**. How does the interest change over time?

2 How much more interest will Dario owe for 5 years than for 1 year? How does this difference compare to the amount of interest Dario would owe for borrowing the money for 4 years?

3 Look at the second **Model It**. Which values stay the same when you use the formula to find the interest for 1 year and 5 years? Which values change?

4 How does the formula $I = Prt$ show a proportional relationship between simple interest and time?

5 The total amount Dario owes is the sum of the interest and the principal. Is the relationship between total amount owed and time proportional? Explain.

6 **Reflect** Think about all the models and strategies you have discussed today. Describe how one of them helped you better understand how to think about and find simple interest.

Apply It

➤ **Use what you learned to solve these problems.**

7 Ava borrows $600 to buy a bike at a yearly simple interest rate of 2.25%. Ava borrows the money for 3 years. How much does Ava pay in simple interest? How much does Ava pay in all? Show your work.

Ava's Bike Purchase

Borrows to Buy a Bike
$600

Yearly Simple Interest
2.25%

SOLUTION _____

8 Zhen borrows $1,200. She borrows the money for 2 years and owes $180 in simple interest. What is the yearly simple interest rate on Zhen's loan? Show your work.

SOLUTION _____

9 A bank offers a savings account with a yearly simple interest rate of 2%. Suppose you deposit $550 into a savings account. How much simple interest will you earn in 4 years? In 4 years and 6 months? Show your work.

SOLUTION _____

Practice Finding Simple Interest

➤ **Study the Example showing how to use the simple interest formula. Then solve problems 1–6.**

Example

Pablo deposits $750 into a bank account. The account earns yearly simple interest at a rate of $3\frac{1}{2}$%. How many years will it take Pablo to earn a total of $105 in simple interest?

Use the simple interest formula and solve for t.

$P = \$750, r = 3.5\%$, and $I = \$105$

$$I = Prt$$
$$105 = (750)(3.5\%)(t)$$
$$105 = (750)(0.035)(t)$$
$$105 = 26.25t$$
$$4 = t$$

It will take 4 years for Pablo to earn $105 in interest.

1   Suppose you deposit $1,200 into a bank account. The account earns yearly simple interest at a rate of $1\frac{3}{4}$%. How many years will it take to earn a total of $126 in simple interest? Show your work.

SOLUTION _____

2   Conan borrows $3,000 at a yearly simple interest rate of 1.6% for 2 years.

He owes _____ in interest. He needs to pay back _____ in all.

> **Vocabulary**
>
> **simple interest**
> a percent of an amount that is borrowed or invested.

3 Jamila deposits $800 in an account that earns yearly simple interest at a rate of 2.65%. How much money is in the account after 3 years and 9 months? Show your work.

SAVINGSBANK

Jamila

DEPOSIT

$800.00

YEARLY SIMPLE
INTEREST RATE

2.65%

SOLUTION _____

4 Carmela borrows $400 and will pay 5.25% yearly simple interest. How much more interest will Carmela owe if she borrows the money for 4 years instead of 2 years? Show your work.

SOLUTION _____

5 Ellie borrows money at a yearly simple interest rate of $6\frac{1}{2}$%. After 4 years, Ellie owes $39 in interest. How much money did Ellie borrow? Show your work.

SOLUTION _____

6 Lilia borrows $400 at a yearly simple interest rate of 6%. She writes the expression $400 + (0.6 \times 400)$ to represent the total amount of money she will pay back for borrowing the money for 1 year. Is Lilia's expression correct? Explain your answer and determine the amount of money Lilia will need to pay back after 1 year.

Develop Solving Problems Involving a Single Percent

➤ **Read and try to solve the problem below.**

Cyrus is hosting a dinner to celebrate Nowruz, the Persian New Year. His groceries cost $150 before he uses a 10%-off coupon. He also orders $60 worth of flowers. Sales tax on the flowers is 6.25%. What is the total amount Cyrus spends?

Groceries	Flowers
Cost: $150	Cost: $60
Coupon: 10% off	Sales Tax: 6.25%

TRY IT

Math Toolkit double number lines, grid paper

➤ **Explore different ways to solve a problem with a single percent.**

Cyrus is hosting a dinner to celebrate Nowruz, the Persian New Year. His groceries cost $150 before he uses a 10%-off coupon. He also orders $60 worth of flowers. Sales tax on the flowers is 6.25%. What is the total amount Cyrus spends?

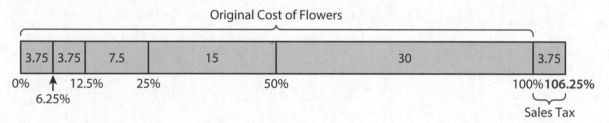

Nowruz celebration

Model It

You can draw bar models to find the percents.

Original Cost of Groceries

15	15	15	15	15	15	15	15	15	15

0% 10% 20% 30% 40% 50% 60% 70% 80% 90% 100%

Coupon

Cyrus pays **90%** of the original cost for groceries.

Original Cost of Flowers

3.75	3.75	7.5	15	30	3.75

0% 6.25% 12.5% 25% 50% 100% 106.25%

Sales Tax

Cyrus pays **106.25%** of the original cost for flowers.

Model It

You can write equations to solve the problem.

Cost of Groceries:

$(100\% - 10\%)150 = (90\%)150$

$= (0.90)(150)$

Cost of Flowers:

$(100\% + 6.25\%)60 = (106.25\%)60$

$= (1.0625)(60)$

Total Cost = Cost of Groceries + Cost of Flowers

$= (0.90)(150) + (1.0625)(60)$

$= 135 + 63.75$

➤ **Use the problem from the previous page to help you understand how to solve a problem with a single percent.**

1 What is the total amount Cyrus spends?

2 Look at the **Model Its**. How do they show that you can multiply 150 by 0.90 to find the discounted cost of the groceries?

3 Hiroaki uses the expression $a - 0.1a$ to represent a 10% discount on an amount a. Allen uses the expression $0.9a$. Is Hiroaki's expression correct? Is Allen's? Explain.

4 Hiroaki uses the expression $a + 0.05a$ to represent an amount increasing by 5%. Allen uses the expression $1.05a$. Explain why both Hiroaki's and Allen's expressions are correct.

5 The expression $(110)(0.80)$ can be used to find the sale price of an item that has an original price of $110. By what percent is the original price marked down? How do you know?

6 **Reflect** Think about all the models and strategies you have discussed today. Describe how one of them helped you better understand how to solve the **Try It** problem.

Apply It

➤ **Use what you learned to solve these problems.**

7　Alanna earns a commission of 8% on her sales. How much commission does Alanna earn on a sale of $32,000? Show your work.

SOLUTION _____

8　Heidi's lunch costs $12.50. Heidi wants to leave a tip of 18%. How much money does Heidi need to pay for lunch, including the tip?

A $2.25

B $10.25

C $14.75

D $22.75

9　Before hibernation, a bear weighs 990 pounds. Its weight decreases by 32% during hibernation. How much does the bear weigh when it comes out of hibernation? Show your work.

Before hibernation:
990 lb
During hibernation:
weight ↓32%

SOLUTION _____

Practice Solving Problems Involving a Single Percent

➤ **Study the Example showing how to solve a problem with a percent. Then solve problems 1–5.**

Example

The sales tax at a hotel is 18%. A standard room costs $98 before tax. What is the total cost of a standard room?

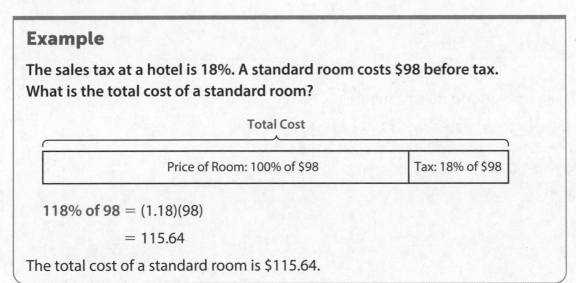

Total Cost

| Price of Room: 100% of $98 | Tax: 18% of $98 |

118% of 98 = (1.18)(98)

= 115.64

The total cost of a standard room is $115.64.

---

1 The hotel in the Example offers a double room for $20 more than a standard room, before tax. What is the total cost of a double room, including tax? Show your work.

SOLUTION _____

2 Darnell wants to limit his screen time. Last week, he spent an average of $3\frac{1}{2}$ h on his phone each day. This week, he reduces his screen time by 5%. To the nearest hour, how much time does Darnell spend on his phone this week? Show your work.

SOLUTION _____

3 Alexis is training for her next 5k race. Her current 5k race time is 40 min. She wants to decrease her time by 20%. What does Alexis want her next 5k race time to be? Show your work.

SOLUTION _____

4 An art store manager buys and sells art supplies.

a. The store manager buys easels for $10.20 each. He marks up the cost by 75% to get the selling price. What is the selling price of each easel? Show your work.

SOLUTION _____

b. The original price of a jar of paint is $1.20. The store manager gets a 10% discount on orders of at least 50 jars of paint. How much does the store manager pay for 50 jars of paint? Show your work.

SOLUTION _____

5 A store is having a buy-one-get-one-30%-off sale. During the sale, Christopher buys two pairs of shoes that each have a regular price of $48. How much does Christopher pay for the two pairs of shoes? Show your work.

SOLUTION _____

Develop Solving Problems Involving Multiple Percents

STORE A

75% OFF GUITARS

➤ **Read and try to solve the problem below.**

The guitar Francisca wants is on sale at two different stores. The original price of the guitar at both stores is $160. At which store is the guitar less expensive? How much less expensive?

STORE B

50% OFF GUITARS

+

ADDITIONAL 30% OFF ALL DISCOUNTED PRICES

TRY IT

Math Toolkit double number lines, grid paper

DISCUSS IT

Ask: How is each percent represented in your solution?

Share: In my solution each percent is represented by . . .

➤ **Explore different ways to solve a problem with multiple percents.**

The guitar Francisca wants is on sale at two different stores. The original price of the guitar at both stores is $160. At Store A, the guitar is 75% off. At Store B, the guitar is 50% off, with an additional 30% off the discounted price. At which store is the guitar less expensive? How much less expensive?

Model It

You can find each percent separately.

Store A

A discount of 75% is the same as paying 25% of the original price.

25% of 160 = (**0.25**)(160)

$\quad\quad\quad\quad= 40$

Store B

The 50%-off price is 100% − 50%, or 50%, of the original price.

50% of 160 = (**0.5**)(160)

$\quad\quad\quad\quad= 80$

An additional 30% discount is applied to the 50%-off price of the guitar.

A discount of 30% is the same as paying 70% of the price.

70% of 80 = (**0.7**)(80)

$\quad\quad\quad\quad= 56$

Model It

You can find multiple percents at one time.

Store A

25% of 160 = (**0.25**)(160)

$\quad\quad\quad\quad= 40$

Store B

70% of **50%** of 160 = (**0.7**)(**0.5**)(160)

$\quad\quad\quad\quad\quad\quad= (0.7)(80)$

$\quad\quad\quad\quad\quad\quad= 56$

➤ **Use the problem from the previous page to help you understand how to solve a problem involving multiple percents.**

1 At which store is the sale price of the guitar less? How much less?

2 Look at the **Model Its**. Why does the expression $(0.7)(0.5)(160)$ represent the price of a guitar at Store B?

3 Look at the second **Model It**. Explain why the sale price at Store B is 35% of the original price.

4 Would the amount Francisca would pay at Store B change if the sale were 30% off the price of the guitar, with an additional 50% off all sale prices? Explain.

5 Explain why a 75% discount followed by an additional 25% discount is not the same as a 100% discount.

6 **Reflect** Think about all the models and strategies you have discussed today. Describe how one of them helped you better understand how to solve the **Try It** problem.

Apply It

➤ **Use what you learned to solve these problems.**

7 A bookstore has 120 science fiction books. It has 30% fewer mysteries than science fiction books. It has 25% more biographies than mysteries. How many biographies are in the bookstore? Show your work.

SOLUTION _____

8 Members of a community garden grow 500 vegetable plant sprouts. They donate 10% of the sprouts to a school. They sell 20% of the remaining sprouts to a local park. They plant 5% of those left in a greenhouse. Then they plant the rest of the sprouts outside. How many sprouts do the members plant outside? Show your work.

SOLUTION _____

9 A store manager buys binoculars for $45 each. He marks up the cost by 40% to get the store price. Then the store has a sale and the store price is reduced by 10%. What is the sale price of the binoculars? Show your work.

SOLUTION _____

Practice Solving Problems Involving Multiple Percents

➤ **Study the Example showing how to solve a problem involving multiple percents. Then solve problems 1–5.**

Example

Store A sells a computer for $1,200. The computer is on sale for 15% off. The sales tax is 5.4%. What is the total cost of the computer?

A discount of 15% is the same as paying **85%**.

Paying a 5.4% sales tax is the same as paying **105.4%**.

   (1.054)(0.85)(1,200) = 1,075.08

The total cost is $1,075.08.

---

1 Store B sells the same computer as in the Example for $1,300. Store B offers a 20% discount on the computer. The tax rate is the same. Which store has the lower total price? How much lower? Show your work.

SOLUTION _____

2 A lacrosse league has 20 teams in its first year. The number of teams in the league increases by 20% in its second year. In the third year, the number of teams decreases by 25% from the second year. How many teams are in the league in the third year? Show your work.

SOLUTION _____

3   Galeno wants to buy a video game at a store having a 20%-off storewide sale. The regular price of the video game is $50. Galeno also has a coupon for an extra 5% off the sale price of any video game. Sales tax on the video game is 5.75%. How much does Galeno pay for the video game? Show your work.

SOLUTION _____

4   Jesse's starting salary is $30,000 a year. He gets a 3% raise after his first year. Then he gets a 10% bonus on his second-year salary. How much is Jesse's bonus? Show your work.

SOLUTION _____

5   Volunteers collect and remove litter from a park. They collect 20 cans. They also collect 50% more glass bottles than cans and 110% more plastic bottles than glass bottles. How many plastic bottles do the volunteers collect? Show your work.

SOLUTION _____

Refine Solving Problems Involving Percents

➤ **Complete the Example below. Then solve problems 1–9.**

Example

Ethan pays $31.50 for a jacket. The amount includes a sales tax of 5%. What is the price of the jacket without the sales tax?

Look at how you could show your work using a diagram.

p = price of the jacket without tax

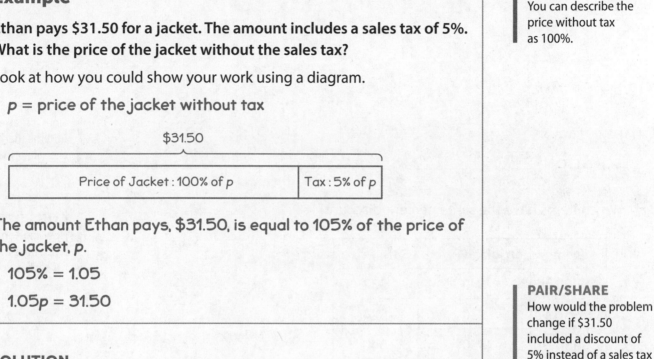

The amount Ethan pays, $31.50, is equal to 105% of the price of the jacket, p.

$105\% = 1.05$

$1.05p = 31.50$

SOLUTION _____

CONSIDER THIS . . .
You can describe the price without tax as 100%.

PAIR/SHARE
How would the problem change if $31.50 included a discount of 5% instead of a sales tax of 5%?

Apply It

1 The total simple interest owed on a loan of $8,000 after 60 months is $1,280. What is the yearly interest rate on the loan? Show your work.

CONSIDER THIS . . .
There are 12 months in a year.

PAIR/SHARE
How would you solve the problem if you wanted to know the monthly interest rate?

SOLUTION _____

2 The owner of a store buys wooden benches for $50 each. She marks up the price by 75%. At the end of the season, she sells the remaining benches for 30% off. How much profit does the owner make on each bench at the end of the season? Show your work.

CONSIDER THIS...
The profit is the difference between the amount the owner pays and the selling price of the bench.

PAIR/SHARE
Does it matter if you find the markup price or the sale price first?

SOLUTION _____

3 Which items have the same percent discount?

CONSIDER THIS...
How can you find the amount of the discount for each item?

Item	Original Price	Sale Price
Sweater	$40	$32
Shorts	$30	$24
Jeans	$50	$40
Shirt	$45	$35

A sweater and shorts only

B sweater, shorts, and shirt only

C jeans and shirt only

D sweater, shorts, and jeans only

Elias chose C as the correct answer. How might he have gotten that answer?

PAIR/SHARE
How can you check your answer?

4 On the first day of training, Aretha holds a plank position for 30 seconds. She increases her time by 20% each day. What is the first day on which Aretha holds a plank for over a minute? Show your work.

Day 1: Holds plank position for **30 seconds**

SOLUTION _____

5 Gabriel pays $37.80 for a ticket to a show. The amount includes an 8% sales tax. What is the price of the ticket without sales tax? Show your work.

SOLUTION _____

6 Jade wants to spend less than $22 on a board game. Which of the following prices are in Jade's budget? Select all that apply.

A 15% off $25

B 30% off $32

C $19.50 plus a 15% shipping fee

D $20.45 plus a 5% shipping fee

E 15% off $25 plus a 5% shipping fee

F 30% off $32 plus an additional 5% off the discounted price

7 Anne deposits $680 in an account that pays 3.5% yearly simple interest. She neither adds more money nor withdraws any money. How much will be in Anne's account after 6 years? Show your work.

SOLUTION _____

8 A store has a sale. Customers can buy one item at full price and take 50% off the cost of a second item with a lesser price. Nikia buys one item with a price of $80 and another item with a price of $120. With the sale, what percent discount does Nikia receive on her total purchase? Show your work.

SOLUTION _____

9 **Math Journal** Is 108% of 2 *greater than, less than,* or *equal to* 1.08% of 200? Explain your reasoning.

✓ **End of Lesson Checklist** —————————————————

☐ **INTERACTIVE GLOSSARY** Find the entry for *simple interest*. Add two important things you learned about simple interest in this lesson.

☐ **SELF CHECK** Go back to the Unit 5 Opener and see what you can check off.

Dear Family,

This week your student is learning about percent change.

A percent is often used to describe how an amount or quantity changes over time. **Percent change** is the amount of change compared to the original, or starting, amount, expressed as a percent.

Percent Change $= \frac{\text{amount of change}}{\text{original amount}} \times 100$

Percent change is either a **percent increase** or a **percent decrease**. Some examples are shown below.

Percent Increase	Percent Decrease
A county increases property taxes by 5%.	A news show reports gasoline prices are 30% less than they were last year.
A city transit system announces fare increases of 8%.	A report shows a 15% population decrease over the last 10 years.

A percent can also be used to describe the amount of error in a measurement or calculation.

Percent Error $= \frac{\text{amount of error}}{\text{correct amount}} \times 100$

Your student will be solving problems like the one below.

Lulu scored 5 goals in her first soccer season and 8 goals in her second. What is the percent increase in the number of goals she scored?

➤ **ONE WAY** to find the percent increase is to use a bar model.

Change in number of goals = 3

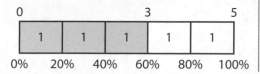

➤ **ANOTHER WAY** is to use an equation.

Original amount: number of goals last year, 5

Percent change $= \frac{8 - 5}{5} \times 100$

$= 60$

Using either method, the percent increase in the number of goals is 60%.

▶ Use the next page to start a conversation about percent change.

Activity Thinking About Percent Change Around You

1975

2010

32 fl oz
$1.30

17 fl oz
$4.60

➤ **Do this activity together to investigate percent change in the real world.**

Have you ever noticed that prices seem to increase over time? A general, continuing increase in prices is called *inflation*.

In 1975, the cost of a bottle of mouthwash was about $1.30 for a 32 fl oz bottle. In 2010, it was about $4.60 for a 17 fl oz bottle.

That means that the size of the bottle decreased by almost 50%, while the price increased by over 250%!

If inflation continues at the same rate, in 2045 an 8 fl oz bottle of mouthwash will cost more than $11!

? Where else do you see change represented as a percent in the world around you?

Explore Percent Change

Previously, you learned how to solve problems involving percents. In this lesson, you will learn about percent change.

➤ **Use what you know to try to solve the problem below.**

Before editing, a movie is 120 min long. The edited movie is 25% shorter. What is the length of the edited movie?

TRY IT

Math Toolkit double number lines, grid paper

◎ **Learning Target** SMP 1, SMP 2, SMP 3, SMP 4, SMP 5, SMP 6, SMP 7
Use proportional relationships to solve multistep ratio and percent problems.

CONNECT IT

1 **Look Back** How many minutes long is the edited movie? How do you know?

2 **Look Ahead** You can use a percent to describe the change in the length of the movie. A **percent change** is a percent that compares the change in a quantity to the original quantity.

$$\text{Percent Change} = \frac{\text{amount of change}}{\text{original amount}} \times 100$$

a. When the new amount is greater than the original amount, the percent change is called a **percent increase**. When the new amount is less than the original amount, the percent change is called a **percent decrease**. Is a discount a *percent increase* or a *percent decrease*? Explain.

b. **Percent error** compares the amount of error to the correct amount. The amount of error is the positive difference between the correct amount and an incorrect amount. You can also think of the positive difference as the absolute value of the difference.

$$\text{Percent Error} = \frac{\text{amount of error}}{\text{correct amount}} \times 100$$

A store sells 10-lb bags of apples. One of the bags actually weighs 9.9 lb. What is the amount of error? What is the correct amount?

3 **Reflect** How are a percent error and a percent change similar? How are they different?

Prepare for Solving Problems Involving Percent Change and Percent Error

1 Think about what you know about how a percent can describe a change in an amount. Fill in each box. Use words, numbers, and pictures. Show as many ideas as you can.

Word	In My Own Words	Example
commission		
markdown		
markup		

2 Anders owns a hat shop. During a sale, he sells all his hats for 20% off. Is this a markup or a markdown? Explain.

3 The original version of a song is 270 seconds long.
The remix is 20% shorter.

a. How many seconds long is the remix of the song?
Show your work.

SOLUTION _____

b. Check your answer to problem 3a. Show your work.

Develop Solving Problems Involving Percent Change

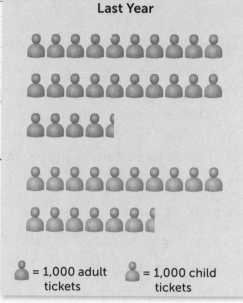

Last Year

 = 1,000 adult tickets   = 1,000 child tickets

➤ **Read and try to solve the problem below.**

A county fair sells adult and child tickets. Last year, the fair sold 24,600 adult tickets and 16,400 child tickets. This year, the number of adult tickets sold increased by 10% and the number of child tickets sold decreased by 20%. What is the overall percent change in ticket sales from last year to this year?

TRY IT

Math Toolkit double number lines, grid paper

DISCUSS IT

Ask: How did you get started finding the percent change?

Share: I got started by . . .

➤ **Explore different ways to find percent increase.**

A county fair sells adult and child tickets. Last year, the fair sold 24,600 adult tickets and 16,400 child tickets. This year, the number of adult tickets sold increased by 10% and the number of child tickets sold decreased by 20%. What is the overall percent change in ticket sales from last year to this year?

Model It

You can compare this year's ticket sales to last year's ticket sales.

Last year's ticket sales

Adults: 24,600

Children: 16,400

Total: 24,600 + 16,400 = **41,000**

This year's ticket sales

Adults: 1.1(24,600) = 27,060

Children: 0.8(16,400) = 13,120

Total: 27,060 + 13,120 = **40,180**

Divide to find this year's ticket sales as a percent of last year's ticket sales.

$$\frac{40,180}{41,000} = 0.98$$

Model It

You can compare the amount of change to last year's ticket sales.

Last year's ticket sales: **41,000**

This year's ticket sales: **40,180**

$$\begin{aligned}
\text{Percent change} &= \frac{\text{amount of change}}{\text{original amount}} \times 100 \\
&= \frac{41,000 - 40,180}{41,000} \times 100 \\
&= \frac{820}{41,000} \times 100 \\
&= 0.02 \times 100
\end{aligned}$$

➤ **Use the problem from the previous page to help you understand how to find a percent change.**

1 What is the overall percent change in the ticket sales? Is this a percent increase or a percent decrease?

2 Look at the first **Model It**. What does 0.98 mean in the context of the problem?

3 Look at the **Model Its**. How are the methods similar? How are they different?

4 The number of adult tickets sold increased by 10%. The number of child tickets sold decreased by 20%. Why is the overall percent change in ticket sales not a 10% decrease?

5 How does the percent change help you understand how the ticket sales changed better than the amount of change alone?

6 **Reflect** Think about all the models and strategies you have discussed today. Describe how one of them helped you better understand percent change.

Apply It

➤ **Use what you learned to solve these problems.**

7. One year, an estimated 598,000 sandhill cranes migrated in March. The next March, an estimated 660,000 sandhill cranes migrated. To the nearest percent, what is the percent change in the number of migrating cranes from the first March to the next? Is this a percent increase or a percent decrease? Show your work.

sandhill cranes

SOLUTION _____

8. A large container of breath mints has a mass of 50 g. A small container has a mass of 10 g. What is the percent decrease from the mass of the large container to the mass of the small container? Show your work.

SOLUTION _____

9. What is the percent change from 40 to 51? Is this a percent increase or a percent decrease? Show your work.

SOLUTION _____

Practice Solving Problems Involving Percent Change

➤ **Study the Example showing percent change. Then solve problems 1–5.**

Example

On Friday, 375 people attended the school concert. On Saturday, 250 people attended the concert. What is the percent change in attendance from Friday to Saturday? Is this a percent increase or a percent decrease?

$$\text{Percent change} = \frac{\text{amount of change}}{\text{original amount}} \times 100$$

$$= \frac{375 - 250}{375} \times 100$$

$$= \frac{125}{375} \times 100$$

$$= 33\frac{1}{3}$$

Fewer people attended on Saturday than on Friday, so the percent change in attendance is a $33\frac{1}{3}$% decrease.

1 On Sunday, 300 people attended the school concert in the Example. What is the percent change in attendance from Saturday to Sunday? Show your work.

SOLUTION _____

2 A payment increases from $700 to $945. What is the percent increase in the payment? Show your work.

> **Vocabulary**
>
> **percent change**
> the amount of change compared to the original (or starting) amount, expressed as a percent.

SOLUTION _____

3 Pilar has 40 shells in her collection. She goes to the beach. She collects 6 more shells in the morning and 3 more shells in the afternoon. What is the percent change in Pilar's shell collection from the beginning of the day to the end? Show your work.

Found in Morning

Found in Afternoon

SOLUTION _____

4 Last year, an organization spent $500 on food for an event 100 people attended. This year, they plan for 120 people to attend the event. Food costs the same per person as it did last year. From last year to this year, what is the percent change in the money the organization spends on food? Show your work.

SOLUTION _____

5 The original cost of a shirt is $40. A store manager marks up the cost by 20% to get the selling price. During a sale, the store manager marks down the cost of the shirt by 20%. What is the percent change from the original cost to the sale price? Is this a percent increase or a percent decrease? Show your work.

SOLUTION _____

Develop Solving Problems Involving Percent Error

➤ **Read and try to solve the problem below.**

A breadmaker buys a bag of flour labeled as containing 5 lb of flour. She weighs the flour in the bag and finds that its actual weight is 4.5 lb. What is the percent error from the labeled weight to the actual weight of flour in the bag?

TRY IT

Math Toolkit double number lines, grid paper

DISCUSS IT

Ask: How are the labeled weight and the actual weight used in your strategy?

Share: In my strategy . . .

➤ **Explore different ways to find percent error.**

A breadmaker buys a bag of flour labeled as containing 5 lb of flour. She weighs the flour in the bag and finds that its actual weight is 4.5 lb. What is the percent error from the labeled weight to the actual weight of flour in the bag?

Model It

You can use a double number line to make sense of the problem.

Amount of error in weight: $5 - 4.5 = 0.5$

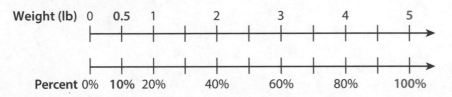

Model It

You can use a formula to find the percent error.

$$\text{Percent error} = \frac{\text{amount of error}}{\text{correct amount}} \times 100$$

$$= \frac{5 - 4.5}{5} \times 100$$

$$= \frac{0.5}{5} \times 100$$

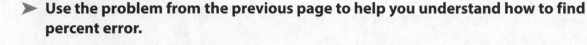

CONNECT IT

➤ **Use the problem from the previous page to help you understand how to find percent error.**

1 Look at the **Model Its**. Where does each one show the amount of error? Where does each one show the correct amount?

2 Why is the correct weight of the bag 5 lb and not 4.5 lb? What is the percent error in the weight?

3 A bag of flour labeled 3 lb actually weighs 3.5 lb. How would you find the percent error for this bag?

4 The 3-lb bag of flour and the 5-lb bag of flour both have an amount of error of 0.5 lb. Why is the percent error different even though the amount of error is the same?

5 **Reflect** Think about all the models and strategies you have discussed today. Describe how one of them helped you better understand how to solve the **Try It** problem.

Apply It

➤ **Use what you learned to solve these problems.**

6   The proper air pressure for Caitlin's bicycle tire is 30 pounds per square inch (psi). The percent error in Caitlin's current tire pressure is 15%. What are the possible current tire pressures for Caitlin's tire? Show your work.

SOLUTION _____

7   Jaime estimates it will take 8.5 h to read a book. It actually takes Jaime 10 h to read the book. What is the percent error in Jaime's estimate? Show your work.

SOLUTION _____

8   A radar gun measures the speed of a car at 45 miles per hour. The actual speed of the car is 40 miles per hour. What is the percent error in the reading of the radar gun? Show your work.

SOLUTION _____

Practice Solving Problems Involving Percent Error

➤ **Study the Example showing how to find percent error. Then solve problems 1–4.**

Example

Students estimate the distance a toy car will roll down a ramp. Greg's estimate is 74 cm. The car rolls 80 cm. What is the percent error of Greg's estimate?

$$\text{Percent error} = \frac{\text{amount of error}}{\text{correct amount}} \times 100$$

$$= \frac{80 - 74}{80} \times 100$$

$$= \frac{6}{80} \times 100$$

$$= 7.5$$

The percent error of Greg's estimate is 7.5%.

---

1 Consider the experiment in the Example.

a. Keiko's estimate for the distance the car will roll is 85 cm. What is the percent error in Keiko's estimate? Show your work.

SOLUTION _____

b. Ian's estimate has a 7% error. What are the possible estimates Ian could have made? Show your work.

> **Vocabulary**
>
> **percent error**
> the difference between the correct value and the incorrect value compared to the correct value, expressed as a percent.

SOLUTION _____

2 Elijah estimates that 54 students will be at the school dance. Angel estimates that 45 students will be. There are actually 48 students at the dance. How much less is the percent error in Angel's estimate than in Elijah's estimate? Show your work.

SOLUTION _____

3 Francisco and Kazuko guess the number of marbles in a jar. Francisco guesses 50 marbles and Kazuko guesses 60 marbles. The actual number of marbles is 55. Kazuko says there is less error in her guess because $\frac{5}{50} = 10\%$ and $\frac{5}{60} = 8.\overline{3}\%$. Explain why Kazuko is incorrect.

4 A sign says the distance to the next exit is 5 mi. The actual distance is 5.2 mi. To the nearest percent, what is the percent error of the sign? Show your work.

SOLUTION _____

Refine Solving Problems Involving Percent Change and Percent Error

➤ **Complete the Example below. Then solve problems 1–9.**

Example

As part of a recycling drive, a school collects cans. The first week of the drive, students collect 25 pounds of cans. The last week, students collect 145 pounds of cans. By what percent do the pounds of cans collected increase from the first to the last week?

Look at how you could use percent change to find the increase.

$$\text{Percent change} = \frac{\text{amount of change}}{\text{original amount}} \times 100$$

$$= \frac{145 - 25}{25} \times 100$$

$$= \frac{120}{25} \times 100$$

SOLUTION _____

CONSIDER THIS ...
You can simplify the quotient before you find the percent.

PAIR/SHARE
How can you check your answer?

Apply It

1 A paper mill cuts poster boards that are 36 in. long. A poster board is acceptable if the percent error of its length is less than 1.5%. What is the range of acceptable lengths? Show your work.

CONSIDER THIS ...
You need two numbers to define a range.

SOLUTION _____

PAIR/SHARE
How would your answer change if an acceptable percent error were less than or equal to 1.5%?

2 The boiling point of water is 212°F at sea level. Andres lives at an elevation of 7,500 ft and finds that water boils at 198°F. What is the percent decrease in the boiling point of water from sea level to 7,500 ft? Give your answer to the nearest tenth of a percent. Show your work.

CONSIDER THIS...
At higher elevations, air pressure decreases, which decreases the boiling point of water.

PAIR/SHARE
When Andres travels to sea level, what is the percent increase in the boiling point of water?

SOLUTION _____

3 Last summer, 80 students signed up for a summer trip to Washington, D.C. This summer, 94 students signed up. To the nearest percent, what is the percent change in the number of students who signed up for the trip?

A 2%

B 14%

C 15%

D 18%

Hailey chose C as the correct answer. How might she have gotten that answer?

CONSIDER THIS...
Is the percent change a *percent increase* or a *percent decrease*?

PAIR/SHARE
How can you check your answer?

4 Elena is organizing her craft supplies. She estimates that her jars will fit 1,000 buttons or 50 large beads. They actually fit 677 buttons or 22 large beads. Does Elena's estimate about the buttons or her estimate about the large beads have less percent error? To the nearest percent, how much less? Show your work.

SOLUTION _____

_____

5 Kevin's weekly salary is $865. He receives a 25% raise. How can Kevin find his new weekly salary? Select all that apply.

A divide 865 by 0.25

B divide 865 by 1.25

C multiply 865 by 0.25

D multiply 865 by 1.25

E add 865 and $\frac{1}{4}$ of 865

F add 865 and $1\frac{1}{4}$ of 865

6 For each of the following situations, is the percent change greater than or equal to 20% and less than 30%? Select *Yes* or *No* for each situation.

	Yes	No
a. A $12 cost increases to $15.	○	○
b. A person's height increases from 52 in. to 61 in.	○	○
c. The temperature falls from 4°F to 3°F.	○	○
d. *n* changes to $\frac{3}{4}n$.	○	○

7 Doubling an amount is the same as a percent increase of _____.

The result of increasing 5 by 200% is _____.

8 Most days, Mr. Romano sells umbrellas for $8. On rainy days, he increases the price by 75%. How much, in dollars, does he charge for umbrellas on rainy days?

9 **Math Journal** A game show has two contestants guess the price of an item. The contestant with the closest guess that does not go above the price of the item wins. Will the winning guess always have the least percent error? Explain why or why not. Support your position with an example.

✔ End of Lesson Checklist

☐ **INTERACTIVE GLOSSARY** Find the entry for *percent change*. Rewrite the definition in your own words using the terms *percent increase* and *percent decrease*.

☐ **SELF CHECK** Go back to the Unit 5 Opener and see what you can check off.

Dear Family,

This week your student is exploring random samples.

Sometimes you want to gather information from a group, or a **population**. Depending on the size of the population, it can be very difficult, or even impossible, to survey every member of the group. It is more practical to survey a smaller subset, or a **sample**, of the group. When you select a sample, you want it to be as much like the entire population as possible. That way, any conclusions you draw from the data are more likely to be true for the whole population.

In a **random sample**, every member of the population has an equal chance of being selected for the sample. A random sample is more likely to be representative of a population than other types of samples. So, you can use a random sample to draw conclusions about the entire population.

Your student will be exploring problems like the one below.

> A dance school director wants to know what type of dance the students at her school like best. Describe how the director could select a random sample of students to survey.

➤ **ONE WAY** to take a random sample is to pull names from a bowl.

- Write the names of all students on slips of paper.
- Put all the slips in a bowl and mix them up.
- Choose slips until you have reached the number of students you want to survey.

➤ **ANOTHER WAY** is to use an alphabetized list.

- List all students in alphabetical order.
- Roll a number cube to select a number 1–6.
- Start with the person on the list with that number. Then select every sixth name on the list.

Using either approach, the dance school director will get a random sample because each student has an equal chance of being chosen for the sample.

 Use the next page to start a conversation about samples of populations.

Activity Thinking About Sampling Around You

Café TSquare
New York, NY
★★★★★

We discovered this hidden gem just outside of Times Square. Lines were a little long, but I think it was totally worth the wait.
Mike D. 👍 245 👎 28

➤ **Do this activity together to investigate sampling in the real world.**

Have you ever read a review for a restaurant online? You cannot always trust the reviews to accurately reflect the opinions of all the people who have eaten at that restaurant.

The reviewers who comment online are not a representative sample of the population of people who have eaten at the restaurant. Because the reviewers voluntarily wrote a review, they likely have a strong positive or negative opinion about the restaurant. A negative review could be from a competitor and a positive review could be from a friend of an employee.

 How could you generate a representative sample of reviewers for a restaurant?

Explore Sampling

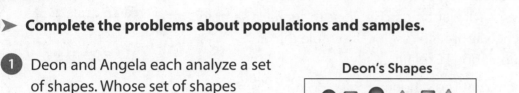

Model It

➤ **Complete the problems about populations and samples.**

1 Deon and Angela each analyze a set of shapes. Whose set of shapes appears to be arranged randomly? Explain.

Deon's Shapes   **Angela's Shapes**

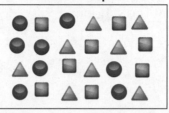

2 Each set of shapes is a **population**. A population is the entire group being studied. Sometimes it can be difficult or take too much time to collect data from every member of a population. In these cases, you can collect data from a **sample**, or smaller set, of the population. The circled group of shapes in each set is a sample.

Deon's Shapes

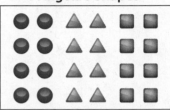

a. How are the populations of shapes the same?

b. How are the samples the same? How are they different?

Angela's Shapes

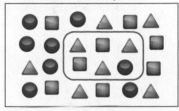

c. A sample that is representative of a population has similar characteristics to the population. Which sample is more representative of the population? Why?

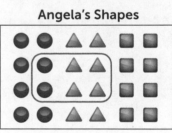

> ### DISCUSS IT
>
> **Ask:** How are a population and a sample related?
>
> **Share:** I think Deon's sample would be more representative of the population if . . .

◎ **Learning Target**   SMP 2, SMP 3, SMP 7
Understand that statistics can be used to gain information about a population by examining a sample of the population; generalizations about a population from a sample are valid only if the sample is representative of that population. Understand that random sampling tends to produce representative samples and support valid inferences.

Model It

➤ **Complete the problems about representative samples.**

3 Issay's school plans to add one of three new elective classes next year: *teen leadership, fashion design,* or *robotics.* Issay wants to know which class the students at his school want most. He plans to survey a sample of the population. Will each approach result in a sample that is representative of the population? Explain.

Elective Class Choices

Teen Leadership ☐

Fashion ☐

Robotics ☐

a. surveying all the teachers at the school

b. surveying all of the students on the student council

c. surveying five students in each math class

d. surveying every fifth student who buys lunch on a certain day

DISCUSS IT

Ask: Which approach do you think Issay should use? Why?

Share: I think another way Issay could get a representative sample is to . . .

4 **Reflect** Why is it important to use a representative sample when you want to learn something about a population?

Name:

Prepare for Random Sampling

1 Think about what you know about statistics and data. Fill in each box. Use words, numbers, and pictures. Show as many ideas as you can.

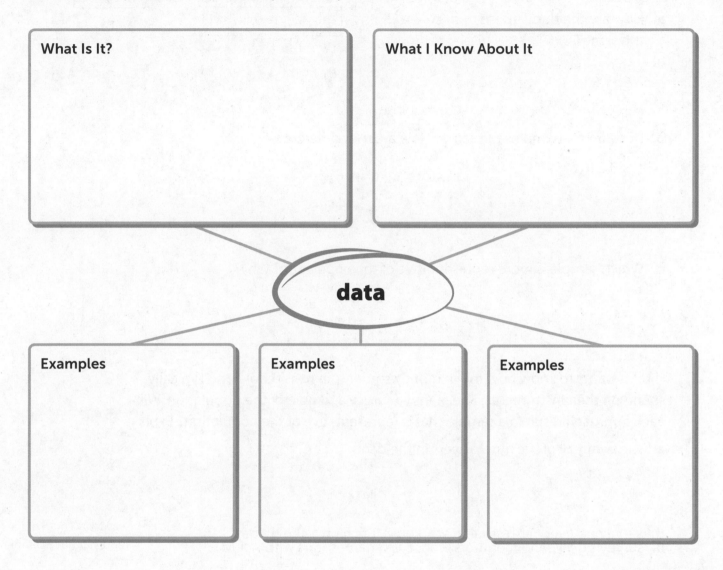

What Is It?

What I Know About It

data

Examples

Examples

Examples

2 Neva asks her friends for their favorite color and number. Neva says that all the favorite numbers are data, but all the favorite colors are not because they are not numbers. Do you agree or disagree? Explain.

➤ **Complete problems 3–4.**

3 The diagrams show the populations of mice at two pet stores. The circled group of mice in each diagram is a sample.

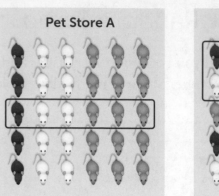

Pet Store A   Pet Store B

a. How are the populations of mice the same?

b. How are the samples the same? How are they different?

c. Which sample is more representative of the population? Why?

4 Hiroko wants to know how much money students in her school band typically spend on their instruments. She plans to survey a sample of the population. Will each approach result in a sample that is representative of the population? Explain.

a. surveying all of the flute players in the band

b. surveying all band members whose first names start with J or M

c. surveying two band members from each school in her city

UNDERSTAND: How can you use samples to gain information about a population?

Develop Understanding of Random Sampling

Model It: Selecting Random Samples

➤ **Try these two problems involving random samples.**

BEAR

BULLDOG

EAGLE

HIPPO

WILDCAT

1 The students at Carlos's middle school will attend a brand-new high school once they reach ninth grade. Carlos plans to survey a **random sample** of the students at his middle school about what the mascot of the new high school should be. With a random sample, every member of a population has an equal chance of being selected.

 a. Suppose Carlos lists every student's name on a slip of paper and mixes the slips in a hat. Then he pulls 20 names out of the hat without looking. Why is this sample a random sample?

 b. Suppose Carlos selects all the members of the school's basketball team for his sample instead. Why is this not a random sample?

2 Is each approach likely to result in a random sample of the students at Carlos's school? Explain.

 a. letting students volunteer to take an online survey

 b. spinning a spinner to select one of the first 10 names in the school directory and then selecting every 10th name after that

 c. assigning each student a number, using a computer program to produce 30 numbers at random, and selecting the students with those numbers

 **DISCUSS IT**

Ask: Why is a random sample likely to be representative of a population?

Share: I think you can use a random sample to learn about a population because . . .

LESSON 22 Understand Random Sampling **475**

Model It: Drawing Conclusions from Random Samples

➤ **Try this problem about drawing conclusions from random samples.**

3 Carlos surveys a random sample of 40 students at his school about the mascot they want. The table shows his results.

Mascot	Number of Votes
Bear	4
Bulldog	10
Eagle	16
Hippo	1
Wildcat	9

a. Based on the sample, should Carlos conclude that there are probably more students at his school who want an eagle mascot than a wildcat mascot? Explain.

b. Of the students surveyed, 25% voted for a bulldog. Should Carlos conclude that exactly 25% of the students at his school would vote for a bulldog? Explain.

DISCUSS IT

Ask: Why can taking a random sample of a population be useful?

Share: I think Carlos could also use his sample data to conclude that . . .

CONNECT IT

➤ **Complete the problems below.**

4 Conclusions about a population are more likely to be correct when they are based on random samples than on samples that are not random. Why?

5 A farmer plants 50 orange trees. How could the farmer select a sample of 5 trees that is likely to be representative of the population of 50 trees?

©Curriculum Associates, LLC Copying is not permitted.

Practice Random Sampling

➤ **Study how the Example shows how to determine whether a survey plan will result in a sample that is representative of the population. Then solve problems 1–4.**

Example

A food service company supplies lunches for 12 different schools. The company wants to learn about the students' favorite lunches. It plans to survey students at one school on a Friday. The company will survey every fourth student who enters the cafeteria during each lunch period. Will this result in a random sample of the population the company wants to learn about? Explain.

You should consider whether each member of the population has an equal chance of being included in the sample.

The population includes the students at the 12 schools the company supplies meals for. The sample includes only students from one school, so not all students have a chance of being included.

The company's plan will not result in a random sample of the population the company wants to learn about.

1 Look at the situation in the Example. How could the company change its approach to get a more representative sample of the population? Explain why the change is likely to result in a more representative sample.

2 A scientist wants to know how far monarch butterflies travel when they migrate. The scientist decides to tag 50 butterflies from one location in California. Are conclusions drawn from this sample likely to be true for all monarch butterflies? Explain.

Vocabulary

population
the entire group of interest. Samples are drawn from populations.

random sample
a sample in which every element in the population has an equal chance of being selected.

sample
a part of a population.

3 The manager of a fitness center wants to add a new class. The manager plans to survey a sample of the fitness center's members to find out which type of class would be most popular.

a. Describe one way the manager could select a random sample of fitness center members.

b. Is the most popular class for members in the sample guaranteed to be the most popular class for all members? Explain.

4 Elisa and Benjamin survey a random sample of 50 students at their school about which superpower they would most like to have. The table shows their data.

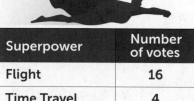

Superpower	Number of votes
Flight	16
Time Travel	4
Mind Reading	10
Super Speed	8
Invisibility	5
Healing	0
Other	7

a. Elisa claims that about 20% of the students at the school would choose mind reading as their superpower. Is this claim supported by the sample data? Explain.

b. Elisa claims that more students at the school would choose invisibility than time travel. Benjamin claims that more students at the school would choose flight than super speed. Whose claim is more strongly supported by the sample data? Explain.

c. Benjamin claims that no students at the school would choose healing as a superpower. Is Benjamin's claim definitely correct? Why or why not?

UNDERSTAND: How can you use samples to gain information about a population?

Refine Ideas About Random Sampling

Apply It

➤ **Complete problems 1–5.**

1 **Evaluate** Members of the Green Club survey a random sample of 20 of the students in Mr. Díaz's math class. They find that 55% of students in the sample recycle plastic bottles. They use their results to design the poster at the right. Describe one reason the poster is misleading.

Only 55% of Washington Middle School students recycle plastic bottles.

DO YOUR PART
Recycle today and every day!

2 **Compare** A baseball league has players who are 12 and 13 years old. Gaspar is considering three plans for selecting a sample of players from the league.

- **Plan 1:** Put the names of the 12-year-old players in a box. Select 10% of the names without looking. Repeat for the 13-year-old players.

- **Plan 2:** Select all the players on the team with the most wins this season.

- **Plan 3:** Assign a two-digit number to each player. Spin a spinner with equal regions 0–9 twice to get a two-digit number. Repeat to select a total of 20 players.

Which plan is least likely to produce a sample that is representative of the league? Explain.

3 **Explain** The producers of a television singing contest post a survey on their website that asks viewers which singer they like best. Alison says that the results will tell the producers which singer viewers like best. Do you agree? Explain.

4 A doctor plans to add evening office hours one day per week. She wants to know which day her patients would most prefer for the evening hours.

PART A What does it mean for a sample of the doctor's patients to be representative of the population?

PART B The doctor uses a computer to make a list of every patient between the ages of 18 and 25. She selects every third name on this list. Is this sample likely to be representative of the population of her patients? Explain.

PART C Describe one way the doctor could select a random sample of her patients.

5 **Math Journal** An assistant at an animal shelter wants to know the typical age of dogs admitted to the shelter. The shelter has admitted 353 dogs. Each dog has an ID number. How could the assistant select a representative sample of the dogs and use it to gain information about the population?

☑ **End of Lesson Checklist**

☐ **INTERACTIVE GLOSSARY** Find the entry for *random sample*. Tell two important things you learned about random samples in this lesson.

Dear Family,

This week your student is learning about using random samples to make inferences and estimates about a population.

You can use data from a random sample to make an estimate or inference about the entire population. Using data from more than one random sample can lead to more accurate estimates.

Your student will be solving problems like the one below.

There are 440 students at Veda's school. Veda asks a random sample of 20 students their favorite genre of book. In the random sample, 7 students prefer fantasy books. Based on this sample, how many students at the entire school should Veda expect to prefer fantasy books?

➤ **ONE WAY** to make an inference is to use a double number line.

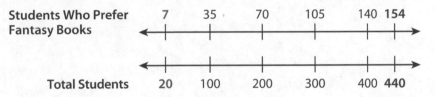

Students Who Prefer Fantasy Books: 7   35   70   105   140   **154**

Total Students: 20   100   200   300   400   **440**

➤ **ANOTHER WAY** is to use the percent of the sample that prefer fantasy books.

$\frac{7}{20} = 0.35$, or **35%**

35% of the students in the random sample prefer fantasy books.

So, about 35% of the **population** should prefer fantasy books.

0.35(440) = 154

Using either method, Veda should expect about 154 students in the school to prefer fantasy books.

▶ Use the next page to start a conversation about random samples.

Activity Thinking About Random Samples Around You

Guess how many

➤ **Do this activity together to investigate random samples in the real world.**

Have you ever tried to guess the number of small objects in a jar? Your guess may have been way off. However, if you had been able to average the guesses from lots of people, your guess might have been close to the true number.

Wisdom of crowds is the idea that collecting information from many different people can result in a better decision than relying on information from one person, even an expert! When you have more sample guesses, you can make a better guess.

 What are some times when you might want to use more than one sample to make an inference?

Explore Random Samples

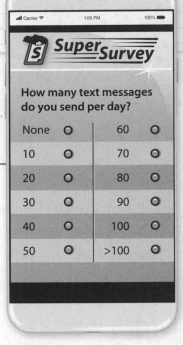

Previously, you learned about random samples. In this lesson, you will learn about using random samples to make estimates.

➤ **Use what you know to try to solve the problem below.**

Vivian surveys a random sample of Grade 7 students in the school band. She asks the students how many text messages they send each day. The median of her sample data is 50.

Edward surveys a random sample of all Grade 7 students. He asks the students how many text messages they send each day. The median of his sample data is 60. Whose result is more likely to be representative of all the Grade 7 students? Why?

TRY IT **Math Toolkit** bags, bowls, buttons, cups, index cards, number cubes

DISCUSS IT

Ask: How did you reach that conclusion?

Share: First, I thought . . .

◎ **Learning Target** SMP 1, SMP 2, SMP 3, SMP 4, SMP 5, SMP 6
Use data from a random sample to draw inferences about a population with an unknown characteristic of interest. Generate multiple samples (or simulated samples) of the same size to gauge the variation in estimates or predictions.

CONNECT IT

1 Look Back Is Vivian's or Edward's result more likely to be representative of the whole grade? Why?

2 Look Ahead While Vivian and Edward surveyed different populations, they both surveyed random samples. You can use data from a random sample to make an estimate or an inference about a population.

a. Sofia surveys a random sample of students in her school. She finds that 20 people in her random sample have pierced ears. Is it reasonable for Sofia to estimate that 20 people in the population of students at her school have pierced ears? Explain.

b. Sofia also finds that 50% of the students in her random sample wear glasses. Why is it a more reasonable inference that about 50% of the students in her school wear glasses than exactly 50% of the students in her school wear glasses?

3 Reflect How is making an inference about a population different from knowing something for certain about a population?

Prepare for Reasoning About Random Samples

1 Think about what you know about random samples. Fill in each box. Use words, numbers, and pictures. Show as many ideas as you can.

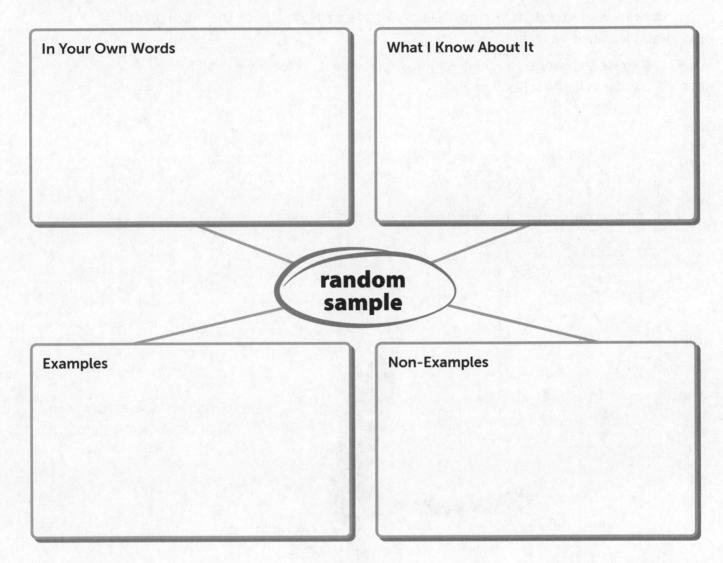

In Your Own Words	What I Know About It

random sample

Examples	Non-Examples

2 José is interested in the favorite activities of the students in his school. He surveys all the members of the school's book club. Did José survey a random sample of all the students in his school? Explain.

3 On the last day of school, all of the students in Jordan and Dara's middle school compete in a long jump contest. Jordan surveys a random sample from all students in the school about how far they can long jump. The mean of her sample data is 11 ft 6 in.

Dara surveys a random sample of Grade 8 students in the school. The mean of his sample data is 12 ft 2 in.

a. Whose answer do you think is more likely to be representative of all the students in the school? Explain.

b. Justify your answer in a different way.

©Curriculum Associates, LLC Copying is not permitted.

Develop Making Inferences from Samples About Populations

➤ **Read and try to solve the problem below.**

There are 406 students at Destiny's school. Destiny surveys 20 randomly chosen students from her school about how they get to school.

Based on the data from the sample, about how many students in the school should Destiny expect to take the subway?

Transportation Method	Frequency
Subway	8
Walk	4
Bus	4
Bike	2
Car	2

TRY IT   **Math Toolkit** double number lines, grid paper

➤ **Explore different ways to use a random sample to make inferences about a population.**

There are 406 students at Destiny's school. Destiny surveys 20 randomly chosen students from her school about how they get to school.

Based on the data from the sample, about how many students in the school should Destiny expect to take the subway?

Transportation Method	Frequency
Subway	8
Walk	4
Bus	4
Bike	2
Car	2

Model It

You can use a double number line to make an inference about the population.

The data come from a random sample, so you can expect them to be representative of the population.

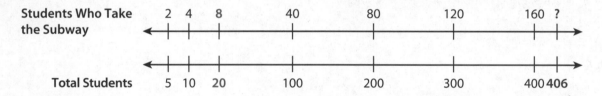

Students Who Take the Subway: 2 4 8 40 80 120 160 ?

Total Students: 5 10 20 100 200 300 400 406

Model It

You can use percents to make an inference about a population.

Find the percent of students in the sample that take the subway.

$\frac{8}{20} = 0.4$, or 40%

So, you can infer that 40% of all the students in the population take the subway.

0.4(406)

➤ **Use the problem from the previous page to help you understand how to use a random sample to make inferences about a population.**

1 Look at the first **Model It**. What two quantities does it show a proportional relationship between?

2 Look at 0.4(406) in the second **Model It**. How is the random sample represented in the expression?

3 Based on Destiny's random sample, about how many students can she expect to take the subway? Is this the same as the result of finding 40% of 406? Explain.

4 Destiny's friends Xavier and Querida also each survey 20 students selected at random from the school. Based on their samples, Xavier infers that about 142 students take the subway to school and Querida infers that about 183 students do. Explain why both of their inferences are reasonable.

5 How can you use proportional reasoning to make an inference about a population from a random sample of that population?

6 **Reflect** Think about all the models and strategies you have discussed today. Describe how one of them helped you better understand how to use a random sample to make inferences about a population.

Apply It

➤ **Use what you learned to solve these problems.**

7 A random sample of Grade 8 students at a school are asked whether they plan to take computer science in high school. Of those asked, 15 students plan to take computer science, 5 do not, and 7 are unsure. There are 326 Grade 8 students in the school. Based on the sample, about how many Grade 8 students in the school plan to take computer science in high school? Show your work.

SOLUTION _____

8 Yolanda asks a random sample of 50 students at her school what they do after school. Of the 50 students, 30 say they play a sport. Based on the sample, about what percent of students at Yolanda's school play a sport after school?

A 15%   **B** 30%

C 50%   **D** 60%

9 There are 5,119 households in Salvador's town. Salvador surveys a random sample of 20 households from his town. He finds that more than one language is spoken in 4 of the households. Based on the sample, in about how many households in the town should Salvador expect more than one language to be spoken? Show your work.

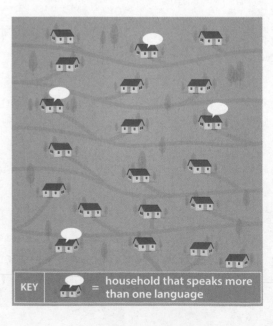

KEY [icon] = household that speaks more than one language

SOLUTION _____

_____

Practice Making Inferences from Samples About Populations

➤ **Study the Example showing how to use a random sample to make an inference about a population. Then solve problems 1–4.**

Example

Garrett is running for class president. He wants to know if he is likely to win, so his friend Jacob surveys a random sample of 10 students in his school. Of the 10 students, 7 say they will vote for Garrett. Suppose all 233 students in the school vote in the election for class president. About how many students should Garrett expect to vote for him?

Since $\frac{7}{10}$ of students in the sample say they will vote for Garrett, he should expect about $\frac{7}{10}$ **of the population** to vote for him.

$$\frac{7}{10}(233) = 163\frac{1}{10}$$

Garrett should expect about 163 students to vote for him.

---

1 Jacob conducts another survey of students in the school in the Example. This time, he surveys a random sample of 30 students.

   a. In Jacob's sample, 24 students say they will vote for Garrett. Based on this sample, about how many students in the school should Garrett expect to vote for him? Show your work.

   SOLUTION _____

   b. Using Jacob's surveys, can Garrett know for certain how many students plan to vote for him? Explain why or why not.

> **Vocabulary**
>
> **random sample**
> a sample in which every element in the population has an equal chance of being selected.

2 Mindy works at a movie theater. One Friday, she collects a random sample of the type of tickets sold in the afternoon and the evening. She estimates that when 400 tickets are sold on a Friday evening, about 100 of them will be senior tickets. Is Mindy's estimate reasonable? Explain.

Time of Day	Adult	Senior
Afternoon	12	48
Evening	45	15

3 Students at a certain high school have to take an arts or technology class. A random sample of 60 students from the high school are surveyed. Each student is asked which class they take. Based on the survey results, which of the following statements are true? Select all that apply.

Class	Number of Students
Dance	19
Electronics	8
Music	7
Painting	15
Photography	11

A There are many excellent dancers at the high school.

B About 25% of the students at the high school take painting.

C Of every 30 students in the high school, about 11 of them take photography.

D Next year, 7 out of every 60 students at the high school will take music.

E In a group of 120 students from the high school, about 16 of the students likely take electronics.

4 Moses writes a paper on fruit for health class. He surveys a random sample of students at his school about their favorite fruit. In his sample 46 students say strawberries. The other 34 students in his sample say a different fruit. There are 506 students in Moses's school. What inference can Moses make about the number of students in his school who would say strawberries are their favorite fruit? Show your work.

SOLUTION _____

Develop Making Inferences from Multiple Samples

➤ **Read and try to solve the problem below.**

Mr. Seda has a bag with 500 marbles. The marbles are either green or yellow. He has 20 students in his class take turns selecting 10 marbles from the bag without looking. Each student records the number of green marbles and then returns the marbles to the bag.

What is a reasonable estimate for the number of green marbles in the bag?

Samples from Mr. Seda's Class

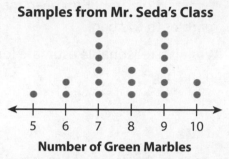

Number of Green Marbles

Math Toolkit double number lines, grid paper

DISCUSS IT

Ask: Why did you choose that strategy to find a reasonable estimate?

Share: I chose that strategy because . . .

➤ **Explore different ways to make inferences about a population from multiple random samples.**

Mr. Seda has a bag with 500 marbles. Some marbles are green, and the rest are yellow. He has 20 students in his class each select 10 marbles from the bag without looking. Each student records the number of green marbles and then returns the marbles to the bag.

What is a reasonable estimate for the number of green marbles in the bag?

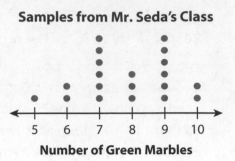

Samples from Mr. Seda's Class

Number of Green Marbles

Analyze It

You can use the mean of the samples to make an inference.

Each sample has **10** marbles. The mean of the number of green marbles in each sample is **7.85**.

You can expect the fraction $\frac{\text{green marbles}}{\text{total marbles}}$ to be about the same for the population and the average of the samples.

Let g represent the number of green marbles in the population.

$$\frac{7.85}{10} = \frac{g}{500}$$

Analyze It

You can use the median of the samples to make an inference.

Use a box plot to organize the samples.

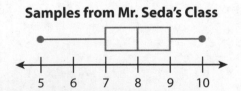

Samples from Mr. Seda's Class

Number of Green Marbles

Each sample has **10** marbles. The median number of green marbles in each sample is **8**.

Let g represent the number of green marbles in the population.

$$\frac{8}{10} = \frac{g}{500}$$

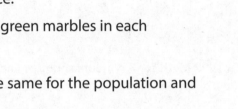

➤ **Use the problem from the previous page to help you understand how to use multiple random samples to make an inference about a population.**

1 Look at the **Analyze Its**. How many green marbles do you estimate are in the bag when you use the mean? What about when you use the median?

2 Why are the estimates different even though both use a measure of center?

3 Are both estimates reasonable? Why?

4 The first student who selected a sample got 6 green marbles in his sample. Why might making an inference from just this one sample be misleading?

5 How can using more than one sample help you make a better inference about a population than using only one sample?

6 **Reflect** Think about all the models and strategies you have discussed today. Describe how one of them helped you better understand how to solve the **Try It** problem.

Apply It

➤ **Use what you learned to solve these problems.**

7 Staff at a recreation center are deciding whether to offer martial arts classes. Each of 15 staff members surveys a random sample of 8 recreation center members about whether they practice martial arts.

Riley uses the median of the results and infers that $\frac{1}{8}$ of the recreation center members practice martial arts. Brian uses the mean and infers that $\frac{1}{5}$ do. Explain why Riley's inference is more reasonable than Brian's.

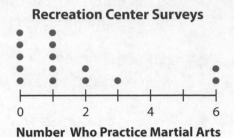

Recreation Center Surveys

Number Who Practice Martial Arts

8 Caleb, Aimee, and Ramón all survey random samples of 40 students in their school about whether they babysit their younger siblings. They use the results to make an inference about what percent of students in the school babysit their younger siblings. Which range of inferences is most reasonable?

A 27.5% to 30%

B 20% to 30%

C 8% to 12%

D 10.3% to 11%

Student Who Conducted Survey	Number of Students Who Babysit Siblings
Caleb	ⅢⅢ ⅢⅢ Ⅰ
Aimee	ⅢⅢ ⅢⅢ ⅠⅠ
Ramón	ⅢⅢ ⅠⅠⅠ

9 Mason has a bag with 171 beads. Some beads are red, some are orange, and the rest are yellow. He selects 8 beads without looking, counts how many are orange, and then puts the beads back in the bag. He does this 12 times. What is a reasonable estimate for the number of orange beads in the bag? Show your work.

Number of Orange Beads	2	3	4	5	6
Frequency	2	5	3	1	1

SOLUTION _____

Practice Making Inferences from Multiple Samples

➤ **Study the Example showing how to use multiple random samples to make an inference about a population. Then solve problems 1–4.**

Example

A box in Mrs. McClary's class has 200 plastic jewels. She has 11 students each select a random sample of 10 jewels, count the number of green jewels, and then return all 10 jewels to the box. Estimate the number of green jewels in the box.

Samples from Mrs. McClary's Class

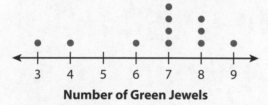

Number of Green Jewels

The median number of green jewels in each sample is 7. There are **10** jewels in a sample. There are **200** jewels in the population.

$$\frac{7}{10} \times 200 = 140$$

A reasonable estimate for the number of green jewels in the box is 140.

1 Use the mean to find an estimate for the number of green jewels in the box in the Example. Show your work.

SOLUTION _____

2 Describe a situation when an inference from the mean and an inference from the median might be very different.

3 Alberto buys a bag of 600 balloons. Some of the balloons are pink, and the rest are green. He wants to estimate the number of pink balloons in the bag. He asks 4 friends to each select a random sample of 10 balloons. Each friend returns the sample before the next friend selects a sample.

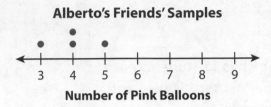

Alberto's Friends' Samples

Number of Pink Balloons

Based on the data, what is a reasonable estimate for the number of pink balloons in the bag? Show your work.

SOLUTION _____

4 A jar holds 3,000 marbles of four different colors. Neena tries to guess the number of marbles of each color. She is allowed to take 4 random samples of 200 marbles each.

	Blue	Green	Red	White
Sample 1	82	42	36	40
Sample 2	70	51	49	30
Sample 3	58	65	45	32
Sample 4	65	62	38	35

Based on Neena's data, which of the following statements are true? Select all that apply.

A The total number of red marbles in the jar is approximately 168.

B There are likely more blue marbles in the jar than any other color.

C There are probably more white marbles than green marbles in the jar.

D Approximately 21% to 33% of the marbles in the jar are green.

E There are probably about twice as many blue marbles as green marbles in the jar.

Refine Reasoning About Random Samples

➤ **Complete the Example below. Then solve problems 1–8.**

Example

There are 150 cards in a bag. Each card is either black or red. Carter selects 5 cards at random, records the number of red cards, and returns the cards. He does this until he has 12 samples of 5 cards.

    Carter's Results: 0, 1, 1, 1, 2, 2, 2, 2, 2, 3, 3, 5

Kwame does the same, but he uses 10 cards in his samples.

    Kwame's Results: 1, 2, 3, 3, 3, 4, 4, 4, 4, 5, 5, 7

What is a reasonable estimate for the number of red cards in the bag?

Look at how you could show your work using percents.

The median number of red cards in Carter's samples is 2.

$\frac{2}{5} = 40\%$

The median number of red cards in Kwame's samples is 4.

$\frac{4}{10} = 40\%$

SOLUTION _____

Apply It

1 A school has 800 students. The staff plans to order a bag for each student. They ask 120 randomly selected students which color bag they prefer. Based on this sample, how many bags of each color should the staff order? Show your work.

Color	Quantity
Blue	48
Black	54
Gray	18

SOLUTION _____

2 A box contains a mix of 800 golf balls. Some are white and the rest are purple. Each student in Mrs. Ramírez's class selects a random sample of 20 golf balls from the box, counts the purple golf balls, and returns the sample to the box.

CONSIDER THIS...
You could use the mean or the median to make an estimate.

Samples from Mrs. Ramírez's Class

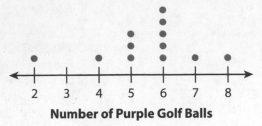

Number of Purple Golf Balls

What is a reasonable estimate for the number of purple golf balls in the box? Show your work.

PAIR/SHARE
How would your confidence in your estimate change if there were 25 students in Ms. Ramírez's class?

SOLUTION _____

3 Mr. Shen selects 20 of his 140 students at random to survey about their pets. His survey indicates that 8 students have a dog, 9 students have a cat, 3 students have another kind of pet, and 5 students have no pet. How many of his students should Mr. Shen expect to have a cat?

CONSIDER THIS...
Some students have more than one pet.

A 9

B 50

C 56

D 63

Nadia chose B as the correct answer. How might she have gotten that answer?

PAIR/SHARE
How can you check your answer?

4 Adsila and Esteban have a bag containing 250 marbles. Each marble is red, black, or white. Adsila and Esteban each select a sample of marbles from the bag, record the percent that are white, and return all the marbles to the bag. They each collect 15 samples. Their results are shown in the box plots. If you could only use one sample to make an estimate of the number of white marbles in the bag, would you rather use one of Adsila's samples or one of Esteban's? Why?

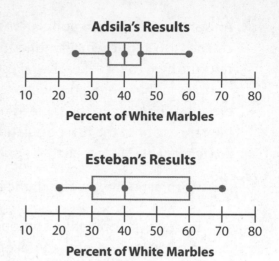

Adsila's Results

Percent of White Marbles

Esteban's Results

Percent of White Marbles

5 Emma has 3 random samples of the same size from a population of 650 people. In one sample, 78% of people have brown eyes. In another, 85% have brown eyes. In the third, 83% have brown eyes. About how many people with brown eyes should she expect are in the population? Show your work.

SOLUTION _____

_____

6 A jar contains 1,800 marbles. James enters a contest to guess the number of any one color of marbles in the jar. He is allowed to take 4 random samples of 200 marbles each.

	Blue	Green	Red	White
Sample 1	41	37	63	49
Sample 2	58	34	54	54
Sample 3	52	29	59	60
Sample 4	47	30	72	51

a. In James's samples, the color _____ has the most variation and the color _____ has the least variation.

b. James can choose which color of marble to make his guess about. Which color do you think he should choose? Why?

7 Aniyah studies the fish populations in a lake. She catches fish, tags them, identifies the type, and returns them to the lake. She takes two random samples in the winter and two in the summer. She organizes her data in the table at the right. Which inferences about the fish populations in the lake are reasonable? Select all that apply.

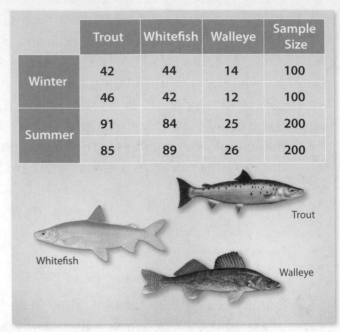

	Trout	Whitefish	Walleye	Sample Size
Winter	42	44	14	100
	46	42	12	100
Summer	91	84	25	200
	85	89	26	200

Trout

Whitefish

Walleye

A The total number of fish in the lake is 600.

B The walleye population comprises anywhere from 12% to 14% of the total population in both the winter and summer.

C The number of whitefish in the lake is greater than the number of trout.

D The ratios of the populations of trout, whitefish, and walleye are relatively stable from the winter to the summer.

E The populations of trout, whitefish, and walleye are approximately twice as large in the summer as in the winter.

8 **Math Journal** Write a word problem about taking a random sample and making an inference about the population. Then explain how to solve your problem.

✓ **End of Lesson Checklist**

☐ **INTERACTIVE GLOSSARY** Write a new entry for *inference*. Tell what you do when you make an *inference* about a population from a random sample.

☐ **SELF CHECK** Go back to the Unit 5 Opener and see what you can check off.

Dear Family,

This week your student is learning about comparing random samples from two populations. Random samples resemble the populations they come from, so you can use samples from two populations to compare the populations. You can use measures of center and variability to compare samples.

Measures of center describe the middle of a set of data with a single value. The mean is the average of the data values. The median is the middle value.

Measures of variability describe the variation in the data with a single value. The range is the difference between the greatest and least values in the data set. The mean absolute deviation (MAD) is the average distance of each data value from the mean. The interquartile range (IQR) is the range of the middle 50% of the data.

Using dot plots or box plots to display two data sets can help you visually compare the data. Your student will be solving problems like the one below.

A consumer agency randomly samples tires from two different companies. The results are shown in the box plots. Which company's tires have a longer life? Which company's tires have a more consistent lifespan?

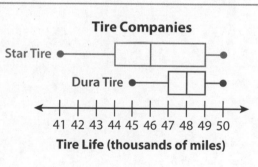

Tire Companies

Star Tire

Dura Tire

41 42 43 44 45 46 47 48 49 50

Tire Life (thousands of miles)

➤ **ONE WAY** to compare the tires is with a measure of center.

The median is shown by the line that divides each box into two parts.

Median for Star Tire: 46,000   Median for Dura Tire: 48,000

➤ **ANOTHER WAY** is to use a measure of variability.

The IQR is the difference between the ends of the box.

IQR for Star Tire: 49 − 44, or 5   IQR for Dura Tire: 49 − 47, or 2

The methods show that tires from Dura Tire tend to have longer lives and more consistent lifespans.

 Use the next page to start a conversation about populations.

Activity Thinking About Populations

➤ **Do this activity together to investigate populations.**

Have you ever seen advertisements for two competing companies that both claim they are the best? Both companies can be right, depending on how you look at it!

For example, two companies that provide internet service might both claim to have the best data network. One company has faster data speeds, but the other company has more reliable connections.

Whether a company is the best depends on what you care about: faster speed on average, or fewer times with dropped connections.

? When else might you want to compare two claims?

Explore Comparing Two Populations

Previously, you learned about using random samples to make inferences about a population. In this lesson, you will learn about using data to compare two populations.

➤ **Use what you know to try to solve the problem below.**

An inspector tests 30 randomly selected batteries from two different brands. The inspector records the life of each battery using dot plots. Which sample has a more consistent battery life? How do you know?

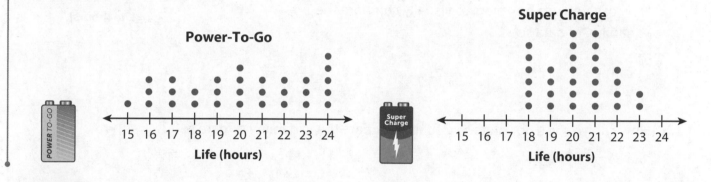

TRY IT

Math Toolkit grid paper, number lines

DISCUSS IT

Ask: How do you know your answer is reasonable?

Share: I know my answer is reasonable because . . .

Learning Targets SMP 1, SMP 2, SMP 3, SMP 4, SMP 5, SMP 6, SMP 7
• Informally assess the degree of visual overlap of two numerical data distributions with similar variabilities, measuring the difference between the centers by expressing it as a multiple of a measure of variability.
• Use measures of center and measures of variability for numerical data from random samples to draw informal comparative inferences about two populations.

CONNECT IT

1 **Look Back** Do the sample Power-To-Go or sample Super Charge batteries have a more consistent battery life? How do you know?

2 **Look Ahead** You can compare the variability of two data sets using both dot plots and box plots. The box plots at the right display the same data about the samples of Power-To-Go and Super Charge batteries as the dot plots you saw previously.

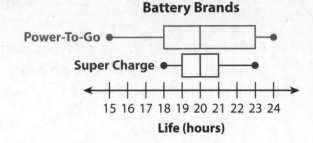

Battery Brands

a. How can you use box plots to visually compare the variability of data sets?

b. How can you use dot plots to visually compare the variability of data sets?

c. You can use median, interquartile range (IQR), mean, and mean absolute deviation (MAD) to describe a data set. Which of those can you use to compare the variability of two data sets?

d. Could you find the mean and MAD of the data sets from the box plots? Could you find the mean and MAD from the dot plots? Explain.

3 **Reflect** How can displaying two data sets on the same number line help you compare them?

Prepare for Comparing Populations

1 Think about what you know about measures of center and variability. Fill in each box. Use words, numbers, and pictures. Show as many ideas as you can.

Word	In My Own Words	Example
median		
interquartile range (IQR)		
mean		
mean absolute deviation (MAD)		

2 How does the box plot show the median and IQR?

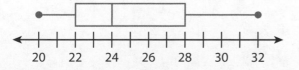

3 The library where Enrico works has a large collection of movies. Enrico takes a random sample of 20 animated movies and another random sample of 20 comedies. He records the run time of each movie using dot plots.

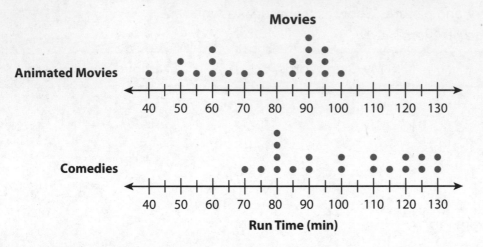

Movies

Animated Movies

Comedies

Run Time (min)

a. Do the animated movies or the comedies have more variability in their run time? Show your work.

SOLUTION _____

b. Check your answer to problem 3a. Show your work.

Develop Comparing Centers of Data Relative to Variability

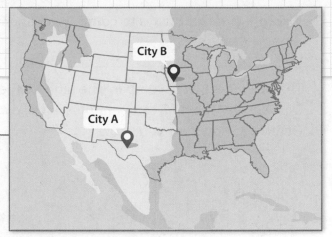

➤ **Read and try to solve the problem below.**

The box plots below compare the high temperatures in two cities in June and in October. Are the high temperatures in the two cities more similar in June or in October? Show how you know.

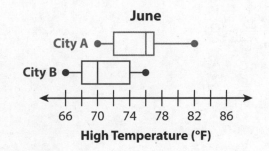

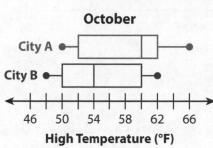

TRY IT

Math Toolkit grid paper, number lines

DISCUSS IT

Ask: What are some ways of comparing two data sets besides comparing their medians?

Share: I can see from the plots that . . .

➤ **Explore different ways to compare the centers of two data sets relative to their variabilities.**

The box plots below compare the high temperatures in two cities in June and in October. Are the high temperatures in the two cities more similar in June or in October? Show how you know.

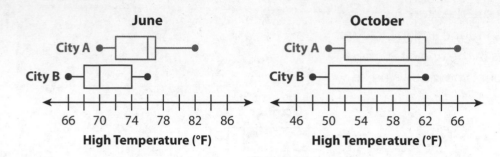

Picture It

You can look at and compare the overlap in the boxes for each month.

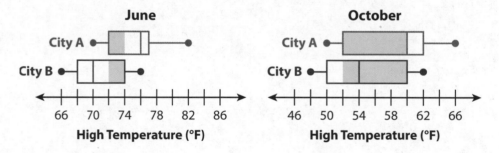

Analyze It

You can show how similar two data sets are by expressing the difference in the medians as a multiple of each IQR.

Difference in the medians for June: $76 - 70 = 6$

IQR for City A in June: $77 - 72 = 5$

The difference in the medians, 6, divided by the IQR for City A, 5, is 1.2.

The difference in the medians is **1.2 times the IQR for City A.**

IQR for City B in June: $74 - 68 = 6$

The difference in the medians is **1 times the IQR for City B.**

Difference in the medians for October: $60 - 54 = 6$

IQR for both cities: 10

The difference in the medians is **0.6 times the IQR for both cities.**

> **Use the problem from the previous page to help you understand how to express the difference in centers of data relative to their variability.**

1 Look at **Picture It**. In which month did the cities have more similar temperatures? How does the overlap of the boxes show how similar the data sets are?

2 Look at **Analyze It**. Both June and October have the same difference in the medians. However, the multiple of the IQRs is lesser in October. Why does it make sense that the multiple is less in October?

3 The less the multiple of the IQR, the more the boxes in the plots overlap. Why?

4 Mean is another measure of center and MAD is another measure of variability. You can express the difference in the means as a multiple of the MADs. The less the multiple of the IQR and the MAD are, the more overlap there will be in the dot plots. Why?

5 How does expressing the difference in centers of two data sets as a multiple of their variabilities indicate how similar or different the data sets are?

6 **Reflect** Think about all the models and strategies you have discussed today. Describe how one of them helped you understand how to express the difference in centers of data relative to their variability.

Apply It

➤ **Use what you learned to solve these problems.**

7 The students in a science class take a quiz before they start a new unit. The mean score is 3 and the MAD is 1.8. After the unit, the students take the quiz again. The mean score is 7.5 and the MAD is 1.5. Suppose you plotted the scores for both quizzes. Would you expect to see a lot of overlap? Explain.

8 The box plots show the number of hours members of two different service groups volunteered last month. Express the difference in the medians as a multiple of the IQR for each group. Show your work.

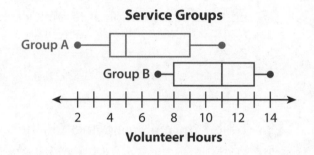

SOLUTION _____

9 At a dog show, the mean weight of the Norfolk Terriers is 11.5 pounds with a MAD of 2. The mean weight of the Cairn Terriers is 13 pounds with a MAD of 1.8. Express the difference in mean weights as a multiple of the MAD for both dog breeds. Show your work.

SOLUTION _____

_____

_____

Practice Comparing Centers of Data Relative to Variability

➤ **Study the Example showing how to compare two data sets. Then solve problems 1–2.**

Example

Serafina is researching how much time advertisements take up on different radio stations. She collects data from 20 music and 20 talk stations. The box plots show the number of minutes each station devotes to ads each hour. Express the difference between the medians as a multiple of each IQR.

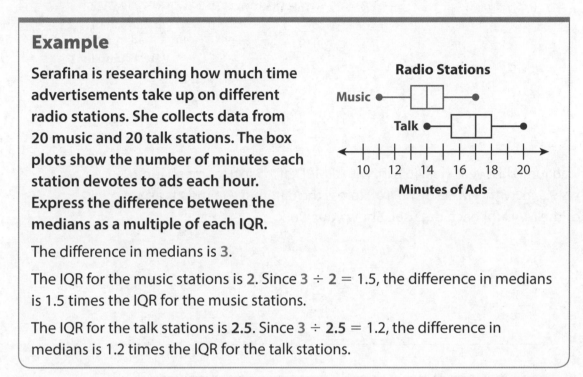

The difference in medians is 3.

The IQR for the music stations is 2. Since $3 \div 2 = 1.5$, the difference in medians is 1.5 times the IQR for the music stations.

The IQR for the talk stations is 2.5. Since $3 \div 2.5 = 1.2$, the difference in medians is 1.2 times the IQR for the talk stations.

1 The box plots show the number of minutes Geraldo and Colin spend on chores each day. Express the difference in the median time spent on chores as a multiple of the IQR for each data set. Show your work.

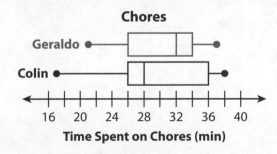

SOLUTION _____

_____

2 The dot plots show the height of Maria's high jumps in track meets over two years.

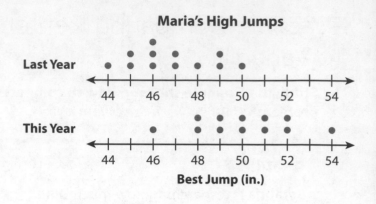

Maria's High Jumps

a. Look at the plots without making any calculations. How would you describe the change in Maria's high jump performance? Why?

b. Maria's mean jump last year was 46.8 in. with a MAD of 1.5 in. Her mean jump this year is 49.9 in. with a MAD of 1.6 in. Express the difference in means as a multiple of the MAD for each data set. Show your work.

SOLUTION _____

_____

c. Do you think that using the median and the IQR, instead of the mean and the MAD, would provide a useful description of how Maria's performance has changed? Explain.

Develop Comparing Two Populations

➤ **Read and try to solve the problem below.**

The principal wants students in all social studies classes to have similar amounts of homework. She selects a random sample of 20 homework assignments each from Mr. Duda's and Ms. Lincoln's lesson plans. Who assigns more homework? How do you know?

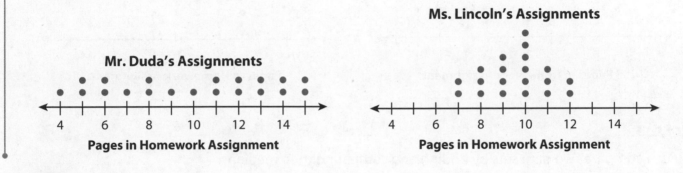

Mr. Duda's Assignments

Pages in Homework Assignment

Ms. Lincoln's Assignments

Pages in Homework Assignment

TRY IT

Math Toolkit counters, grid paper, number lines

DISCUSS IT

Ask: How is your strategy similar to mine? How is it different?

Share: My strategy is similar to yours . . . It is different . . .

➤ **Explore different ways to compare two populations by using random samples from each population.**

The principal wants students in all social studies classes to have similar amounts of homework. She selects a random sample of 20 homework assignments each from Mr. Duda's and Ms. Lincoln's lesson plans. Who assigns more homework? How do you know?

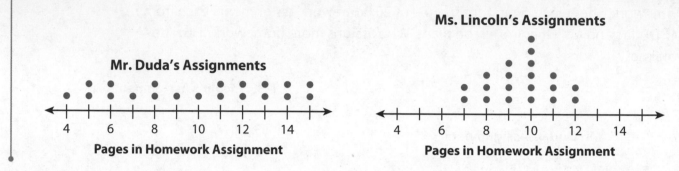

Picture It

You can compare two data sets by finding and comparing their medians.

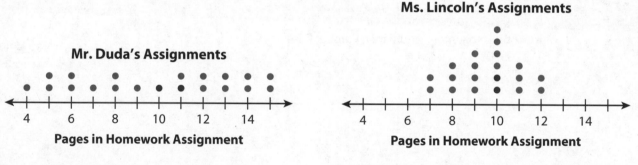

The median of Mr. Duda's sample is **10.5**.

The median of Ms. Lincoln's sample is **10**.

Analyze It

You can compare two data sets by finding and comparing their means.

Mr. Duda

Mean of sample: 9.9

Inferred mean of population: about 9.9

Ms. Lincoln

Mean of sample: 9.55

Inferred mean of population: about 9.55

➤ **Use the problem from the previous page to help you understand how to use random samples to compare two populations.**

1 Look at **Analyze It**. Why are the inferences about Mr. Duda's and Ms. Lincoln's samples reasonable?

2 Look at **Picture It**. Based on the medians of the samples, who gives more homework? Does your answer change if you make an inference from the means instead of the medians? Explain.

3 The median of Ms. Lincoln's sample is greater than the mean of Mr. Duda's sample. Can you infer that Ms. Lincoln gives more homework? Explain.

4 When can you compare an inference about one population to an inference about another population?

5 **Reflect** Think about all the models and strategies you have discussed today. Describe how one of them helped you better understand how to compare two populations.

Apply It

➤ **Use what you learned to solve these problems.**

6 Roberto and Amata each have a bag of 360 marbles. Roberto draws 10 marbles from his bag, records the number that are green, and replaces the marbles. He does this 20 times. Amata does the same with her bag. Do you expect that Roberto's or Amata's bag has more green marbles? About how many more? Show your work.

Mean Number of Green Marbles	
Roberto's Samples	4.9
Amata's Samples	2

SOLUTION _____

7 The box plots show the number of pretzels in random samples of 30 snack bags from two brands. Which brand has more pretzels in a typical bag? Which brand has a more consistent number of pretzels in each bag? Explain how you can use the data from the random samples to tell.

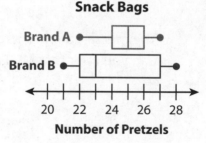

Snack Bags

Brand A
Brand B

20 22 24 26 28
Number of Pretzels

8 River County has 15,000 likely voters. A survey of 100 randomly selected voters in River County finds that 60 plan to vote to re-elect the current governor. Lake County has 12,000 likely voters. A survey of 125 randomly selected voters in Lake County finds that 90 plan to vote to re-elect the current governor. In which county can the current governor expect to get more votes? Show your work.

SOLUTION _____

Name: _____

Practice Comparing Two Populations

➤ **Study the Example showing how to use sample data to compare two populations. Then solve problems 1–3.**

Example

Random samples of dentists in the United States are asked which toothpaste brand he or she uses. Each sample has 100 dentists in it. About what percent of all dentists in the United States can you infer use each brand?

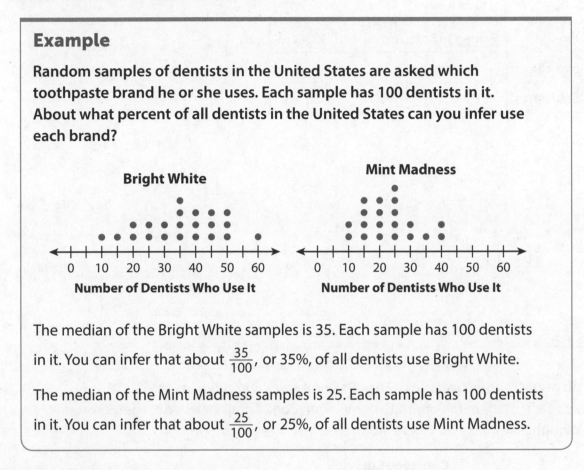

The median of the Bright White samples is 35. Each sample has 100 dentists in it. You can infer that about $\frac{35}{100}$, or 35%, of all dentists use Bright White.

The median of the Mint Madness samples is 25. Each sample has 100 dentists in it. You can infer that about $\frac{25}{100}$, or 25%, of all dentists use Mint Madness.

---

1 Refer to the data in the Example.

a. There are about 200,000 dentists in the United States. About how many dentists in the United States can you infer use Mint Madness? Show your work.

SOLUTION _____

b. Mint Madness wants to advertise their toothpaste as "chosen by at least 50,000 dentists." Based on the data, is this claim definitely true? Explain.

2 There are 279 Grade 7 students and 225 Grade 8 students in Noor's school. Noor asks a random sample of 25 students from each grade which night they plan to attend the school play. Can she expect more Grade 7 or Grade 8 students at the play on Friday night? About how many more? Show your work.

	Friday	Saturday	Will Not Go
Grade 7 Students	7	13	5
Grade 8 Students	8	9	8

SOLUTION _____

3 Company A surveys a random sample of 20 of its employees about how many minutes it takes each of them to commute home after work. Company B does the same with a random sample of 20 of its employees.

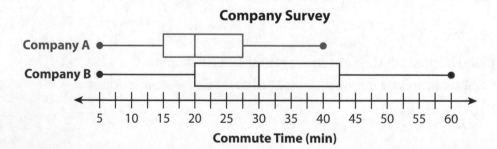

Company Survey

Which company's employees probably have less variability in their commute times? Explain how you made your inference.

Refine Comparing Populations

➤ **Complete the Example below. Then solve problems 1–8.**

Example

A city has had both a baseball team and a football team for 21 seasons. The box plot at the right shows the percent of games won each season. Which team has had a better record? Which team has performed more consistently?

Teams

Baseball

Football

15   25   35   45   55   65

Percent of Games Won in Season

Look at how you could show your work using median and IQR.

The baseball team has a median of 45% and an IQR of 10. The football team has a median of 35% and an IQR of 25.

SOLUTION _____

_____

CONSIDER THIS...
How do percents let you compare the teams' records even though a baseball season has more games than a football season?

PAIR/SHARE
How does the difference in the medians compare to the IQR of each data set?

Apply It

1 A lightbulb manufacturer tests random samples of 200 green light bulbs each. It also tests random samples of 200 yellow light bulbs each. The mean number of defective green bulbs is 5. The mean number of defective yellow bulbs is 6.6.

In a shipment of 1,000 bulbs of each color, would you expect more defective green bulbs or yellow bulbs? About how many more? Show your work.

CONSIDER THIS...
The number of defective green light bulbs does not impact the number of defective yellow light bulbs.

PAIR/SHARE
How might your inference change if there were 500 light bulbs in each sample?

SOLUTION _____

2 These box plots show the daily high temperatures in two cities over a two-week period. Express the difference between the median temperatures as a multiple of the IQR for each city. Show your work.

CONSIDER THIS . . .
The IQR of a data set is the difference between the upper and lower quartiles.

London

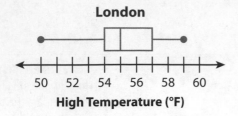

High Temperature (°F)

Honolulu

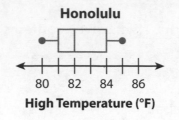

High Temperature (°F)

PAIR/SHARE
How would the data sets look if you graphed them on the same number line?

SOLUTION _____

_____

3 Suppose the data sets described below were plotted on dot plots. Which pair of data sets would show the most visual overlap?

CONSIDER THIS . . .
A greater MAD means that the average data point is farther from the mean.

A Data set 1: mean: 40; MAD: 4

Data set 2: mean: 40; MAD: 8

B Data set 1: mean: 30, MAD: 5

Data set 2: mean: 30, MAD: 6

C Data set 1: mean: 20, MAD: 4

Data set 2: mean: 20; MAD: 2

D Data set 1: mean: 10, MAD: 1

Data set 2: mean: 10, MAD: 4

Lola chose D as the correct answer. How might she have gotten that answer?

PAIR/SHARE
Both data sets in each pair have the same mean. How does that affect your answer?

4 For one year, Kyle records how many pages are in each book he reads. For the fiction books, the median number of pages is 239 and the IQR is 25. For the nonfiction books, the median number of pages is 254 and the IQR is 30.

The difference in medians is _____ times the IQR for the fiction books.

The difference in medians is _____ times the IQR for the nonfiction books.

5 Bus drivers in a certain city take 25 random samples of the number of riders on their routes during the day. Which inferences can you make based on these samples? Select all that apply.

A On both routes, about 75% of the rides have more than 30 riders.

B The route B bus has a more consistent number of riders.

C On a given day, the route A bus is more likely to have fewer than 40 riders than the route B bus is.

D The typical number of riders is greater on a route A bus than on a route B bus.

E The route A bus has between 30 and 55 riders more often than the route B bus does.

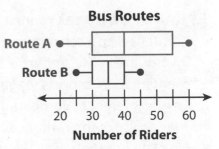

6 The plots show the heights of students on a college's women's basketball team and women's diving team. The difference between the medians is $2\frac{2}{3}$ times the IQR for both teams.

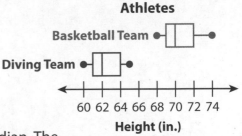

Suppose three students join the diving team and change the median. The students have heights 66 in., 67 in., and 70 in. Does the difference between the medians become a greater or lesser multiple of the basketball team's IQR? Why?

7 These box plots show attendance at a random sample of 40 games in each of two baseball leagues. Jorge says that there is no real difference between attendance at North League games and attendance at South League games. Use the data sets to make a counterargument.

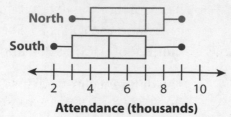

Baseball Leagues

North

South

Attendance (thousands)

8 **Math Journal** Winona takes 10 random samples of sentences in a science magazine and records how many words are in the sentence. She does the same for sentences in a sports magazine. Use Winona's data to make inferences comparing the length and the variability of the sentences in the two magazines. Explain how you used Winona's data to make your inferences.

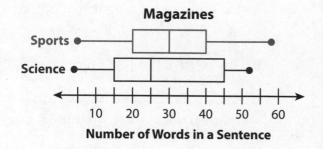

Magazines

Sports

Science

Number of Words in a Sentence

✓ End of Lesson Checklist

☐ **INTERACTIVE GLOSSARY** Write a new entry for *consistent*. Tell what makes a data set *consistent*.

☐ **SELF CHECK** Go back to the Unit 5 Opener and see what you can check off.

Study an Example Problem and Solution

➤ **Read this problem involving random samples of two populations. Then look at one student's solution to this problem on the following pages.**

Analyzing Hawk Data

Adriana and Isaiah are wildlife biologists. They collected data from a random sample of adult red-tailed hawks in the western United States. Read this email from Adriana, and then help Isaiah analyze the data.

| Delete | Archive | Reply | Reply All | Forward |

To: Isaiah
Subject: Hawk Data

Hi Isaiah,

The DNA testing on our hawks is complete, so we now know which ones are female and hich ones are male.

Attached is a copy of our data. I could use your help analyzing it. Please choose the mass data or the wing-length data for your analysis, and I will do the other data set.

I want to use the data to make an inference that can help us predict whether an adult red-tailed hawk is female or male based on its mass or wing length.

Female

Male

WHAT YOU SHOULD DO:
- Use a measure of center (median or mean) to compare the sizes of female and male red-tailed hawks.
- Use dot plots or box plots to analyze the amount of overlap in the distributions of the female and male populations.
- Make an inference based on the sample data that can be used to predict whether an adult red-tailed hawk is female or male.

Thanks!

Adriana

Attachments:

Female Hawks		Male Hawks	
Mass (g)	Wing Length (mm)	Mass (g)	Wing Length (mm)
1,522	433	908	374
1,015	390	917	378

See page DS1 for the complete data set.

Male and female red-tailed hawks look a lot alike. It can be difficult to tell them apart without taking measurements or using a DNA test.

One Student's Solution

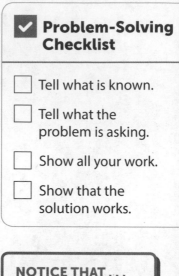

✓ Problem-Solving Checklist

☐ Tell what is known.

☐ Tell what the problem is asking.

☐ Show all your work.

☐ Show that the solution works.

NOTICE THAT . . .
For a data set with an even number of values, the median is the mean of the two middle values when the data are listed from least to greatest.

NOTICE THAT . . .
The lower quartile (Q1), the median, and the upper quartile (Q3) divide a data set into four parts that each represent about 25% of the data.

First, I have to choose one of the data sets to analyze.

I will pick the wing-length data.

Next, I need to use a measure of center to compare the sizes of female and male red-tailed hawks.

I will use the median to compare the wing lengths.

Females: 390, 391, 394, 397, 402, 404, 410, 412, 415, ⟨416, 418⟩ 422, 422, 423, 428, 430, 430, 431, 432, 433

Median: $\frac{(416 + 418)}{2} = 417$

Males: 356, 362, 364, 368, 374, 374, 377, 378, 378, ⟨379, 383⟩ 383, 385, 385, 386, 388, 390, 393, 408, 409

Median: $\frac{(379 + 383)}{2} = 381$

The sample data indicate that female red-tailed hawks have a median wing length of 417 mm, and male red-tailed hawks have a median wing length of 381 mm. So, females typically have longer wings than males.

Now, I will calculate the values that I need to make data displays of the distributions.

I will use box plots to model the distributions, so I need to find the quartiles of each data set.

median ↓

Females: 390, 391, 394, 397, | 402, 404, | 410, 412, 415, 416, 418, 422, 422, 423, | 428, 430, | 430, 431, 432, 433

Q1: $\frac{(402 + 404)}{2} = 403$ Q3: $\frac{(428 + 430)}{2} = 429$

median ↓

Males: 356, 362, 364, 368, | 374, 374, | 377, 378, 378, 379, 383, 383, 385, 385, | 386, 388, | 390, 393, 408, 409

Q1: $\frac{(374 + 374)}{2} = 374$ Q3: $\frac{(386 + 388)}{2} = 387$

Now, I can make data displays to show how much overlap there is in the distributions.

I can use the median and quartiles to make the box plots.

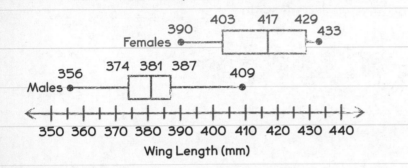

Then, I can analyze the amount of overlap in the distributions.

The box plots show that there is some overlap in the distributions. The upper 25% of the **males** data overlaps with the bottom 25% of the **females** data.

Finally, I will make an inference that can be used to predict whether an adult red-tailed hawk is female or male.

From the box plots of the sample data, I can see that all of the female hawks have a wing length of 390 mm or greater and most of the male hawks have a wing length less than 390 mm.

I will use this observation to make my inference:

If a red-tailed hawk has a wing length of at least 390 mm, it is likely to be female. Otherwise, it is likely to be male.

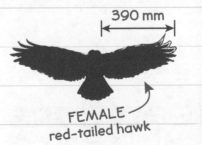

FEMALE red-tailed hawk

NOTICE THAT . . .
It is not possible to say for certain that a red-tailed hawk with a wing length of 390 mm or greater is female. However, based on the data from this random sample, a hawk with this wing length is likely to be female.

Try Another Approach

➤ **There are many ways to solve problems. Think about how you might solve the Analyzing Hawk Data problem in a different way.**

Analyzing Hawk Data

Adriana and Isaiah are wildlife biologists. They collected data from a random sample of adult red-tailed hawks in the western United States. Read this email from Adriana, and then help Isaiah analyze the data.

🗑 Delete 🗑 Archive | ✉ Reply ✉ Reply All ✉ Forward

To: Isaiah
Subject: Hawk Data

Hi Isaiah,

The DNA testing on our hawks is complete, so we now know which ones are female and which ones are male.

Attached is a copy of our data. I could use your help analyzing it. Please choose the mass data or the wing-length data for your analysis, and I will do the other data set.

I want to use the data to make an inference that can help us predict whether an adult red-tailed hawk is female or male based on its mass or wing length.

Female

WHAT YOU SHOULD DO:
• Use a measure of center (median or mean) to compare the sizes of female and male red-tailed hawks.
• Use dot plots or box plots to analyze the amount of overlap in the distributions of the female and male populations.
• Make an inference based on the sample data that can be used to predict whether an adult red-tailed hawk is female or male.

Male

Thanks!

Adriana

Attachments:

Female Hawks		Male Hawks	
Mass (g)	Wing Length (mm)	Mass (g)	Wing Length (mm)
1,522	433	908	374
1,015	390	917	378

See page DS1 for the complete data set.

Math in Action

Plan It

➤ **Answer these questions to help you start thinking about a plan.**

   a. Which data set will you analyze, the mass data or the wing-length data?

   b. Which measure of center will you use to compare the sizes of female and male red-tailed hawks? Why will you use that measure?

Solve It

➤ **Find a different solution for the Analyzing Hawk Data problem. Show all your work on a separate sheet of paper. You may want to use the Problem-Solving Tips to get started.**

PROBLEM-SOLVING TIPS

Math Toolkit double number lines, grid paper, number lines

Key Terms

population	sample	mean
median	percent	random sample
distribution		

Questions

- How can your data display help you make an inference that can be used to predict whether a red-tailed hawk is female or male?

- Can an inference based on the sample data predict with certainty whether a particular red-tailed hawk is female or male? Explain.

Reflect

Use Mathematical Practices As you work through the problem, discuss these questions with a partner.

- **Use Models** Would dot plots be a good choice for analyzing the amount of overlap in the distributions of the females data and the males data? Why or why not?

- **Critique Reasoning** Think about your partner's inference and the reasoning used to make it. Do you think the inference is reasonable based on the sample data? Explain.

Discuss Models and Strategies

➤ **Read the problem. Write a solution on a separate sheet of paper. Remember, there can be lots of ways to solve a problem.**

Counting Bears

Efia is a wildlife biologist studying the black bears and grizzly bears in a national park. She is using a marking technique to estimate the population of each type of bear. Read this email from Efia to her assistant Bridget, and help Bridget complete the list of tasks.

| 🗑 Delete | 🗑 Archive | | ✉ Reply | ✉ Reply All | ✉ Forward |

To: Bridget
Subject: Population Estimates

Hi Bridget,

Our lab results came back, so we can start making our population estimates. I have attached a copy of the data.

For each of our samples, we can estimate the population of black or grizzly bears in the park by treating the fraction of marked bears in the sample as equal to the fraction of marked bears in the population. Marked bears are bears we already identified in any previous sample for a given year.

$$\frac{\text{Number of marked bears in sample}}{\text{Number of bears in sample}} = \frac{\text{Number of marked bears in population}}{\text{Estimated number of bears in population}}$$

Note: This will not work for the first sample of each year because there are no marked bears for those samples.

YOUR TASKS:
- Choose the black bear or grizzly bear data. I will work with the other data set.
- For the bear you pick, use the sample data to estimate the population in the park for each year of the study. Let me know how you determined your estimates.
- Tell me whether you think we should take five samples or fewer next year, and explain why.

Efia

Attachments:

First Year of Study			
Sample	Bears in Sample	Marked Bears in Sample	Marked Bears in Population
1	20	0	0
2	10	5	20

See page DS2 for the complete data set.

Plan It and Solve It

➤ **Find a solution to the Counting Bears problem.**

Write a detailed plan and support your answer. Be sure to include:

- the type of bear you picked.

- reasonable estimates of the number of black bears or grizzly bears in the park for each year of the study.

- an explanation of how you determined your estimates.

- your opinion about whether five samples or fewer samples should be taken next year to estimate the population and a reason for your opinion.

PROBLEM-SOLVING TIPS

Math Toolkit double number lines, grid paper, number lines

Key Terms

population	sample	variability
mean	median	

Questions

- For the first year of the study, how can you use the equation from the email and the data from sample 2 to estimate the population?

- How can you use the population estimates from samples 2 through 5 to produce a single reasonable estimate of the population for each year?

Reflect

Use Mathematical Practices As you work through the problem, discuss these questions with a partner.

- **Reason Mathematically** How much variation is there in your population estimates from samples 2, 3, 4, and 5 for a given year? How does this affect whether you think fewer samples should be taken next year?

- **Make an Argument** Do you think the population increased, decreased, or stayed about the same between the two years of the study? Explain.

When a bear rubs against a hair trap, it leaves a bit of its fur behind, which can be DNA tested. This allows biologists to identify specific bears in a population.

Persevere On Your Own

➤ **Read the problem. Write a solution on a separate sheet of paper.**

Monitoring Sea Otters

Elon is a wildlife biologist studying the California sea otter. These otters are listed as threatened under the Endangered Species Act of 1977. Read about the requirements that must be met before this species can be removed from the threatened list, and then help Elon make a recommendation.

Endangered Species | SPECIES DIRECTORY | MAP | RECOVERY PLANS | ☰

California Sea Otter

Status: **Threatened**

The California sea otter can be removed from the threatened list if its population index stays above 3,090 for 3 years in a row. But even then, officials might decide to keep it on the list for longer.

The **population index** for a given year is the mean of the total populations for that year and the two previous years. For example, the population index for 2015 is the mean of the total populations for 2013, 2014, and 2015.

California Sea Otters			
Year	Adults	Pups	Total Population
2013	2,498	463	2,961
2014	2,469	478	2,947
2015	2,742	512	3,254
2016	3,170	445	3,615
2017	2,283	405	2,688
2018	2,519	562	3,081
2019	2,692	425	3,117

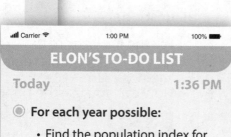

.ıll Carrier 🛜   1:00 PM   100% ▰

ELON'S TO-DO LIST

Today   1:36 PM

◉ **For each year possible:**
- Find the population index for the California sea otter
- Find the percent change in the population index compared to the previous year
- Find the percent change in either the adult or pup population compared to the previous year

◉ **Recommend whether the California sea otter should be removed from the threatened list (must explain my reasoning)**

Solve It

➤ **Find a solution to the Monitoring Sea Otters problem.**

- Calculate the population index for the California sea otter for the years 2015 to 2019.

- Calculate the percent change in the population index compared to the previous year for the years 2016 to 2019.

- Choose either the adult population or the pup population. For the years 2014 to 2019, calculate the percent change in that population compared to the previous year.

- Make a recommendation based on your calculations about whether the California sea otter should be removed from the threatened list, and explain your reasoning.

Reflect

Use Mathematical Practices After you complete the problem, choose one of these questions to discuss with a partner.

- **Make an Argument** Did the percent change in the population index over time influence your recommendation about whether to remove the California sea otter from the threatened list? Explain.

- **Reason Mathematically** Does the population index for California sea otters show more variability than the total population numbers? How do you know?

During the 1930s, the population of California sea otters fell to a low of about 50 animals.

In this unit you learned to . . .

Skill	Lesson(s)
Calculate simple interest.	20
Solve percent problems involving markups, markdowns, tips, tax, and commission.	20
Solve percent problems involving percent change or percent error.	21
Identify random samples.	22, 23
Make statistical inferences from random samples.	23
Compare data using measures of center and variability.	24
Agree or disagree with ideas in discussions about random samples and explain why.	22, 23, 24

Think about what you have learned.

➤ **Use words, numbers, and drawings.**

1 One topic I could use in my everyday life is _____ because . . .

2 I worked hardest to learn how to . . .

3 I would like to learn more about how to . . .

Vocabulary Review

➤ **Review the unit vocabulary. Put a check mark by items you can use in speaking and writing. Look up the meaning of any terms you do not know.**

Math Vocabulary		Academic Vocabulary
☐ commission	☐ percent increase	☐ discount
☐ gratuity	☐ population	☐ inference
☐ markdown	☐ random sample	☐ original
☐ markup	☐ sample	☐ representative
☐ percent decrease	☐ simple interest	

➤ **Use the unit vocabulary to answer the questions.**

1 Use at least three math or academic vocabulary terms to describe a year-end sale at a store. Underline each term you use.

2 How is a sample similar to and different from a population?

3 How are samples and random samples similar and different? Use at least two math or academic vocabulary terms in your answer. Underline each term you use.

4 Explain commission, gratuity, and simple interest and what they have in common.

➤ **Use what you have learned to complete these problems.**

1 At the end of January, Garrett had $176 in his savings account. By the end of February, he had $217. To the nearest percent, what is the percent change in the amount of money in Garrett's savings account?

A 19% **B** 23%

C 41% **D** 81%

2 The price of a new drone is $289. Sales tax is 9%. What is the total cost of the drone in dollars, including tax? Record your answer on the grid. Then fill in the bubbles.

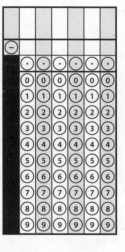

3 The owner of a game shop plans to survey a sample of game players to find the most popular kind of game. Which is the best way the manager could select a random sample of game players?

A Survey every customer that buys a card game.

B Survey every 3rd customer that buys a video game.

C Survey every 5th person that walks by his store on the street.

D Survey every 10th customer at his store.

4 The box plots show the number of minutes Shayla and Roderick spend practicing the guitar. Which statements describe the data? Choose all the correct answers.

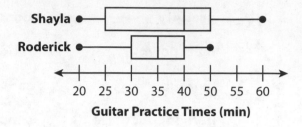

Guitar Practice Times (min)

A The IQR for Shayla is 25.

B The IQR for Roderick is 35.

C The difference in medians is 5.

D The difference in medians is 20.

E The difference in medians is 0.2 times the IQR for Shayla's data.

5 Decide if the percent change for each of the situations is between 40% and 50%. Choose *Yes* or *No* for each situation.

	Yes	No
a. The number of students increases from 11 to 19 students.	◯	◯
b. A $25 shirt is on sale for $13.	◯	◯
c. A puppy's weight increases from 8 lb to 11 lb.	◯	◯
d. A sunflower grows from 13 in. to 26 in.	◯	◯

6 Brady and Gregory own different smoothie shops. They both survey a random sample of customers about their favorite smoothie ingredient. The results are shown in the table. What inference can Brady make about the percent of his customers who consider bananas their favorite smoothie ingredient? What inference can Gregory make? Show your work.

Favorite Smoothie Ingredient	Frequency (Brady's Sample)	Frequency (Gregory's Sample)
Bananas	147	89
Yogurt	48	19
Peanut Butter	45	17

SOLUTION _____

_____

7 YourRide and NextCar are ride-sharing apps. YourRide surveys a random sample of 25 of its app users about how long they waited for their last ride. NextCar does the same with a random sample of 25 of its app users. Which app's users have less variability in their wait times? Use a measure of variability to explain your reasoning. Show your work.

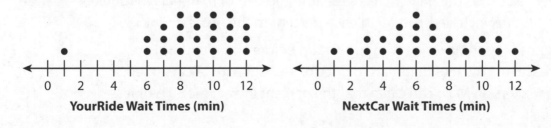

YourRide Wait Times (min)   NextCar Wait Times (min)

SOLUTION _____

_____

Performance Task

➤ **Answer the questions and show all your work on separate paper.**

- A local store, Makers on Main, sells tinker kits. The table below shows the cost of materials needed to make each tinker kit.

Tinker Kits				
Name of Kit	Cost of Materials	Price of Kit with Markup, Before Tax	Price of Kit with Markup, After 8% Tax	Percent Increase from Cost of Materials
Paint Sprayer	$13.00			
Mini Robot	$16.50			
Drink Warmer	$15.25			
Personalized Patch	$9.00			

The store's manager needs to set prices for each tinker kit with the requirements:

- Before tax is included, each kit's price must have a markup of 30% to 35% over the cost of materials. This price is rounded to the nearest increment of $0.25.

- An 8% tax must be added to each kit's price after the markup has been included.

Makers on Main claims that the percent increase from cost of materials is 50% or less. The manager calculates the percent increase from the cost of materials to the price of each kit with tax included, rounding each percent to the nearest tenth.

Determine the price of each tinker kit with its markup before and after tax. Find the percent increase from cost of materials to price of each kit with tax included. Explain whether Makers on Main can claim that the percent increase is 50% or less.

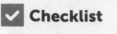

Checklist

Did you . . .

☐ calculate price of each tinker kit before and after tax, rounding correctly when necessary?

☐ find the percent increase, accurate to the nearest tenth?

☐ explain whether the advertisement is true?

Reflect

Use Mathematical Practices After you complete the task, choose one of the following questions to answer.

- **Use Reasoning** How do your strategies for calculating markup and tax compare?

- **Argue and Critique** How did you decide whether Makers on Main's claim is true?

Unit 6

Geometry

Solids, Triangles, and Angles

✓ **Self Check** | **Before starting this unit, check off the skills you know below. As you complete each lesson, see how many more skills you can check off!**

I can . . .	Before	After
Solve problems involving area and surface area.	☐	☐
Solve problems involving volume.	☐	☐
Describe plane sections of prisms, pyramids, and cylinders.	☐	☐
Solve problems with angles.	☐	☐
Draw triangles and quadrilaterals to meet given conditions.	☐	☐
Listen carefully during discussion in order to understand and explain another person's ideas.	☐	☐

Prepare for Solids, Triangles, and Angles

➤ **Think about what you already know about geometric figures. Compare two-dimensional and three-dimensional figures by writing words from the box in the Venn diagram.**

prism	pyramid	dimension	surface area	area	volume
trapezoid	triangle	angle	base	side	composite

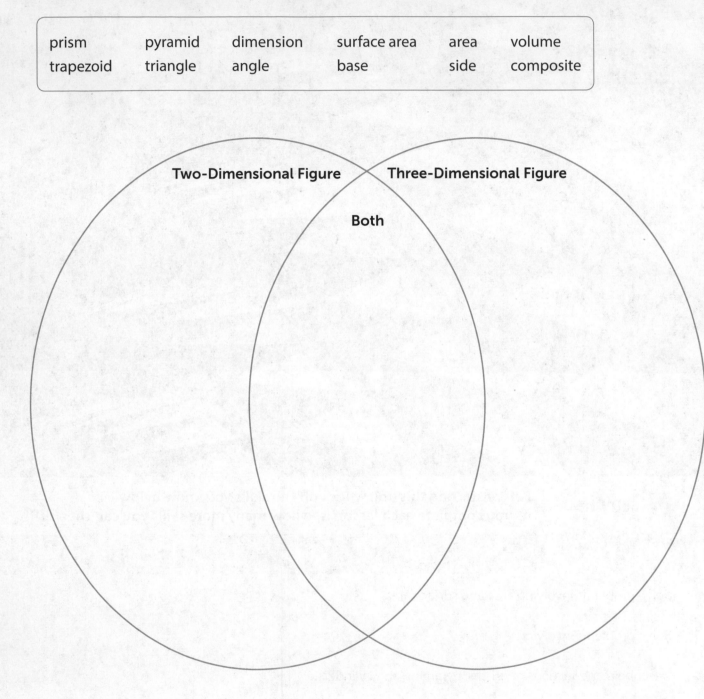

Meet with a partner and compare your answers. Discuss any answers you do not agree on. You may revise or add to your work as needed. With your partner, add more words to the Venn diagram.

Dear Family,

This week your student is learning how to use area and surface area to solve a variety of problems.

Some figures are made up of two or more other shapes, such as rectangles, squares, and triangles. One way to find the area of a figure like this is to find the area of those other shapes and add the areas together. In places where shapes overlap, you can make adjustments so that no area is added more than once.

The surface area of a three-dimensional figure is the sum of the areas of all its faces. You can find the surface area of any prism by finding the area of each face and then adding the areas. Your student will be solving problems like the one below.

What is the area of the figure at the right?

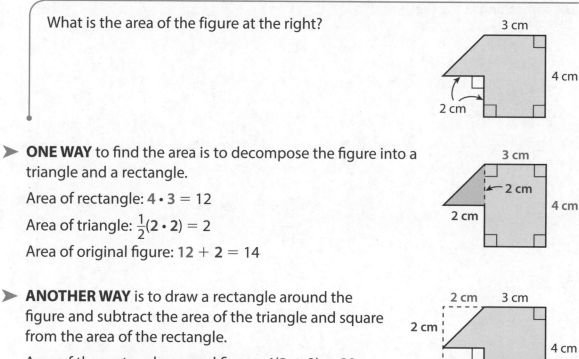

➤ **ONE WAY** to find the area is to decompose the figure into a triangle and a rectangle.

Area of rectangle: $4 \cdot 3 = 12$

Area of triangle: $\frac{1}{2}(2 \cdot 2) = 2$

Area of original figure: $12 + 2 = 14$

➤ **ANOTHER WAY** is to draw a rectangle around the figure and subtract the area of the triangle and square from the area of the rectangle.

Area of the rectangle around figure: $4(2 + 3) = 20$

Area of unshaded square: $2 \cdot 2 = 4$

Area of unshaded triangle: $\frac{1}{2}(2 \cdot 2) = 2$

Area of original figure: $20 - 4 - 2 = 14$

Both methods show that the area of the figure is 14 cm².

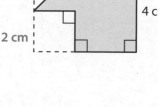

 Use the next page to start a conversation about area.

Activity Thinking About Area

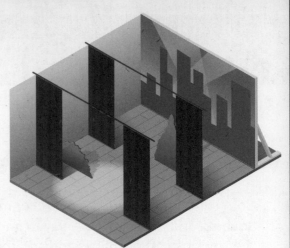

➤ **Do this activity together to investigate area in the real world.**

Have you ever seen a play or a musical?

Sometimes theater productions have elaborate sets that transform the stage into a particular setting.

The set designer has the challenge of designing all the pieces of the set so they not only help to tell the story but are also practical and affordable to build.

Set designers sometimes need to figure out the total amount of wallpaper or paint needed to cover an unusually shaped set piece. They can use the areas of smaller shapes that make up the area of the set piece to calculate how much wallpaper or paint they will need.

 When else would you want to know the area of something in the real world?

Explore Finding Composite Areas

Previously, you learned about area and surface area. In this lesson, you will learn about solving problems that involve area and surface area of composite figures.

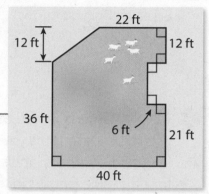

➤ **Use what you know to try to solve the problem below.**

Tyler's family builds a new pen on their dairy goat farm. The diagram represents the new pen. Each goat needs at least 50 ft² of space. What is the greatest number of goats the new pen can hold?

TRY IT

Math Toolkit grid paper, tracing paper

DISCUSS IT

Ask: How is the way you found the greatest number of goats similar to the way I did? How is it different?

Share: My method is similar to yours because . . . It is different because . . .

LESSON 25 Solve Problems Involving Area and Surface Area   **543**

CONNECT IT

1 **Look Back** What is the greatest number of goats the new pen can hold? Explain how you know.

2 **Look Ahead** To find the number of goats that can fit in the pen, you may have used the side lengths you knew to find an unknown side length. Sometimes a side length in a figure is labeled with a variable. You may be able to write expressions for other side lengths in terms of the variable.

  a. How do you know that $24 - x$ represents the length of $\overline{DE}$?

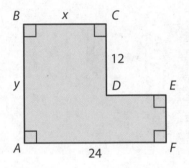

  b. Write an expression for the length of $\overline{EF}$ in terms of y.

  c. Explain how the expression $12x + 24(y - 12)$ represents the area of the figure.

  d. Explain how $24y - 12(24 - x)$ also represents the area of the figure.

3 **Reflect** How do you know that the expression $z + 17$ represents the length of $\overline{JR}$?

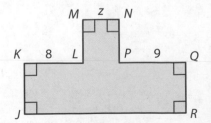

Name:

Prepare for Solving Problems Involving Area and Surface Area

① Think about what you know about three-dimensional figures and surface area. Fill in each box. Use words, numbers, and pictures. Show as many ideas as you can.

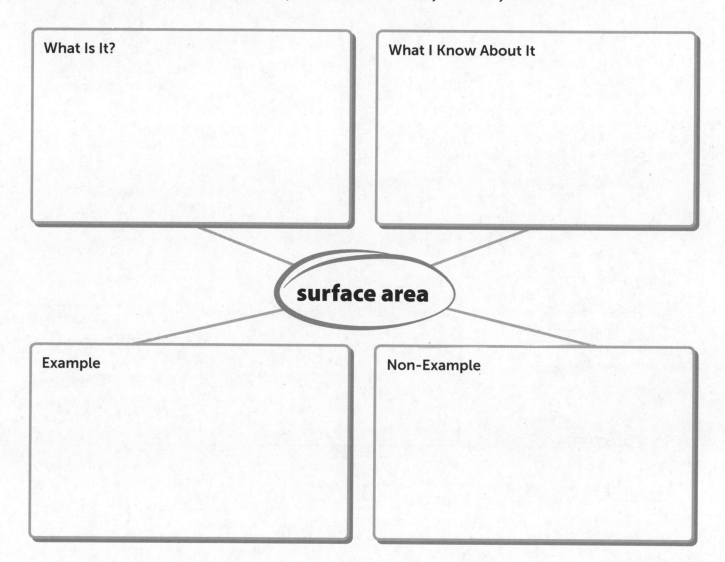

What Is It?

What I Know About It

surface area

Example

Non-Example

② Muna claims that the expression (8)(16) + (8)(12) + (16)(12) represents the surface area, in square inches, of the right rectangular prism shown. Is Muna correct? Explain.

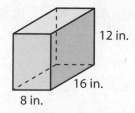

12 in.

16 in.

8 in.

3 A kitchen floor needs new tile. The shaded region in the diagram represents the floor that needs tile. The new tile costs $5.40 per square foot.

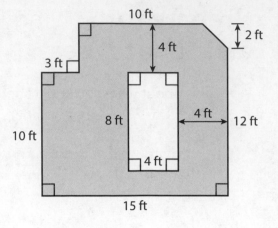

a. What is the total cost of the new tile for the kitchen? Show your work.

SOLUTION _____

b. Check your answer to problem 3a. Show your work.

Develop Solving Problems Involving Area

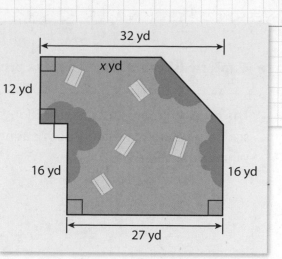

➤ **Read and try to solve the problem below.**

The diagram represents an outdoor eating space at a school. The area of the outdoor eating space is 750 yd². What is the value of x?

TRY IT

Math Toolkit grid paper, tracing paper

DISCUSS IT

Ask: What did you do first to find the value of x?

Share: First, I . . .

➤ **Explore different ways to solve problems involving area.**

The diagram represents an outdoor eating space at a school. The area of the outdoor eating space is 750 yd². What is the value of x?

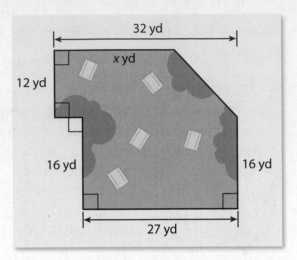

Picture It

You can decompose a composite figure into smaller shapes.

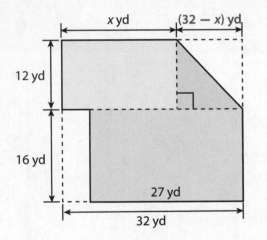

Model It

You can write and solve an equation to find an unknown measurement.

The sum of the areas of the two rectangles and the triangle is equal to the area of the eating space.

$$(x \cdot 12) + (27 \cdot 16) + \frac{1}{2}(32 - x)(12) = 750$$

$$12x + 432 + 6(32 - x) = 750$$

$$12x + 432 + 192 - 6x = 750$$

$$6x + 624 = 750$$

$$6x = 126$$

▶ **Use the problem from the previous page to help you understand how to solve problems involving area.**

1 Look at the shaded triangle in **Picture It**. Why can you use the expression $32 - x$ to represent the base of the triangle in yards?

2 Look at the first equation in **Model It**. Explain why the expression $\frac{1}{2}(32 - x)(12)$ represents the area of the shaded triangle.

3 Why does the sum of the areas of the two rectangles and the triangle equal the area of the composite figure?

4 What is the value of x? How does decomposing the figure help you find the value of x?

5 How can you use the area of a figure to find an unknown side length of the figure?

6 **Reflect** Think about all the models and strategies you have discussed today. Describe how one of them helped you better understand how to solve the **Try It** problem.

Apply It

➤ **Use what you learned to solve these problems.**

7 The diagram shows a plan for a deck. The area of the deck is 511 ft². What is the value of *x*? Show your work.

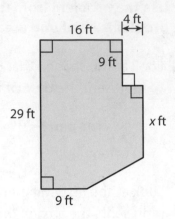

SOLUTION _____

8 Portions of three rectangles are shaded as shown. What is the area of the shaded region? Show your work.

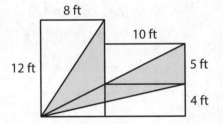

SOLUTION _____

9 The area of the shaded region of the figure is 48 units². What is *n*? Show your work.

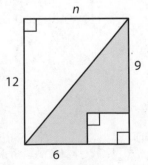

SOLUTION _____

Practice Solving Problems Involving Area

➤ **Study the Example showing how to solve a problem involving area. Then solve problems 1–5.**

Example

Each side of a square is divided into three equal sections. The square is then shaded as shown. What is the area of the shaded part?

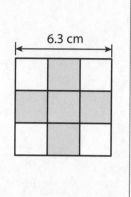
6.3 cm

You can think of the shaded region as 5 small squares of equal size.

Each side of the larger square is divided into thirds. So, each small square has side length 6.3 ÷ 3, or 2.1 cm.

So, each small square has area (2.1)(2.1), or 4.41 cm².

So, the area of the shaded region is 5(4.41), or 22.05 cm².

1 What is the area of the unshaded part of the square in the Example? Show your work.

SOLUTION _____

2 A portion of a rectangle is shaded as shown. The area of the shaded region is 78 in.². What is the value of x? Show your work.

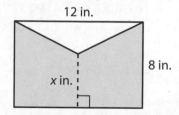
12 in.

8 in.

x in.

SOLUTION _____

3 An art class plans to paint part of a rectangular wall in the cafeteria and leave the rest of the wall white, as shown. The painted section will take up $\frac{2}{3}$ of the area of the wall. What is x? Show your work.

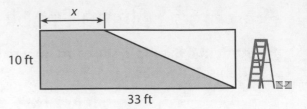

10 ft

33 ft

SOLUTION _____

4 The figure has area 193.5 cm². Which equation can be used to find the value of n, in centimeters?

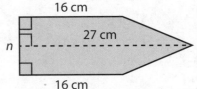

16 cm

27 cm

n

16 cm

A $16n + \frac{1}{2}(11n) = 193.5$

B $16n + \frac{1}{2}(16)(11) = 193.5$

C $27n - \frac{1}{2}(16n) = 193.5$

D $27n - \frac{1}{2}(16)(11) = 193.5$

5 The diagram shows the plan for a lawn. A landscaper needs to buy grass seed to cover the lawn. One bag of grass seed covers an area of 900 yd². How many bags of seed does the landscaper need to buy to cover the lawn? Show your work.

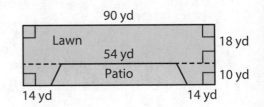

90 yd

Lawn

54 yd

18 yd

Patio

10 yd

14 yd

14 yd

SOLUTION _____

Develop Solving Problems Involving Surface Area

➤ **Read and try to solve the problem below.**

The right rectangular prism and the right triangular prism have the same surface area. What is the height in inches, *h*, of the triangular prism?

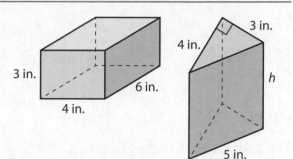

  TRY IT

Math Toolkit geometric solids, grid paper, isometric dot paper

➤ **Explore different ways to solve problems involving surface area.**

The right rectangular prism and the right triangular prism have the same surface area. What is the height in inches, *h*, of the triangular prism?

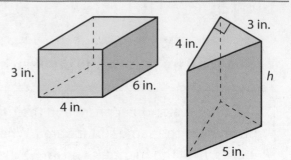

Picture It

You can draw the faces of a prism with their dimensions.

The bases of the triangular prism are the same shape and size.

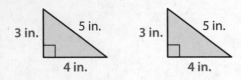

The other three faces of the triangular prism are rectangles.

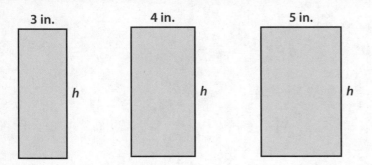

Model It

You can write and solve an equation to find an unknown measurement.

Surface area of rectangular prism: $2(4 \cdot 6) + 2(4 \cdot 3) + 2(6 \cdot 3) = 108$

Surface area of triangular prism: $2\left(\frac{1}{2}\right)(4 \cdot 3) + 3h + 4h + 5h = 12 + 12h$

Surface area of rectangular prism = Surface area of triangular prism

$$108 = 12 + 12h$$

$$96 = 12h$$

➤ **Use the problem from the previous page to help you understand how to solve problems involving surface area.**

1 Look at the expression for the surface area of the triangular prism in **Model It**.

Why is $\left(\frac{1}{2}\right)(4 \cdot 3)$ the only part of the expression that is multiplied by 2?

2 What is the height of the triangular prism? How does knowing the surface area of the prism help you find the height?

3 Another rectangular prism has bases with area 14 cm² each. Each of the other faces has area 15 cm². Why is this enough information to find the surface area of the prism?

4 **Reflect** Think about all the models and strategies you have discussed today. Describe how one of them helped you better understand how to solve problems involving surface area.

Apply It

➤ **Use what you learned to solve these problems.**

Large Popcorn   **Small Popcorn**

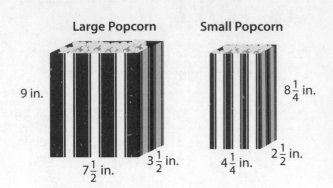

5 A company makes popcorn bags in two sizes. Each bag is shaped like a right rectangular prism, but it is open at the top. How many more square inches of paper are needed to make a large bag than a small bag? Show your work.

9 in. $3\frac{1}{2}$ in. $7\frac{1}{2}$ in. $8\frac{1}{4}$ in. $4\frac{1}{4}$ in. $2\frac{1}{2}$ in.

SOLUTION _____

6 Grace needs to cover a box shaped like a right rectangular prism with wrapping paper. Grace needs 10% more paper than the surface area of the box. How many square inches of wrapping paper does she need? Show your work.

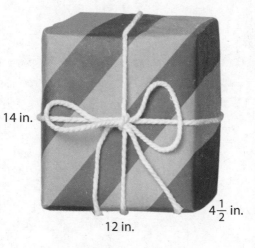

14 in.   12 in. $4\frac{1}{2}$ in.

SOLUTION _____

7 The surface area of the right triangular prism is 376.8 cm². What is the value of x? Show your work.

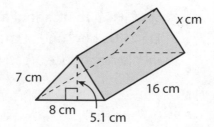

x cm   7 cm   8 cm   5.1 cm   16 cm

SOLUTION _____

Practice Solving Problems Involving Surface Area

➤ **Study the Example showing how to solve a problem involving surface area. Then solve problems 1–5.**

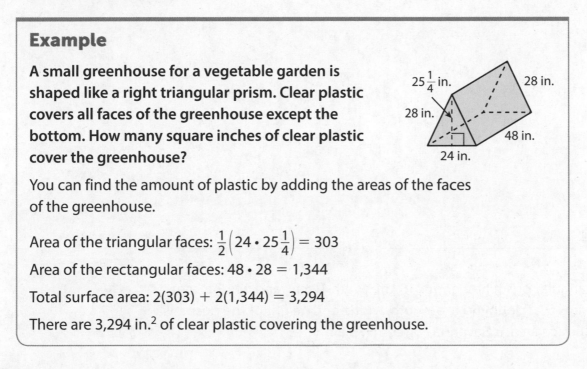

Example

A small greenhouse for a vegetable garden is shaped like a right triangular prism. Clear plastic covers all faces of the greenhouse except the bottom. How many square inches of clear plastic cover the greenhouse?

$25\frac{1}{4}$ in.   28 in.

28 in.

48 in.

24 in.

You can find the amount of plastic by adding the areas of the faces of the greenhouse.

Area of the triangular faces: $\frac{1}{2}\left(24 \cdot 25\frac{1}{4}\right) = 303$

Area of the rectangular faces: $48 \cdot 28 = 1{,}344$

Total surface area: $2(303) + 2(1{,}344) = 3{,}294$

There are 3,294 in.^{2} of clear plastic covering the greenhouse.

---

1 **a.** The expression $2(303) + 2(1{,}344)$ can be used to find the area of the plastic in the Example. Why is each term multiplied by 2?

b. Teresa writes the expression $2(303 + 1{,}344 + 1{,}152)$ to find the total surface area of the greenhouse, including the bottom. Explain why her expression is incorrect.

2 A right rectangular prism has length 10 in. and width 8 in. The surface area of the prism is 376 in.^{2}. Which equation can be used to find the height in inches, h, of the prism?

A $80h = 376$

B $160 + 18h = 376$

C $80 + 18h = 376$

D $160 + 36h = 376$

3 The swimming pool at an apartment complex is shaped like a right prism. The bottom and sides of the pool need to be repainted. One gallon of paint covers up to 125 ft². Paint can only be purchased in whole gallons. How many gallons of paint will the painters need to purchase? Show your work.

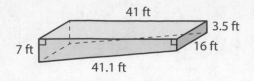

41 ft
3.5 ft
7 ft
16 ft
41.1 ft

SOLUTION _____

4 A right rectangular prism has length 15 cm, width 10 cm, and height 5 cm. Savanna claims that doubling the length, width, and height of the prism will double its surface area. Is Savanna correct? Explain.

5 The awning for a window is shaped like a right triangular prism. The fabric of the awning covers one rectangular and two triangular faces of the prism, as shown. The fabric for the awning costs $0.55 per square foot. What is the cost of fabric for the awning? Show your work.

3.6 ft
3 ft
8 ft
2 ft

SOLUTION _____

Develop Solving Problems Involving Surface Area of Composite Figures

➤ **Read and try to solve the problem below.**

A company sells cardboard scratching blocks for cats. The block is shaped like a right rectangular prism with a rectangular hole cut through its center. A cat can scratch on any face of the block, including the bottom and inside faces. What is the total area of the block's scratching surface?

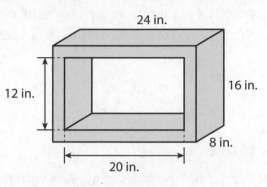

24 in.

16 in.

12 in.

8 in.

20 in.

 TRY IT

Math Toolkit dot paper, geometric solids, grid paper, isometric dot paper

➤ **Explore different ways to solve problems involving surface area of composite figures.**

A company sells cardboard scratching blocks for cats. The block is shaped like a right rectangular prism with a rectangular hole cut through its center. A cat can scratch on any face of the block, including the bottom and inside faces. What is the total area of the block's scratching surface?

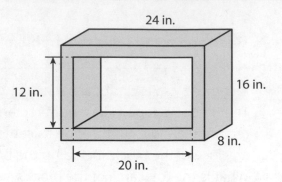

Picture It

You can draw the faces of a figure with their dimensions.

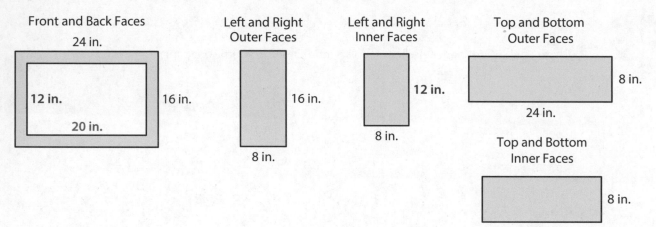

Front and Back Faces	Left and Right Outer Faces	Left and Right Inner Faces	Top and Bottom Outer Faces

Top and Bottom Inner Faces

Model It

You can think of the total surface area as the area of the outside surfaces plus the area of the inside surfaces.

Total surface area = area of outer faces + area of inner faces

Outer Faces		Inner Faces	
Left and right	2(8 · 16)	Left and right	2(8 · **12**)
Top and bottom	2(24 · 8)	Top and bottom	2(**20** · 8)
Front and back	2[(24 · 16) − (**20 · 12**)]		

➤ **Use the problem from the previous page to help you understand how to solve problems involving surface area of composite figures.**

1 Look at the drawing of the front and back faces in **Picture It**. How does **Model It** show how to find their area?

2 What is the total area of the block's scratching surface? Would the surface area of the block be greater or less if it did not have a hole? Explain.

3 You can think of the block as a rectangular prism that had a smaller rectangular prism cut out of it. Felipe claims that you can add the surface areas of the two prisms to find the total surface area of the block. Why is Felipe incorrect?

4 How is finding the surface area of a three-dimensional figure with a hole in it like finding the surface area of a solid three-dimensional figure? How is it different?

5 **Reflect** Think about all the models and strategies you have discussed today. Describe how one of them helped you better understand how to solve the **Try It** problem.

Apply It

➤ **Use what you learned to solve these problems.**

6 A garden shed is shaped like a right prism. The shed has one 7 ft-by-6 ft rectangular door and two 3 ft-by-1$\frac{1}{2}$ ft rectangular windows. The outer walls will be painted, but not the roof, door, or windows. What is the total surface area to be painted? Show your work.

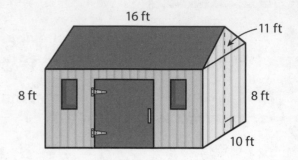

SOLUTION _____

7 The three-dimensional figure shown is composed of right prisms. What is the total surface area of the figure?

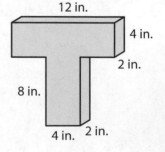

A 510 in.²

B 642 in.²

C 606 in.²

D 678 in.²

8 Tyrone makes a wooden letter T to hang on his bedroom wall. The T is a right prism. Tyrone plans to cover all the faces except the back with fabric. How many square inches of fabric will he need? Show your work.

SOLUTION _____

Practice Solving Problems Involving Surface Area of Composite Figures

➤ Study the Example showing how to solve problems involving surface area of composite figures. Then solve problems 1–4.

Example

The three-dimensional figure shown is composed of right prisms. What is the total surface area of the figure?

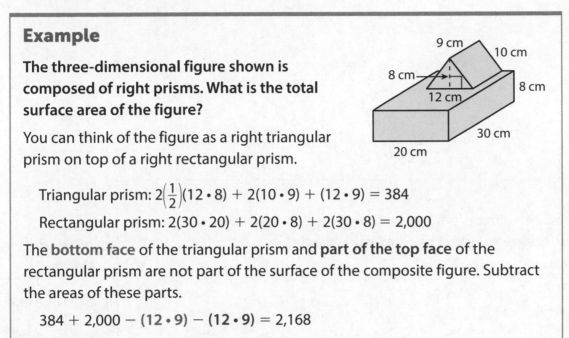

You can think of the figure as a right triangular prism on top of a right rectangular prism.

Triangular prism: $2\left(\frac{1}{2}\right)(12 \cdot 8) + 2(10 \cdot 9) + (12 \cdot 9) = 384$

Rectangular prism: $2(30 \cdot 20) + 2(20 \cdot 8) + 2(30 \cdot 8) = 2{,}000$

The **bottom face** of the triangular prism and **part of the top face** of the rectangular prism are not part of the surface of the composite figure. Subtract the areas of these parts.

$384 + 2{,}000 - (12 \cdot 9) - (12 \cdot 9) = 2{,}168$

The total surface area of the figure is 2,168 cm².

1 **a.** Why is $(12 \cdot 9)$ subtracted twice in the expression for the surface area of the figure from the Example?

b. Consider the figure in the Example. Suppose the triangular prism was moved so that a triangular base touches the rectangular prism instead. Would the total surface area of the figure increase or decrease? Explain your reasoning.

2 All faces of a bench except the two faces that rest on the ground will be coated with a water-resistant paint. The bench is a right prism. What is the total area to be coated with the paint? Show your work.

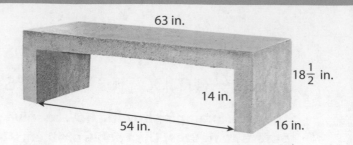

63 in.

$18\frac{1}{2}$ in.

14 in.

54 in.

16 in.

SOLUTION _____

3 All sides of the three-dimensional figure shown meet at right angles. What is the surface area of the three-dimensional figure? Show your work.

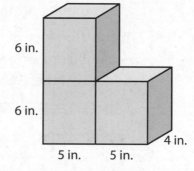

6 in.

6 in.

5 in.   5 in.

4 in.

SOLUTION _____

4 Indira makes a wooden box without a lid. All the faces of the box meet at right angles. Indira plans to paint all surfaces of the box, including the inside and outside. The interior of the box has length 13 in., width 8 in., and depth 7 in. Indira can cover up to 1,350 in.^{2} with $\frac{1}{2}$ cup of paint. Will she need more than $\frac{1}{2}$ cup of paint to cover the box? Explain how you know.

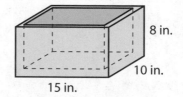

8 in.

10 in.

15 in.

Refine Solving Problems Involving Area and Surface Area

➤ **Complete the Example below. Then solve problems 1–9.**

Example

The four walls in a classroom need to be painted. The room is 27 ft long, 32 ft wide, and 10 ft high. The room has two windows, each with width 3 ft 9 in. and height 2 ft 1 in. The door has width 3 ft and height 6 ft 10 in. One gallon can of paint covers about 400 ft². Estimate the number of gallon cans of paint needed for the walls.

Look at how you could show your work using rounding.

Round dimensions to the nearest foot and find each area.

Area of the walls: $2(27 \cdot 10) + 2(32 \cdot 10) = 1{,}180$

Area of the door: $2(4 \cdot 2) = 16$

Area of the windows: $(3 \cdot 7) = 21$

Area of walls minus area of doors and windows:

$1{,}180 - 16 - 21 = 1{,}143$

SOLUTION _____

PAIR/SHARE
How would your estimate change if the ceiling of the classroom also needed to be painted? Why?

Apply It

1 The right prism has surface area 536.4 cm². What is the value of x? Show your work.

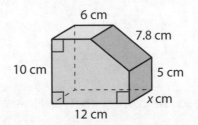

6 cm
7.8 cm
10 cm
5 cm
x cm
12 cm

CONSIDER THIS...
The front face can be decomposed into two rectangles and a triangle.

PAIR/SHARE
How can you check that you accounted for all the faces of the prism?

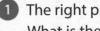

SOLUTION _____

2 Ignacio makes a display shelf from 4 wooden boards. All angles formed by the boards are right angles. Ignacio plans to stain all faces of the shelf, except the back face, which will be against the wall. What is the total area Ignacio will stain? Show your work.

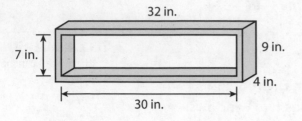

SOLUTION _____

3 The figure at the right has area 125 cm². Which equation can be used to find the value of x?

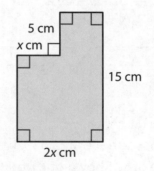

5 cm
x cm
15 cm
2x cm

A $125 = 30x - 5$

B $35x = 125$

C $25x = 125$

D $125 \div 15 = 2x$

Josephine chose B as the correct answer. How might she have gotten that answer?

4 The center of a rectangular courtyard has a circular fountain with radius 3 ft. All paths in the courtyard are 4 ft wide. Each path will be covered with gravel. The gravel needed to cover 1 ft² weighs about 15 lb. Ju-long estimates that the gravel needed to cover the paths will weigh less than 2,000 lb. Is Ju-long's estimate reasonable? Explain.

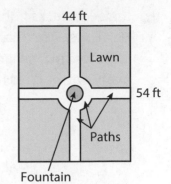

44 ft

Lawn

54 ft

Paths

Fountain

5 The prism shown is made of two cubes. What is its total surface area? Show your work.

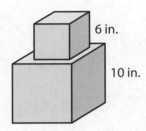

6 in.

10 in.

SOLUTION _____

6 The diagram shows a plan for a rectangular house with an attached porch. The combined area of the house and the porch is 733 ft². What is the value of x? Show your work.

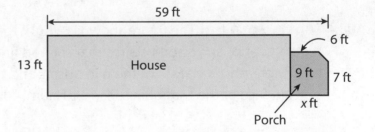

59 ft

13 ft

House

6 ft

9 ft

7 ft

x ft

Porch

SOLUTION _____

7 Kadeem stacks right rectangular prisms like the one shown. He aligns each prism on top of the previous prism to make a larger prism. The larger prism has surface area 288 in.². How many prisms does Kadeem stack? Show your work.

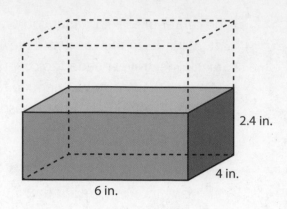

2.4 in.

4 in.

6 in.

SOLUTION _____

8 The right prism has surface area 132 cm². What is x?

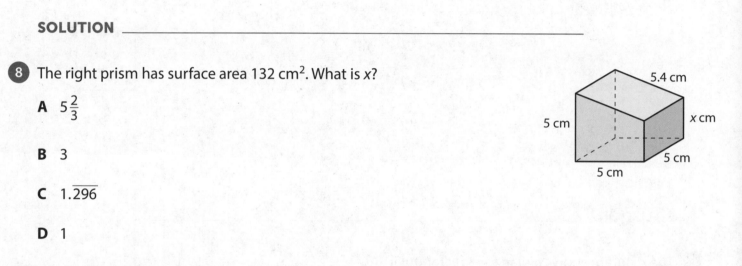

5.4 cm

5 cm

x cm

5 cm

5 cm

A $5\frac{2}{3}$

B 3

C $1.\overline{296}$

D 1

9 **Math Journal** The figure shown is a right triangular prism on top of a right rectangular prism. Naomi claims that she can find the surface area of the figure by adding the surface areas of the two prisms and then subtracting the area of the bottom face of the triangular prism. Is Naomi correct? Explain.

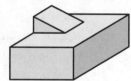

✓ End of Lesson Checklist

☐ **INTERACTIVE GLOSSARY** Write a new entry for *claim*. Tell what you do when you *claim* something about a three-dimensional figure.

☐ **SELF CHECK** Go back to the Unit 6 Opener and see what you can check off.

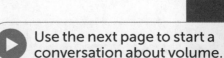

Solve Problems Involving Volume

Dear Family,

This week your student is learning to solve problems involving volumes of three-dimensional figures. The volume of a three-dimensional figure can mean the amount of space the figure occupies or the amount of space inside the figure. Volume is measured in cubic units, like cubic inches (in.³) or cubic centimeters (cm³).

You can find the volume of a right prism by multiplying the area of its base by its height. You can also use the volume of a figure to find an unknown dimension. Your student will be solving problems like the one below.

> The drawing shows a birdhouse Fernando built.
> What is the volume the birdhouse occupies?

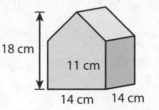

18 cm

11 cm

14 cm   14 cm

➤ **ONE WAY** to find the volume is to decompose the figure into other prisms and add the volumes of those prisms.

Volume = **triangular prism** + **rectangular prism**
       volume   **volume**

$$= \frac{1}{2}(14)(7)(14) + (14)(11)(14)$$

$$= 2{,}842$$

7 cm

14 cm   14 cm

11 cm

14 cm   14 cm

➤ **ANOTHER WAY** is to find the area of the base of the prism and then multiply it by the height of the prism.

Area of base = **area of triangle** + **area of rectangle**

$$= \frac{1}{2}(14)(7) + (14)(11)$$

$$= 203$$

7 cm

11 cm

14 cm

Now multiply the area of the base by the height of the prism, 14.

Volume of prism: (203)(14) = 2,842

Both methods show that the volume the birdhouse occupies is 2,842 cm³.

> ▶ Use the next page to start a conversation about volume.

Activity Thinking About Volume

➤ **Do this activity together to investigate volume in the real world.**

Water Tank

Have you ever wondered where firefighters get the water they use to put out fires? Some fire engines have a water tank to store water. When the water supply in the tank runs out, firefighters can use other sources of water, like fire hydrants.

Water tanks need to hold as much water as possible while fitting in the space available in the fire engine.

Not all fire engines use tanks with the same shape. The most common shape is a rectangular or T-shaped tank, which is made of right rectangular prisms.

Some water tanks can hold 134 cubic feet, or 1,000 gallons, of water!

? Where else do you use volume in the real world?

Explore Finding Volumes of Right Prisms

Previously, you learned about surface area of three-dimensional figures. In this lesson, you will learn about volume.

➤ **Use what you know to try to solve the problem below.**

The figure at the right is a right rectangular prism. The volume of the shaded part is 102 in.³. What is the volume of the right rectangular prism? How do you know?

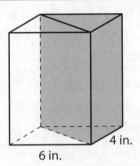

4 in.

6 in.

 TRY IT  **Math Toolkit** geometric solids, grid paper, isometric dot paper

DISCUSS IT

Ask: What was the first thing you did to solve the problem?

Share: First, I . . .

◎ **Learning Target** SMP 1, SMP 2, SMP 3, SMP 4, SMP 5, SMP 6, SMP 8
Solve real-world and mathematical problems involving area, volume and surface area of two- and three-dimensional objects composed of triangles, quadrilaterals, polygons, cubes, and right prisms.

CONNECT IT

1 **Look Back** What is the volume of the right rectangular prism? How do you know?

2 **Look Ahead** In the **Try It**, a right rectangular prism was divided into two right triangular prisms. The right rectangular prism at the right is also divided into two identical right triangular prisms. It has volume 72 cm³.

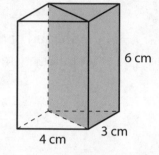

6 cm

3 cm

4 cm

a. What is half of the volume of the right rectangular prism?

b. What is the area of the base of each right triangular prism? How does it compare to the base of the right rectangular prism?

c. You can use the formula $V = Bh$ to find the volume of any right prism. Why does the expression $\left(\frac{1}{2} \cdot 4 \cdot 3\right)(6)$ represent the volume of each right triangular prism in the figure?

d. What is the volume of each right triangular prism? How does that compare to the volume of the right rectangular prism?

e. Another prism has the same base as the one shown, but has a height of 3 cm. How does the volume of that prism compare to the one shown?

3 **Reflect** Why can you double the volume of a right prism by doubling either the height or the area of the base?

Prepare for Solving Problems Involving Volume

1 Think about what you know about volume and three-dimensional figures. Fill in each box. Use words, numbers, and pictures. Show as many ideas as you can.

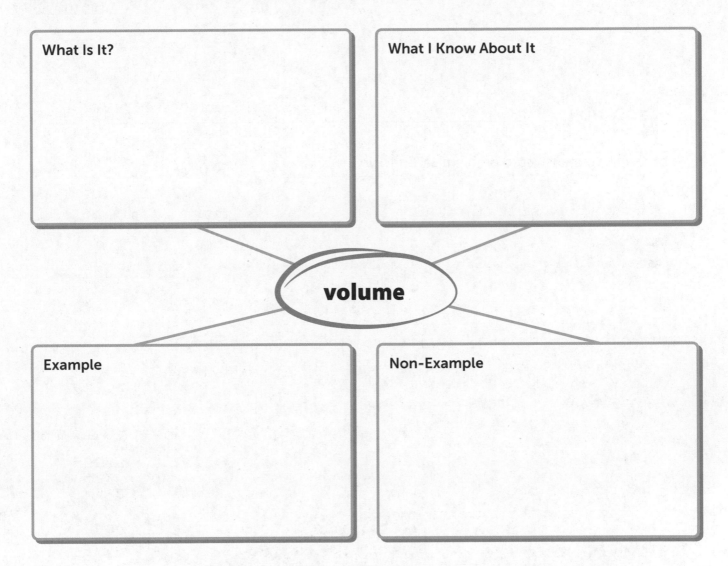

What Is It?

What I Know About It

volume

Example

Non-Example

2 Badru claims that any two right rectangular prisms with the same length, width, and height have the same volume. Do you agree? Justify your answer.

3 The shaded part of the cube is $\frac{1}{16}$ in.^{3}.

  a. What is the volume of the cube? Show your work.

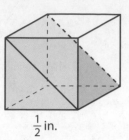

$\frac{1}{2}$ in.

SOLUTION _____

  b. Check your answer to problem 3a. Show your work.

houses made of cubes in Rotterdam, Netherlands

Develop Solving Problems Involving Volume of Right Prisms

➤ **Read and try to solve the problem below.**

Troy uses colored sand to make sand art. The storage container for his sand is shaped like a right square prism. He pours some of the sand into a display container shaped like a right triangular prism. When he is done, the height of the sand left in the storage container is 4 in. What is the height of the sand in the display container?

Storage Container

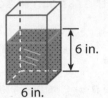

6 in.

6 in.

Display Container

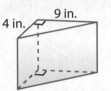

9 in.

4 in.

TRY IT

Math Toolkit dot paper, geometric solids, grid paper, isometric dot paper

DISCUSS IT

Ask: How did you use what you know about prisms?

Share: I used what I know about prisms to . . .

➤ **Explore different ways to use volumes of right prisms.**

Troy uses colored sand to make sand art. The storage container for his sand is shaped like a right square prism. He pours some of the sand into a display container shaped like a right triangular prism. When he is done, the height of the sand left in the storage container is 4 in. What is the height of the sand in the display container?

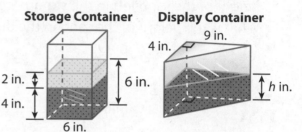

Picture It

You can use a drawing to make sense of the problem.

You can think of the sand removed from the storage container as a right square prism with height 2 in.

This sand is poured into the triangular display container. The sand changes shape, but its total volume stays the same. Let *h* represent the unknown height.

Model It

You can use a formula to find the unknown height.

The area of the base of the storage container is (**6 • 6**) in.²

The area of the base of the display container is $\left(\frac{1}{2} \cdot 9 \cdot 4\right)$ in.²

Volume of sand removed from storage container:

$V = Bh$

$\quad = (6 \cdot 6)(2)$

$\quad = 72$

Volume of sand poured into display container:

$V = Bh$

$72 = \left(\frac{1}{2} \cdot 9 \cdot 4\right)h$

$72 = 18h$

➤ **Use the problem from the previous page to help you understand how to use volumes of right prisms.**

1 Look at **Picture It**. Why can you think of the sand removed from the storage container as a square prism with height 2 in.?

2 Look at **Model It**. How does knowing the volume of sand removed from the storage container help you find the height of the sand in the display container?

3 What is the height of the sand in the display container? Why can you find it by using the equation $(6 \cdot 6 \cdot 2) = \frac{1}{2}(9 \cdot 4)h$?

4 Sometimes you know the dimensions of a prism and need to find the volume. Sometimes you know the volume of a prism and need to find a dimension. How can you use the formula $V = Bh$ in either situation?

5 **Reflect** Think about all the models and strategies you have discussed today. Describe how one of them helped you better understand how to solve the **Try It** problem.

Apply It

➤ **Use what you learned to solve these problems.**

6 The volume of the right trapezoidal prism is 60 cm³. What is its height? Show your work.

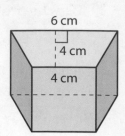

6 cm

4 cm

4 cm

SOLUTION _____

7 The diagram shows the bases of three right prisms.

    a. Suppose the prisms all have the same height. Which prism has the greatest volume? Explain.

                                                      A   B   C

    b. Suppose the prisms all have the same volume. Which prism has the greatest height? Explain.

8 This camping tent has the shape of a right triangular prism. The volume the tent occupies is 46.8 ft³. What is the width, *x*, of the opening of the tent? Show your work.

3 ft

6.5 ft

x

SOLUTION _____

Name:

Practice Solving Problems Involving Volume of Right Prisms

▶ **Study the Example showing how to solve a problem about the volume of a right prism. Then solve problems 1–5.**

Example

The right triangular prism shown has volume 240 m³. What is x?

The base of the prism is a right triangle. Use the volume formula for a prism.

$$V = Bh$$

$$240 = \left(\frac{1}{2} \cdot x \cdot 4\right)(12)$$

$$240 = 24x$$

$$10 = x$$

x is 10 m.

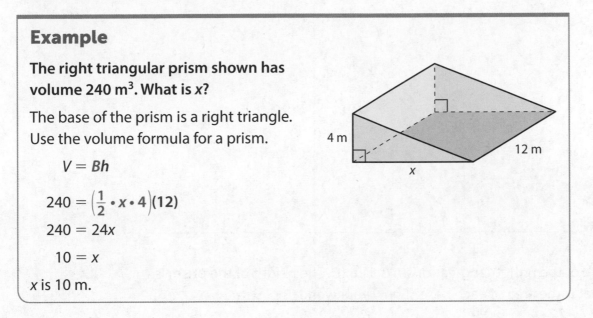

4 m

12 m

x

1 Another right triangular prism has the same base as the prism in the Example. The height of this prism is 8 m. What is the volume of the prism? Show your work.

SOLUTION _____

2 Suppose you double the length, width, and height of a rectangular prism. What is the volume of the new prism in terms of the original prism? How do you know?

3 Pure gold is formed into bricks that are right trapezoidal prisms. The dimensions of a gold brick are shown. What is the volume of the gold brick? Show your work.

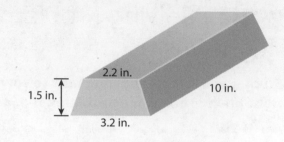

SOLUTION _____

4 The volume of the right triangular prism is 91.8 ft³. The height of the prism is 10.8 ft. What is the area of each base? Show your work.

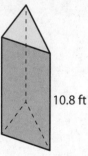

10.8 ft

SOLUTION _____

5 A right rectangular prism has a square base with sides $\frac{1}{2}$ in. long. The volume of the prism is $\frac{3}{8}$ in.³. What is the height of the prism? Show your work.

SOLUTION _____

Develop Solving Problems Involving Volume of Composite Figures

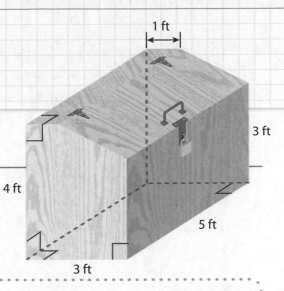

➤ **Read and try to solve the problem below.**

Alita designs a storage bin for horse feed. Her design is at the right. What will be the volume the storage bin occupies?

 TRY IT

Math Toolkit dot paper, geometric solids, grid paper, isometric dot paper

➤ **Explore different ways to find the volume of a composite figure.**

Alita designs a storage bin for horse feed. Her design is at the right. What will be the volume the storage bin occupies?

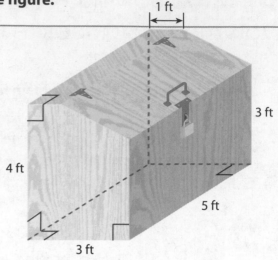

1 ft

3 ft

4 ft

5 ft

3 ft

Model It

You can decompose a prism into smaller prisms.

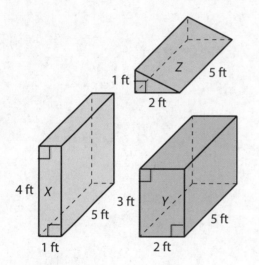

Volume of bin = **Volume of** + **Volume of** + **Volume of**
                Prism X   **Prism Y**   **Prism Z**

$$= (1 \cdot 4)(5) + (2 \cdot 3)(5) + \left(\frac{1}{2} \cdot 2 \cdot 1\right)(5)$$

$$= 20 + 30 + 5$$

Model It

You can decompose the base of a prism into two-dimensional figures.

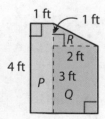

1 ft   1 ft

4 ft

R

2 ft

P   3 ft

Q

Area of base of bin = **Area of P** + **Area of Q** + Area of R

$$= (1 \cdot 4) + (2 \cdot 3) + \frac{1}{2}(2 \cdot 1)$$

$$= 4 + 6 + 1$$

$$= 11$$

The area of the base of the bin is 11 ft². The height of the bin is 5 ft.

Volume of the bin = Bh

$$= 11 \cdot 5$$

➤ **Use the problem from the previous page to help you understand how to find the volume of composite figures.**

1 Look at the first **Model It**. How can dividing the storage bin into prisms help you find its volume?

2 Look at the **Model Its**. How are the strategies for finding the volume the storage bin occupies similar? How are they different?

3 What is the volume the storage bin occupies? How could you use subtraction rather than addition to find the volume?

4 How is finding the volume of a composite three-dimensional figure like finding the area of a composite two-dimensional figure?

5 **Reflect** Think about all the models and strategies you have discussed today. Describe how one of them helped you better understand finding volumes of composite figures.

Apply It

➤ **Use what you learned to solve these problems.**

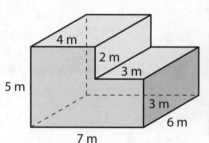

6 One part of a robotic arm is made from a right rectangular prism with a smaller right rectangular prism cut out of it, as shown. What is the volume occupied by the robotic arm part? Show your work.

SOLUTION _____

7 All faces of the prism meet at right angles. Which expressions represent the volume of the prism in cubic meters? Select all that apply.

A $(4 \cdot 5)(6) + (3 \cdot 3)(6)$

B $(2 \cdot 7 + 3 \cdot 7)(6)$

C $(3 \cdot 3 \cdot 6) + (3 \cdot 7 \cdot 6) + (2 \cdot 7 \cdot 6)$

D $(4 \cdot 2 + 7 \cdot 3)(6)$

E $(5 \cdot 7 \cdot 6) - (2 \cdot 3 \cdot 6)$

8 All faces of the prism meet at right angles. What is the volume of the prism? Show your work.

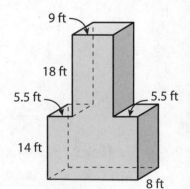

SOLUTION _____

Practice Solving Problems Involving Volume of Composite Figures

➤ **Study the Example showing how to find the volume of a composite figure. Then solve problems 1–4.**

Example

What is the volume of the right prism?

The base of the prism is a pentagon. You can think of the pentagon as a triangle and a rectangle to find its area.

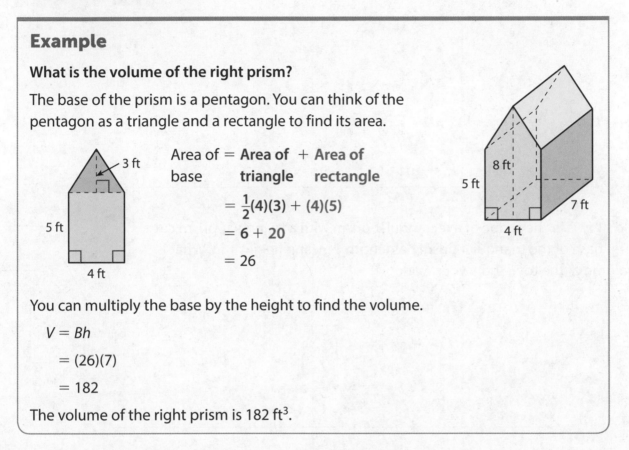

Area of = **Area of** + **Area of**
base   **triangle**   **rectangle**

$= \frac{1}{2}(4)(3) + (4)(5)$

$= 6 + 20$

$= 26$

You can multiply the base by the height to find the volume.

$V = Bh$

$= (26)(7)$

$= 182$

The volume of the right prism is 182 ft³.

---

1 Juan solved the problem in the Example by dividing the figure into a triangular prism and a rectangular prism. Show how to find the volume this way.

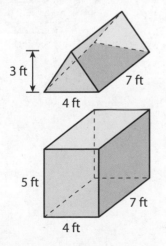

2 What is the volume of space occupied by the birdhouse?
Show your work.

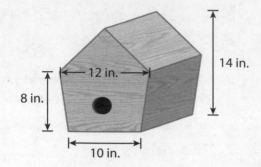

SOLUTION _____

3 A child's toy is in the shape of a rectangular prism with a triangular prism cut
out. The base of the triangular prism has length 1 in. and height 1 in. What is
the volume of the toy? Show your work.

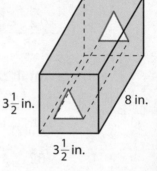

SOLUTION _____

4 Tessa has a plan for a set of stairs made of concrete, as shown. Each stair
is the same width and taller than the previous one by the same amount.
What is the volume of concrete needed for the set of stairs?
Show your work.

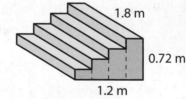

SOLUTION _____

Refine Solving Problems Involving Volume

➤ **Complete the Example below. Then solve problems 1–9.**

Example

The surface area of the right rectangular prism is 62 cm². What is the volume of the prism?

Look at how you could show your work using the surface area to find the height of the prism.

$$2(3 \cdot h) + 2(2 \cdot h) + 2(3 \cdot 2) = 62$$
$$6h + 4h + 12h = 62$$
$$10h + 12 = 62$$
$$10h = 50$$
$$h = 5$$

The height of the prism is 5 cm and the area of the base is 6 cm².

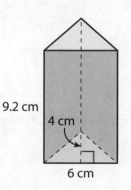

h

3 cm   2 cm

SOLUTION _____

CONSIDER THIS...
You can use the same measurements to find both the surface area and the volume of a prism.

PAIR/SHARE
What is another expression you could write for the surface area of the prism?

Apply It

1 Fadil makes a candle. He has a block of wax shaped like a rectangular prism 8 cm long, 6 cm wide, and 2 cm high. He melts the block of wax and pours it into the mold shown. What is the height of the empty space in the mold after Fadil adds the wax? Show your work.

9.2 cm

4 cm

6 cm

CONSIDER THIS...
The volume of the wax does not change when it is melted and poured into the mold.

PAIR/SHARE
How could you find the maximum volume of wax that Fadil could pour into the mold?

SOLUTION _____

2 The surface area of the right triangular prism is 120 ft². What is the volume of the prism? Show your work.

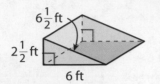

6½ ft
2½ ft
6 ft

SOLUTION _____

3 What is the volume of the composite figure?

A 68 cm³

B 376 cm³

C 408 cm³

D 588 cm³

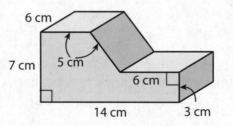

6 cm
7 cm 5 cm
6 cm
14 cm   3 cm

Rolando chose A as the correct answer. How might he have gotten that answer?

4 Jia designs a vase in the shape of a triangular prism. She decides to make a smaller version of the vase. She decreases the area of the base by 50%. She decreases the height by 50%. By what percent does the volume of the vase change? Show your work.

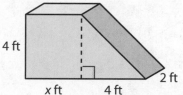

SOLUTION _____

5 Which expressions represent the volume of the figure in cubic feet? Select all that apply.

A $\frac{1}{2} \cdot 4(x + x + 4)$

B $2(4x + 8)$

C $\left(\frac{1}{2} \cdot 4 \cdot 4\right)(2) + (4x)(2)$

D $4(x + 4)(2)$

E $2(4x + 2x)$

6 Which prisms, if any, have the same volume? Show your work.

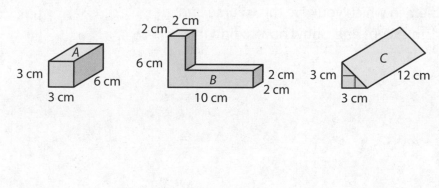

SOLUTION _____

7 Amelia has a music box that is shaped like a right rectangular prism. She wants to pack the music box into a container, with 1 in. of packing material between each face of the music box and the container. A bag contains 200 in.³ of packing material. How many bags of packing material will Amelia need? Show your work.

8 in.

10 in.

6 in.

SOLUTION _____

8 The volume of the right prism is 120 ft³. What is the surface area of the prism, in square feet?

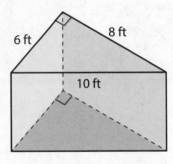

6 ft

8 ft

10 ft

9 **Math Journal** Write a problem in which you give the volume and all the dimensions of a right prism except one. Show how to find the unknown dimension.

✓ End of Lesson Checklist

☐ **INTERACTIVE GLOSSARY** Write a new entry for *strategy*. Tell what you do when you use a *strategy* to solve a problem.

☐ **SELF CHECK** Go back to the Unit 6 Opener and see what you can check off.

Dear Family,

This week your student is learning about plane sections. A **plane section** is a two-dimensional shape that is exposed when a plane slices through a three-dimensional figure. The shape and size of a plane section depend on the angle at which the plane slices and how many faces of the figure the plane slices through.

A plane section of a three-dimensional figure is not always the same shape as one of the faces of the figure, as shown below.

Plane Parallel to Base

Plane Perpendicular to Base

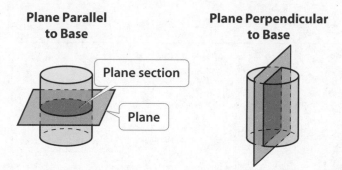

A horizontal slice through the **cylinder** results in a circular plane section. A vertical slice through the same cylinder results in a rectangular plane section.

Your student will be solving problems like the one below.

How can you slice the square pyramid shown to get a square plane section?

➤ **ONE WAY** to find a plane section is to picture slicing a figure with a plane.

➤ **ANOTHER WAY** is to picture the faces that result after slicing a figure.

Both methods show that you can slice the pyramid parallel to its base to get a square plane section.

▶ Use the next page to start a conversation about plane sections.

Activity Thinking About Plane Sections

➤ **Do this activity together to investigate plane sections in the real world.**

Have you ever made something out of wood?

Carpenters build and repair wooden structures, furniture, and other objects.

Carpenters often make cuts of different sizes and angles with saws and other equipment. This means the faces of wood scraps, or the leftover wood, can be all kinds of geometric shapes!

? Where else do you see plane sections in the real world?

Explore Plane Sections of Three-Dimensional Figures

Previously, you learned about surface area and volume of three-dimensional figures. In this lesson, you will learn about plane sections of three-dimensional figures.

traditional tagine cooking pot from Morocco

➤ **Use what you know to try to solve the problem below.**

Jamal is learning to make a tagine pot. He first needs to cut a piece from a block of clay shaped like a right square prism. The dashed segments show three ways Jamal could slice through the clay with a wire. Each slice leaves a flat surface. What is the shape of each surface?

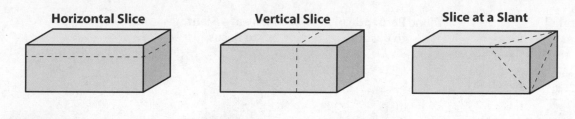

Horizontal Slice   **Vertical Slice**   **Slice at a Slant**

TRY IT

🖊 **Math Toolkit** geometric solids, isometric dot paper

DISCUSS IT

Ask: What did you do first to find the shape each slice makes? Why?

Share: First, I . . . because . . .

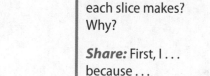

Learning Target   SMP 1, SMP 2, SMP 3, SMP 4, SMP 5, SMP 6, SMP 7
Describe the two-dimensional figures that result from slicing three-dimensional figures, as in plane sections of right rectangular prisms and right rectangular pyramids.

CONNECT IT

1 **Look Back** What shape is the flat surface made by each of Jamal's slices? Is each two-dimensional shape the same as one of the faces of the block? Explain.

2 **Look Ahead** When you make a straight cut through a three-dimensional figure, you expose a two-dimensional shape called a **plane section**. You can think of a plane section as the intersection of a plane and a three-dimensional figure. A plane is a two-dimensional surface that extends forever. Below are three ways a plane can slice through a right **cylinder**.

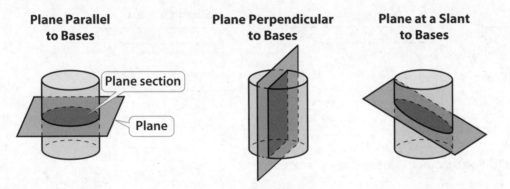

Plane Parallel to Bases · Plane section · Plane · Plane Perpendicular to Bases · Plane at a Slant to Bases

a. When a plane slices the right cylinder parallel to its bases, what shape is the plane section it makes?

b. When a plane slices the right cylinder perpendicular to its bases, what shape is the plane section it makes?

c. When a plane slices the right cylinder at a slant to its bases, what shape is the plane section it makes?

3 **Reflect** Why might not all plane sections that result from a plane slicing a three-dimensional figure have the same shapes?

Prepare for Describing Plane Sections of Three-Dimensional Figures

1 Think about what you know about two- and three-dimensional geometric figures. Fill in each box. Use words, numbers, and pictures. Show as many ideas as you can.

Word	In My Own Words	Illustration
parallel (∥)		
perpendicular (⊥)		
prism		
pyramid		

2 Which face or faces of the right rectangular prism are parallel to the front face? Which face or faces are perpendicular to the front face?

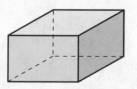

3 Ashwini is helping her uncle make a set of wooden blocks for her younger brother. The dashed segments show three ways Ashwini's uncle could slice through a piece of wood shaped like a right triangular prism.

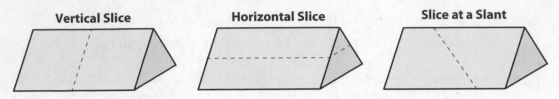

Vertical Slice   Horizontal Slice   Slice at a Slant

a. Each slice leaves a flat surface. What is the shape of each surface?

b. Show the shape of the surface made by each slice.

Develop Describing Plane Sections of Three-Dimensional Figures

➤ **Read and try to solve the problem below.**

How can you slice each of these three-dimensional figures to get a rectangular plane section?

Right Rectangular Prism

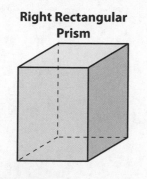

Right Rectangular Pyramid

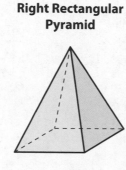

Right Cylinder

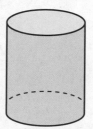

 TRY IT

Math Toolkit geometric solids, isometric dot paper

DISCUSS IT

Ask: How do you know that your slices result in rectangular plane sections?

Share: I know they result in rectangles because . . .

➤ **Explore different ways to describe plane sections of three-dimensional figures.**

How can you slice each of these three-dimensional figures to get a rectangular plane section?

Right Rectangular Prism

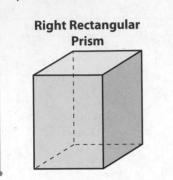

Right Rectangular Pyramid

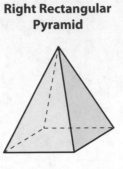

Right Cylinder

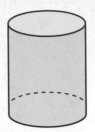

Picture It

You can picture slicing a figure with a plane.

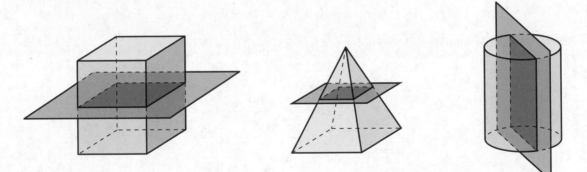

Picture It

You can picture separating the two pieces that result from the slice.

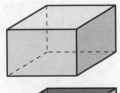

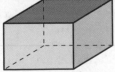

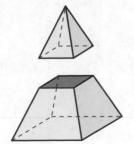

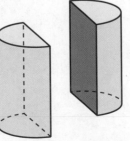

➤ **Use the problem from the previous page to help you understand how to describe plane sections of three-dimensional figures.**

1 Look at the **Picture Its**. How does the plane section of the rectangular prism compare to the base of the prism? How does the plane section of the rectangular pyramid compare to the base of the pyramid?

2 Describe how you can slice each of the three-dimensional figures to get a rectangular plane section.

3 Is there a way to slice the right cylinder parallel to its bases and get a rectangular plane section? Explain.

4 Is a plane section of a three-dimensional figure always the same shape as one of its bases or faces? Explain.

5 How can you slice a right prism, right pyramid, or right cylinder so that the plane section is the same shape as a base of the figure?

6 **Reflect** Think about all the models and strategies you have discussed today. Describe how one of them helped you better understand how to solve the **Try It** problem.

Apply It

➤ **Use what you learned to solve these problems.**

7 A woodworker is making a coat rack. She starts by cutting a right cylindrical piece of wood. Her cut is neither parallel nor perpendicular to the bases of the cylinder. Which figure shows the shape of the plane section that results from the woodworker's cut?

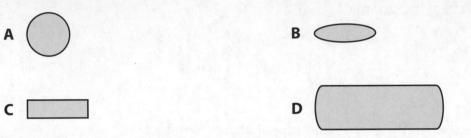

A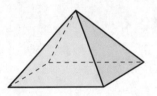

B

C

D

8 Eduardo claims that if you slice a right rectangular pyramid perpendicular to its base, the plane section will always be a triangle. If he is correct, explain why. If he is incorrect, give a counterexample.

9 Show and describe two different types of slices you could make to the right triangular prism so that the plane section is triangular.

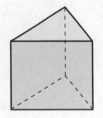

Practice Describing Plane Sections of Three-Dimensional Figures

➤ **Study the Example showing how to describe a plane section of a three-dimensional figure. Then solve problems 1–5.**

Example

Carson has modeling clay in the shape of a right cylinder with circular bases. He slices the cylinder parallel to its bases. What shape is the plane section resulting from the slice?

You can draw a picture to show the plane section.

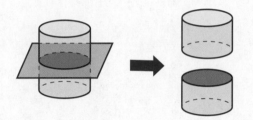

The drawing shows a plane parallel to the bases of the cylinder. The cut surface is the same shape as each base.

The plane section resulting from the slice is a circle.

---

1 Carson has another cylinder of modeling clay like the one in the Example. He slices through it so that the slice is perpendicular to the bases of the cylinder. Will this slice result in a circular plane section? Explain.

2 Samuel claims that when you slice a right square pyramid, there are only two possible shapes the plane section can be. Is Samuel correct? Explain why or give a counterexample.

3 Fiona has a block of cheese shaped like a right rectangular prism. She slices it vertically along a diagonal of the top face, as shown. Show and describe the plane section that results from Fiona's slice.

4 Can the three-dimensional figure be sliced to result in a triangular plane section? Select *Yes* or *No* for each three-dimensional figure.

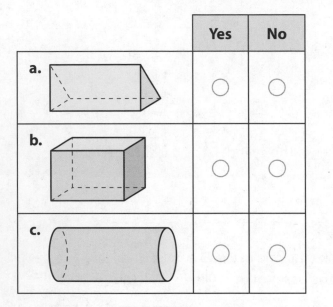

	Yes	No
a.	○	○
b.	○	○
c.	○	○

5 Which slices will always result in a square plane section? Select all that apply.

A Slicing a cube parallel to one of its faces

B Slicing a right square pyramid parallel to its base

C Slicing a cube perpendicular to one of its faces

D Slicing a right square pyramid perpendicular to its base

E Slicing a cube at an angle neither parallel nor perpendicular to any of its faces

F Slicing a right square pyramid at an angle neither parallel nor perpendicular to any of its faces

Refine Describing Plane Sections of Three-Dimensional Figures

➤ **Complete the Example below. Then solve problems 1–9.**

Example

Bao slices a right rectangular pyramid so that the slice goes through each face of the pyramid, as shown. What shape is the plane section that results from Bao's slice?

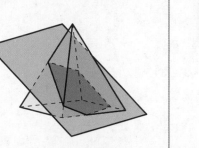

Look at how you could show your work by separating the pieces after the slice.

Separate the two parts of the pyramid.

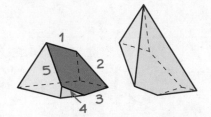

Count the sides of the plane section.

SOLUTION _____

Apply It

1 A plane slices the three rectangular faces of a right triangular prism but neither of its bases. The plane is not parallel to the bases of the prism. Show and describe the plane section that results from the slice.

② Suppose you want to slice a three-dimensional figure so the resulting plane section is the triangle shown. What are two different types of figures you could slice? Show and describe how you need to slice each figure.

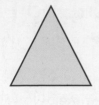

CONSIDER THIS...
Would the slice of each three-dimensional figure need to be parallel to a base, perpendicular to a base, or neither?

PAIR/SHARE
What is an example of a three-dimensional figure that could not be sliced to result in the triangular plane section?

③ Alejandro slices a right rectangular prism along the dashed line shown. The slice is perpendicular to the bottom face of the prism. Which figure shows the shape of the plane section that results from Alejandro's slice?

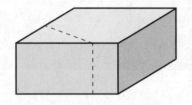

CONSIDER THIS...
Which faces of the prism does Alejandro slice?

A

B

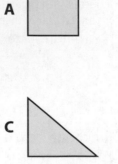

C

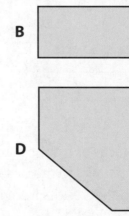

D

Dalila chose C as the correct answer. How might she have gotten that answer?

PAIR/SHARE
How could you describe the shape of the plane section?

④ Michael has modeling clay in the shape of a right rectangular prism, a right triangular prism, and a right rectangular pyramid. He slices the pieces of clay either parallel or perpendicular to a base. Which plane sections could result from one of these slices? Select all that apply.

A A triangle could result from one of the slices through the rectangular prism.

B A rectangle could result from one of the slices through the rectangular prism.

C A triangle could result from one of the slices through the triangular prism.

D A rectangle could result from one of the slices through the triangular prism.

E A triangle could result from one of the slices through the pyramid.

F A rectangle could result from one of the slices through the pyramid.

⑤ A plane slices a right cylinder at a slant to its bases. Jennifer draws Figure *A* to show the shape of the plane section that results. Hasina draws Figure *B* to show the shape of the plane section that results. Who is correct? Explain.

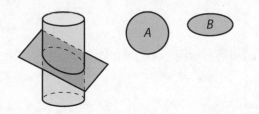

⑥ A plane slices a right rectangular prism as shown. What shape is the plane section that results from the slice? Explain how you know.

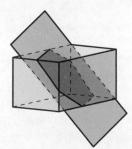

7 A right rectangular prism is sliced by a plane perpendicular to its bases. A right cylinder is sliced the same way. Which statement about the plane sections that result is correct?

    A Both plane sections have two pairs of parallel sides.

    B The plane section of the prism has only straight sides, but the plane section of the cylinder does not.

    C The plane section of the prism has four right angles, but the plane section of the cylinder does not.

    D Both plane sections are the same shape as the bases of the three-dimensional figures from which they resulted.

8 A plane slices a right triangular prism parallel to its bases. The area of the plane section that results is 18 cm². The height of the original prism is 8 cm. What is the volume of the original prism? Explain how you know.

9 **Math Journal** Show and describe two different types of slices you could make to the right square pyramid so that the plane section is a quadrilateral.

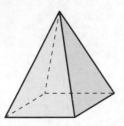

✔ End of Lesson Checklist

    ☐ **INTERACTIVE GLOSSARY** Find the entry for *plane section*. Add two important things you learned about plane sections in this lesson.

    ☐ **SELF CHECK** Go back to the Unit 6 Opener and see what you can check off.

Find Unknown Angle Measures

Dear Family,

This week your student is learning about problem solving with angles.

You can use the special relationships that exist among angles to solve problems that involve angles and to find unknown angle measures.

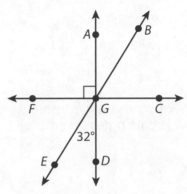

- **Adjacent angles** are two angles that share a vertex and a side and do not overlap. $\angle FGA$ and $\angle AGB$ are adjacent angles.

- A **straight angle** measures 180°. $\angle FGC$ is a straight angle.

- **Complementary angles** are two angles whose measures sum to 90°. They do not need to be adjacent. $\angle AGB$ and $\angle BGC$ are complementary angles.

- **Supplementary angles** are two angles whose measures sum to 180°. They do not need to be adjacent. $\angle FGB$ and $\angle BGC$ are supplementary angles.

- **Vertical angles** are the opposite angles formed when two lines intersect. $\angle FGD$ and $\angle AGB$ are vertical angles. Vertical angles have the same measure.

The notation $m\angle EGD = 32°$ means the measure of $\angle EGD$ is 32°. Your student will be solving problems like the one below.

In the figure at the right, $\angle ACF$ and $\angle BCD$ are straight angles. What is $m\angle DCF$?

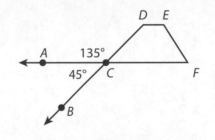

➤ **ONE WAY** to find an unknown angle measure is to use the relationship between supplementary angles.

$\angle ACD$ and $\angle DCF$ are supplementary angles, so $m\angle ACD + m\angle DCF = 180°$. Since $135° + m\angle DCF = 180°$, $m\angle DCF = 45°$.

➤ **ANOTHER WAY** is to use the relationship between vertical angles.

$\angle DCF$ and $\angle BCA$ are vertical angles.

$m\angle DCF = m\angle BCA$

$m\angle DCF = 45°$

Both methods show that the measure of $\angle DCF$ is 45°.

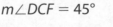 Use the next page to start a conversation about angles.

Activity Thinking About Angles

➤ **Do this activity together to investigate angles in the real world.**

Have you ever played soccer and watched the ball go out of bounds? A corner kick is used to restart the game when this happens.

On a soccer field, the goal line and the sideline form a right angle. A player takes a corner kick from the vertex of this angle.

The path of the ball separates the right angle of the goal line and the sideline into two complementary angles!

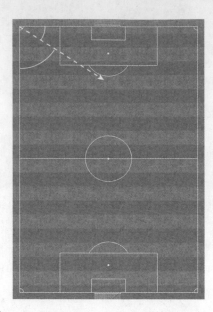

? Where do you see complementary, supplementary, or vertical angles in real life?

Explore Finding Unknown Angle Measures

Previously, you learned about types of angles. In this lesson, you will learn about special angle relationships.

➤ **Use what you know to try to solve the problem below.**

Some stained-glass windows have geometric designs. The diagram shows part of a stained-glass design where several pieces are joined together. In the diagram, $\overleftrightarrow{AD}$, $\overleftrightarrow{CF}$, and $\overleftrightarrow{BG}$ intersect at point E and $\overleftrightarrow{AD}$ is perpendicular to $\overleftrightarrow{CF}$. What is the value of x?

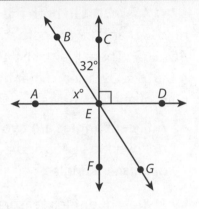

TRY IT

Math Toolkit dot paper, grid paper

Learning Target SMP 1, SMP 2, SMP 3, SMP 4, SMP 5, SMP 6, SMP 8
Use facts about supplementary, complementary, vertical, and adjacent angles in a multi-step problem to write and solve simple equations for an unknown angle in a figure.

CONNECT IT

1 **Look Back** What is the value of x? What angle relationship did you use to find the value of x?

2 **Look Ahead** In both the figure from the **Try It** and the figure at the right, $\overleftrightarrow{AD}$ and $\overleftrightarrow{CF}$ are perpendicular lines. Another way to write this is $\overleftrightarrow{AD} \perp \overleftrightarrow{CF}$. There is also shorter notation for angles. The notation $m\angle BEC = 32°$ means that the measure of $\angle BEC$ is 32°. Some angles and pairs of related angles have special names.

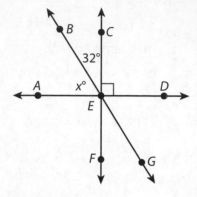

a. **Adjacent angles** are two angles that share a vertex and a side and do not overlap. $\angle AEB$ and $\angle AEF$ are adjacent angles. Name another pair of adjacent angles.

b. A **straight angle** measures 180°. The sides of a straight angle form a straight line. Name a straight angle.

c. Two angles whose measures sum to 90° are **complementary angles**. Explain how the diagram shows that $\angle AEB$ and $\angle BEC$ are complementary angles.

d. Two angles whose measures sum to 180° are **supplementary angles**. Explain how the diagram shows that $\angle BEF$ and $\angle BEC$ are supplementary angles.

e. **Vertical angles** are the opposite angles formed when two lines intersect. $\angle BEC$ and $\angle FEG$ are vertical angles. Name another pair of vertical angles.

3 **Reflect** Supplementary angles and complementary angles do not have to be adjacent. Use the diagram to name a pair of supplementary angles that are not adjacent. How do you know they are supplementary?

Name:

Prepare for Finding Unknown Angle Measures

1 Think about what you know about angles and their measures. Fill in each box.
Use words, numbers, and pictures. Show as many ideas as you can.

Word	In My Own Words	Example
angle		
acute angle		
obtuse angle		

2 Identify one acute angle and one obtuse angle in the figure at the right.

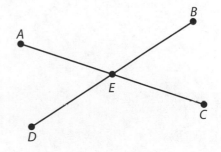

3 In the figure, $\overleftrightarrow{JM}$, $\overleftrightarrow{KN}$, and $\overleftrightarrow{PL}$ intersect at point Q and $\overleftrightarrow{JM}$ is perpendicular to $\overleftrightarrow{KN}$.

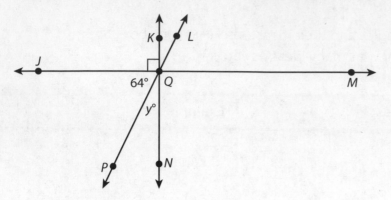

a. What is the value of y? Show your work.

SOLUTION _____

b. Check your answer to problem 3a. Show your work.

Develop Using Supplementary and Vertical Angles

➤ **Read and try to solve the problem below.**

In the figure, $\overleftrightarrow{RV}$, $\overleftrightarrow{WS}$, and $\overleftrightarrow{QT}$ intersect at point P.
What is the value of x?

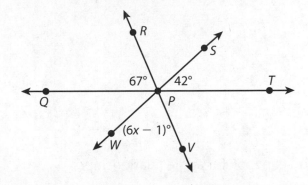

TRY IT

Math Toolkit dot paper, grid paper

DISCUSS IT

Ask: What angle relationships did you use to help you find the value of x?

Share: The angle relationships I used were . . .

➤ **Explore different ways to use supplementary and vertical angles.**

In the figure, $\overleftrightarrow{RV}$, $\overleftrightarrow{WS}$, and $\overleftrightarrow{QT}$ intersect at point P.
What is the value of x?

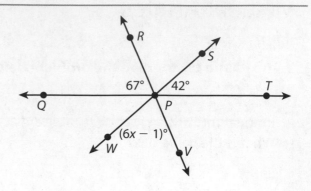

Analyze It

You can look for angle relationships.

Angles that form a straight angle have measures that sum to 180°.

These sets of three angles form straight angles.

$\angle QPR$, $\angle RPS$, and $\angle SPT$

$\angle RPS$, $\angle SPT$, and $\angle TPV$

Vertical angles have the same measure.

These pairs of angles are vertical angles.

$\angle RPS$ and $\angle WPV$

$\angle QPR$ and $\angle TPV$

Model It

You can write and solve equations to find x.

You can use the fact that $\angle QPR$, $\angle RPS$, and $\angle SPT$ form a straight angle to find $m\angle RPS$.

$$m\angle QPR + m\angle RPS + m\angle SPT = 180°$$
$$67° + m\angle RPS + 42° = 180°$$
$$m\angle RPS = 71°$$

Since $\angle WPV$ and $\angle RPS$ are vertical angles, they have the same measure.

$$m\angle WPV = m\angle RPS$$
$$6x - 1 = 71$$
$$6x = 72$$

> **Use the problem from the previous page to help you understand how to find an unknown angle measure.**

1 Look at **Analyze It**. What is another set of three angles that form a straight angle? What is another pair of vertical angles?

2 What is the value of *x*?

3 Explain how you can use straight angles to find *m*∠*TPV*.

4 Explain how you can find *m*∠*TPV* using the fact that vertical angles have equal measures.

5 The figure at the right shows two lines intersecting to form four angles. Use the figure to explain why vertical angles have the same measure.

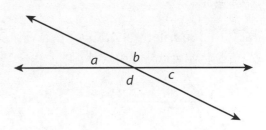

6 **Reflect** Think about all the models and strategies you have discussed today. Describe how one of them helped you better understand how to find an unknown angle measure.

Apply It

➤ **Use what you learned to solve these problems.**

7 $\angle A$ and $\angle B$ are vertical angles. $m\angle A = (4x + 6)°$ and $m\angle B = (7x - 66)°$. What are $m\angle A$ and $m\angle B$? Show your work.

SOLUTION _____

8 In the figure at the right, $\overline{RS}$ is extended as shown. Find $m\angle QSR$.

A 26°

B 34°

C 50°

D 96°

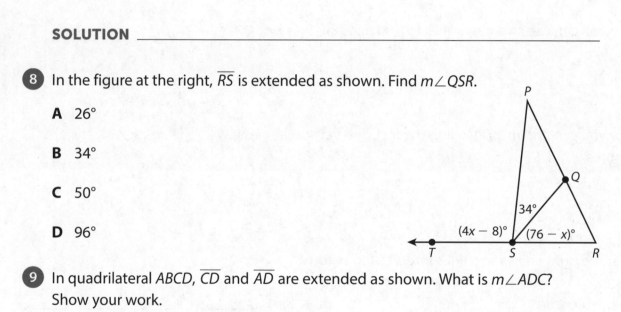

9 In quadrilateral $ABCD$, $\overline{CD}$ and $\overline{AD}$ are extended as shown. What is $m\angle ADC$? Show your work.

SOLUTION _____

Practice Using Supplementary and Vertical Angles

➤ **Study the Example showing how to solve problems using supplementary and vertical angles. Then solve problems 1–5.**

Example

$\overleftrightarrow{AB}$ and $\overleftrightarrow{CD}$ meet at point *E*. What is $m\angle AEC$?

$\angle AED$ and $\angle DEB$ are supplementary angles.

$$(2x - 17) + (x + 32) = 180$$
$$3x + 15 = 180$$
$$3x = 165$$
$$x = 55$$

$\angle DEB$ and $\angle AEC$ are vertical angles.

$$m\angle AEC = m\angle DEB$$
$$= (x + 32)°$$
$$= (55 + 32)°$$
$$= 87°$$

So, $m\angle AEC = 87°$.

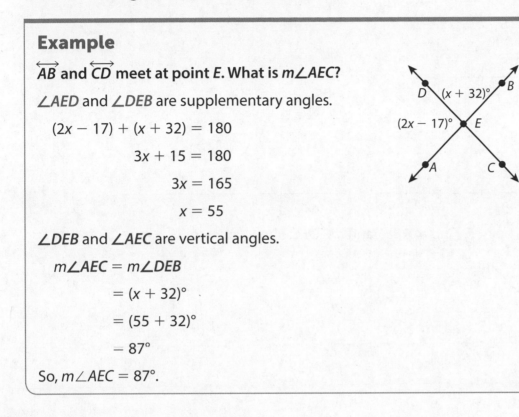

1 Look at the figure in the Example.

a. What is $m\angle CEB$? Show your work.

SOLUTION _____

b. Describe how to find $m\angle CEB$ another way.

2 How can a pair of angles be both vertical and supplementary?

3 ∠ECB and ∠DCA are straight angles. What is m∠DCB? Show your work.

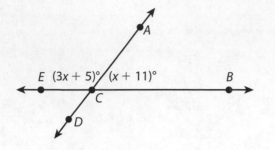

SOLUTION _____

4 $\overline{AC}$ and $\overline{DB}$ intersect at point E. Find m∠BEC and m∠DEC. Show your work.

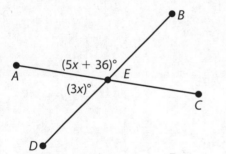

SOLUTION _____

5 Two angles are supplementary and their measures have a ratio of 1 : 3. Find the measures of the angles. Show your work.

SOLUTION _____

Develop Using Complementary and Adjacent Angles

➤ **Read and try to solve the problem below.**

In the figure, $\overleftrightarrow{FD}$, $\overleftrightarrow{BE}$, and $\overrightarrow{AC}$ intersect at point A and $\overrightarrow{AC} \perp \overleftrightarrow{BE}$. Find $m\angle FAB$.

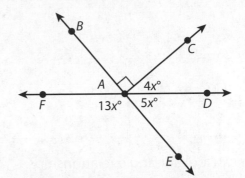

TRY IT

Math Toolkit dot paper, grid paper

DISCUSS IT

Ask: What did you do first to find the angle measure?

Share: First, I . . .

➤ **Explore different ways to find an unknown angle measure.**

In the figure, $\overleftrightarrow{FD}$, $\overleftrightarrow{BE}$, and $\overrightarrow{AC}$ intersect at point A and $\overrightarrow{AC} \perp \overleftrightarrow{BE}$. Find $m\angle FAB$.

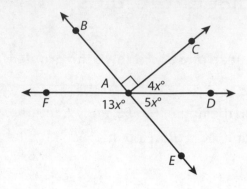

Analyze It

You can look for angle relationships.

These angle pairs are complementary.

$\angle CAD$ and $\angle DAE$

$\angle FAB$ and $\angle CAD$

These angle pairs are vertical angles.

$\angle FAB$ and $\angle DAE$

$\angle FAE$ and $\angle BAD$

Model It

You can use angle relationships to write and solve equations.

You can use complementary angle relationships to solve for x.

$$m\angle CAD + m\angle DAE = 90°$$
$$4x + 5x = 90$$
$$9x = 90$$
$$x = 10$$

You can use vertical angle relationships and the value of x to find $m\angle FAB$.

$$m\angle FAB = m\angle DAE$$
$$= 5x°$$

➤ **Use the problem from the previous page to help you understand how to find an unknown angle measure.**

1 Look at **Analyze It**. Explain how you know ∠CAD and ∠DAE are complementary angles.

2 ∠FAB and ∠CAD are not adjacent. How can you show that they are complementary angles?

3 What is m∠FAB?

4 Suppose ∠R and ∠S are complementary angles, and ∠R and ∠T are also complementary angles. What do you know about m∠S and m∠T? Explain.

5 In the figure at the right, $\overleftrightarrow{JL}$ and $\overleftrightarrow{KN}$ intersect at point P. Describe how to use m∠KPL to find m∠JPK, m∠MPN, and m∠NPJ.

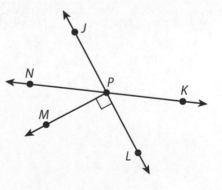

6 **Reflect** Think about all the models and strategies you have discussed today. Describe how one of them helped you better understand how to solve the **Try It** problem.

Apply It

➤ **Use what you learned to solve these problems.**

7 $\angle P$ and $\angle Q$ are complementary angles. $\angle Q$ and $\angle R$ are vertical angles. $m\angle P = 4x°$ and $m\angle Q = (3x - 8)°$. What is $m\angle R$? Show your work.

SOLUTION _____

8 In the figure, $\overleftrightarrow{DE}$ intersects $\overleftrightarrow{AG}$ at point H and $\overleftrightarrow{DE} \perp \overrightarrow{HK}$. Find the value of x.

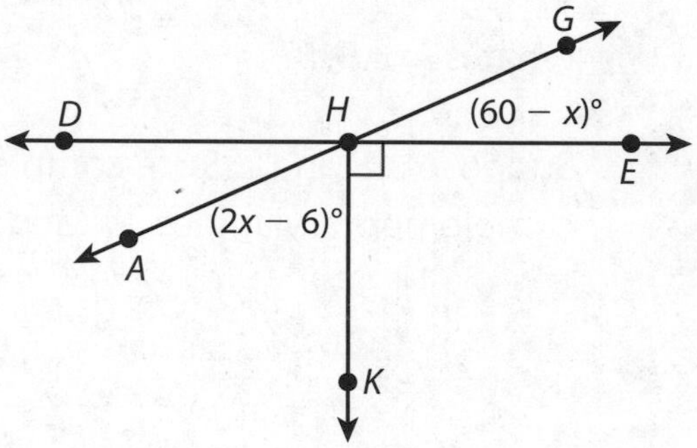

A 126

B 66

C 36

D 22

9 In rectangle $KLMN$, $\overline{NK}$ and $\overline{MK}$ are extended as shown. What is $m\angle PKQ$? Show your work.

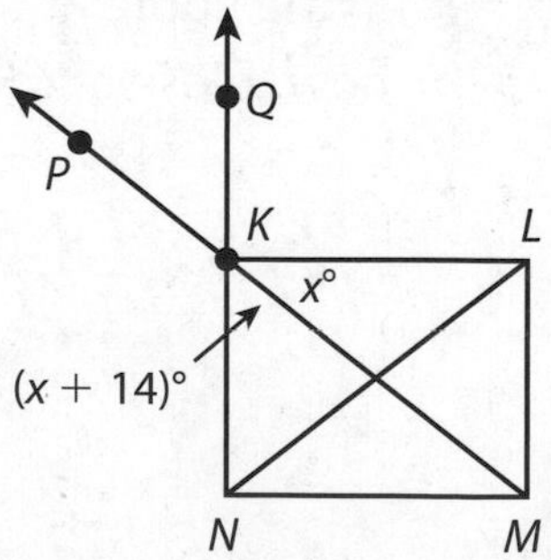

SOLUTION _____

Practice Using Complementary and Adjacent Angles

➤ **Study the Example showing how to solve problems using complementary and vertical angles. Then solve problems 1–6.**

Example

In rectangle *PRST*, $\overline{ST}$ and $\overline{RT}$ are extended as shown. What is $m\angle UTV$?

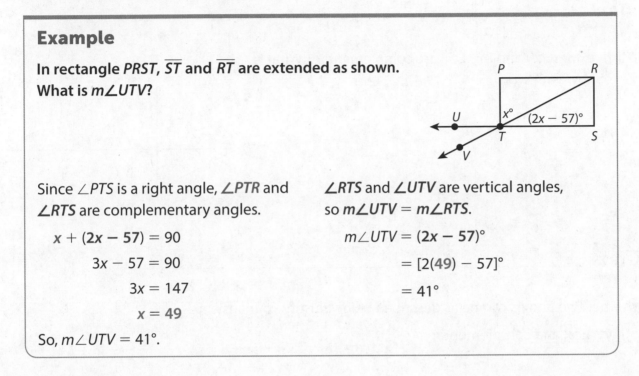

Since $\angle PTS$ is a right angle, $\angle PTR$ and $\angle RTS$ are complementary angles.

$$x + (2x - 57) = 90$$
$$3x - 57 = 90$$
$$3x = 147$$
$$x = 49$$

$\angle RTS$ and $\angle UTV$ are vertical angles, so $m\angle UTV = m\angle RTS$.

$$m\angle UTV = (2x - 57)°$$
$$= [2(49) - 57]°$$
$$= 41°$$

So, $m\angle UTV = 41°$.

1 Look at the Example.

a. Name another pair of complementary angles and another pair of vertical angles.

b. Find $m\angle VTS$ and $m\angle UTR$. Show your work.

SOLUTION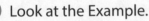

2 $m\angle a = 18°$. $\angle a$ and $\angle b$ are complementary angles. $\angle b$ and $\angle c$ are supplementary angles. So, $m\angle c$ is _____ .

Vocabulary

complementary angles
two angles whose measures sum to 90°.

supplementary angles
two angles whose measures sum to 180°.

vertical angles
opposite angles formed when two lines intersect. Vertical angles have the same measure.

3 Two angles are complementary. The measure of one angle is 35°. What is the measure of the other angle? Show your work.

SOLUTION _____

4 In the figure, $m\angle EDH$ and $m\angle EGF$ are complementary. What is $m\angle EDH$? Show your work.

G

$(9x + 9)°$

$(39 - 2x)°$

D E F

H

SOLUTION _____

5 Tell whether two angles can be as described below. Justify your answers.

   a. both vertical and complementary

   b. both complementary and supplementary

6 A quilter uses complementary angles to cut fabric. One angle has half the measure of the other complementary angle. What are the measures of the angles? Show your work.

SOLUTION _____

Refine Finding Unknown Angle Measures

➤ **Complete the Example below. Then solve problems 1–10.**

Example

In the figure, $\overleftrightarrow{AC}$ and $\overrightarrow{BC}$ intersect at point C. $\angle 2$ and $\angle 3$ are complementary angles. Find $m\angle 1$, $m\angle 2$, $m\angle 3$, and $m\angle 4$.

Look at how you could show your work using angle relationships.

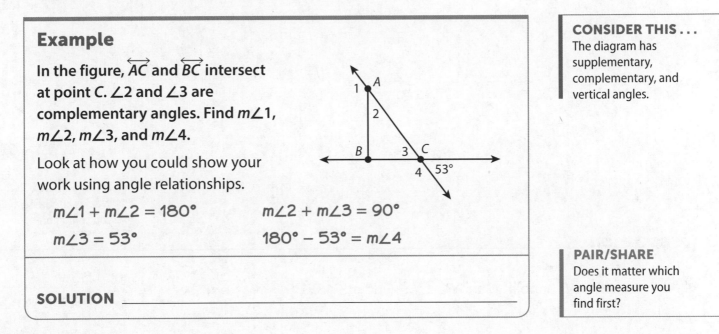

$m\angle 1 + m\angle 2 = 180°$ $m\angle 2 + m\angle 3 = 90°$

$m\angle 3 = 53°$ $180° - 53° = m\angle 4$

SOLUTION _____

CONSIDER THIS...
The diagram has supplementary, complementary, and vertical angles.

PAIR/SHARE
Does it matter which angle measure you find first?

Apply It

1 $\angle FAC$ is a straight angle and $\angle BAD$ is a right angle. Find $m\angle FAE$. Show your work.

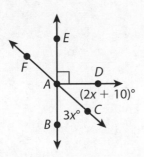

CONSIDER THIS...
Which angles are supplementary?

SOLUTION _____

PAIR/SHARE
How can you check your answer?

2 $\overleftrightarrow{PQ}$ intersects $\overleftrightarrow{SR}$ at point *T*. Find $m\angle RTQ$. Show your work.

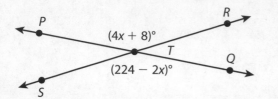

CONSIDER THIS...
How are $\angle PTR$ and $\angle STQ$ related?

PAIR/SHARE
What is another way you could find $m\angle RTQ$?

SOLUTION _____

3 $\overleftrightarrow{BE}$ intersects $\overleftrightarrow{AD}$ at point *G* and $\overleftrightarrow{FC} \perp \overleftrightarrow{BE}$. Find $m\angle AGE$.

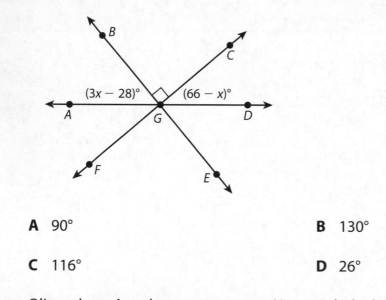

CONSIDER THIS...
Can identifying vertical angles help you solve the problem?

A 90°

B 130°

C 116°

D 26°

Oliver chose A as the correct answer. How might he have gotten that answer?

PAIR/SHARE
Could you solve the problem if you did not know that $\overleftrightarrow{FC}$ and $\overleftrightarrow{BE}$ are perpendicular? Why or why not?

4 The opposite angles formed when two lines intersect are _____ angles.

5 Four straight lines, *k*, *ℓ*, *m*, and *n*, intersect as shown. Lines *k* and *n* are perpendicular. Find the value of *x*.

A 28

B 42

C 58

D 87

6 Tell whether each statement is *True* or *False*.

	True	False
a. The sum of the measures of two supplementary angles is 90°.	○	○
b. If the measure of an acute angle is *x*°, then the measure of its complementary angle is $(90 - x)°$.	○	○
c. Two adjacent angles are always complementary or supplementary.	○	○
d. Vertical angles can be adjacent angles.	○	○
e. Acute angles can have both a complementary angle and a supplementary angle.	○	○
f. Obtuse angles can have both a complementary angle and a supplementary angle.	○	○

7 ∠*MNP* is a straight angle. Is △*NQR* an *acute triangle*, *right triangle*, or *obtuse triangle*? Explain.

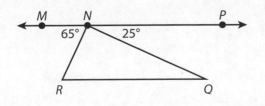

8 ∠R and ∠T are supplementary angles. Can they both be acute angles? Explain why or why not.

9 ∠J and ∠K are vertical angles. ∠J and ∠L are supplementary angles. m∠K = 71°. What is m∠L in degrees?

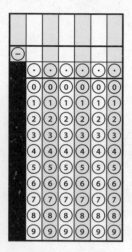

10 **Math Journal** Three lines intersect as shown in the figure at the right. Find the values of x, y, and z. Explain your thinking.

35°

x°

z°

y°

✓ **End of Lesson Checklist**

  ☐ **INTERACTIVE GLOSSARY** Find the entries for *complementary angles*, *supplementary angles*, and *vertical angles*. Rewrite the definitions in your own words.

  ☐ **SELF CHECK** Go back to the Unit 6 Opener and see what you can check off.

Dear Family,

This week your student is learning about conditions for drawing triangles and quadrilaterals. Triangles have three sides and three angles. Quadrilaterals have four sides and four angles. You can try to draw a triangle or quadrilateral with a given combination of side lengths or angle measures.

Your student will learn that:

- Some combinations of three sides lengths can form a triangle, while other combinations cannot.

- When you know all the side lengths of a triangle, there is only one possible triangle you can make. This means the triangle is a *unique triangle*.

- When you know three angle measures, either there are no triangles you can make with those measures or there are many possible triangles.

- When you know all the side lengths of a quadrilateral, you can draw more than one quadrilateral.

Your student will be solving problems like the one below.

Is it possible to make a triangle with each set of side lengths?

　　3, 3, 4　　　　3, 3, 7

▶ **ONE WAY** to decide if a given set of side lengths can make a triangle is to try drawing figures with the given side lengths.

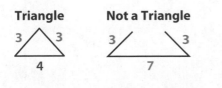

Triangle	Not a Triangle

▶ **ANOTHER WAY** is to compare the sum of two side lengths to the third side length.

For side lengths to make a triangle, the sum of the two shorter lengths must be greater than the longest side length.

$$3 + 3 > 4 \qquad 3 + 3 < 7$$
$$6 > 4 \qquad\qquad 6 < 7$$

Both methods show that it is possible to draw a triangle with side lengths 3, 3, and 4, but not with side lengths 3, 3, and 7.

▶ Use the next page to start a conversation about triangles.

Activity Thinking About Triangles

➤ **Do this activity together to investigate triangles in real life.**

Have you ever seen a ladder leaning against a building or wall?

A ladder forms a triangle with the ground and the wall it leans against. However, there is more than one possible triangle the ladder can make.

Extension ladders can change length, so the only constant condition is the right angle between the wall and the ground. You can change the ladder length or the angle between the top of the ladder and the wall to make many different triangles!

? Where else do you see triangles in your everyday life?

Explore Drawing Triangles

Previously, you learned to identify different types of triangles and quadrilaterals. In this lesson, you will learn about drawing triangles and quadrilaterals that satisfy certain conditions.

➤ **Use what you know to try to solve the problem below.**

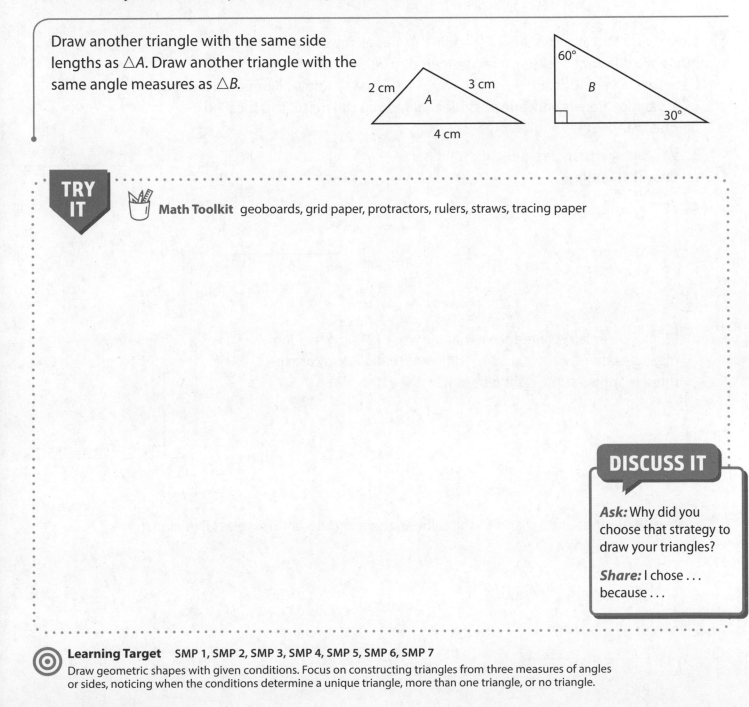

Draw another triangle with the same side lengths as △A. Draw another triangle with the same angle measures as △B.

TRY IT

Math Toolkit geoboards, grid paper, protractors, rulers, straws, tracing paper

DISCUSS IT

Ask: Why did you choose that strategy to draw your triangles?

Share: I chose . . . because . . .

◎ **Learning Target** SMP 1, SMP 2, SMP 3, SMP 4, SMP 5, SMP 6, SMP 7
Draw geometric shapes with given conditions. Focus on constructing triangles from three measures of angles or sides, noticing when the conditions determine a unique triangle, more than one triangle, or no triangle.

CONNECT IT

1 **Look Back** How are the triangles you drew like △A and △B? How are they different from △A and △B?

2 **Look Ahead** You can draw a triangle that has all the same side lengths as △A but is in a different position. It is considered to be the same triangle as △A because you can turn and flip it to cover △A. When you know all three side lengths of a triangle, there is only one possible triangle you can make. This is called a unique triangle.

a. Why are the triangles at the right the same unique triangle?

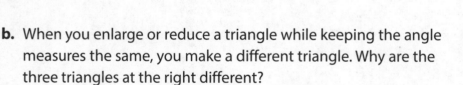

b. When you enlarge or reduce a triangle while keeping the angle measures the same, you make a different triangle. Why are the three triangles at the right different?

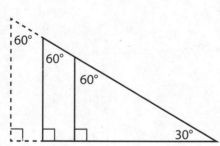

3 **Reflect** Are these two triangles the same triangle or different triangles? Explain.

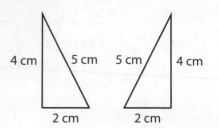

Prepare for Drawing Plane Figures with Given Conditions

1 Think about what you know about triangles. Fill in each box. Use words, numbers, and pictures. Show as many ideas as you can.

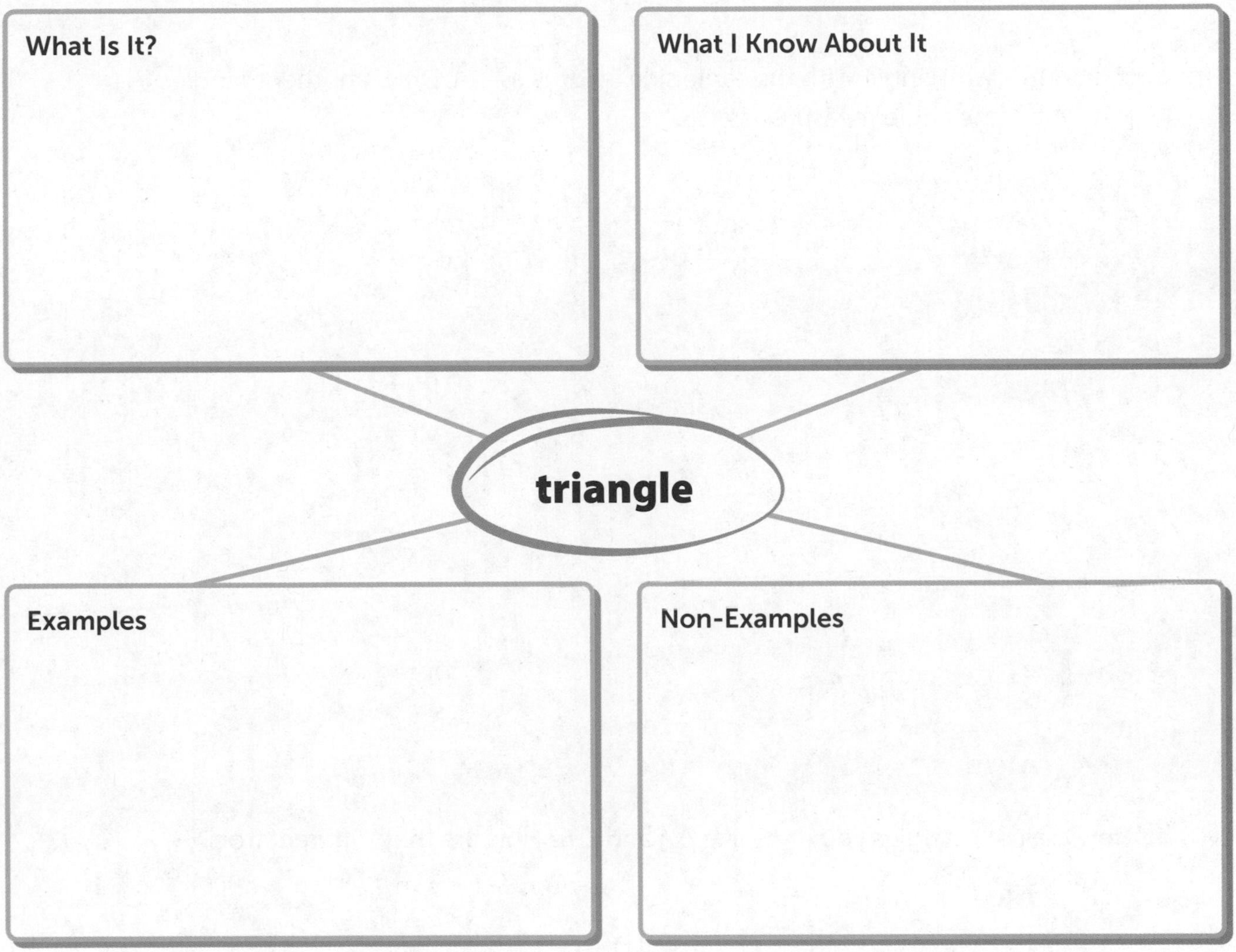

What Is It?	**What I Know About It**

triangle

Examples	**Non-Examples**

2 Chase draws the figure shown. Is it a triangle? Explain.

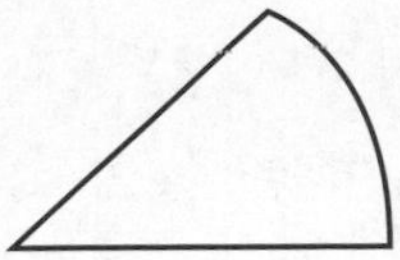

3 Look at the triangles.

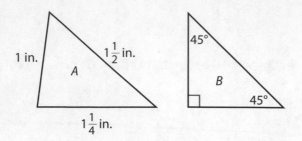

a. Draw another triangle with the same side lengths as △A. Draw another triangle with the same angle measures as △B.

b. How are the triangles you drew like △A and △B? How are they different from △A and △B?

Tablet	Translation
𝍸 𝍶 𝍶	3, 5, 7
𝍸 𝍶 ⟨	3, 5, 10
𝍸 𝍶 ⟨	3, 7, 10

Develop Drawing Triangles from Side Lengths

➤ **Read and try to solve the problem below.**

Imani translates an ancient cuneiform tablet. She finds that it includes the three sets of three numbers below.

3, 5, 10   3, 7, 10   3, 5, 7

Imani thinks each set of numbers describes the side lengths of triangular stone sculptures. Could Imani be correct? Support your conclusion with drawings.

TRY IT

 Math Toolkit geoboards, grid paper, rulers, straws, toothpicks, tracing paper

DISCUSS IT

Ask: How would you explain what the problem is asking in your own words?

Share: The problem is asking . . .

➤ **Explore different ways to determine if a given set of side lengths can make a triangle.**

Imani translates an ancient cuneiform tablet. She finds that it includes the three sets of three numbers below.

  3, 5, 10   3, 7, 10   3, 5, 7

Imani thinks each set of numbers describes the side lengths of triangular stone sculptures. Could Imani be correct? Support your conclusion with drawings.

Picture It

You can try to draw triangles with the given side lengths.

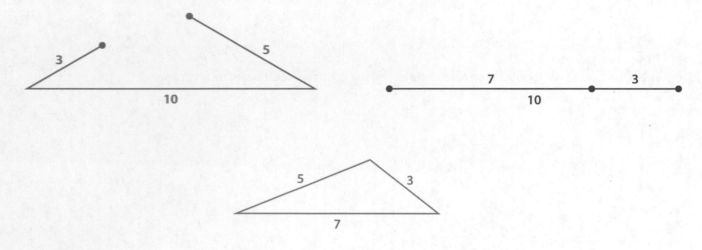

Analyze It

You can compare the sum of the lengths of two sides to the length of the third.

3, 5, 10	3, 7, 10	3, 5, 7
$3 + 5 < 10$	$3 + 7 = 10$	$3 + 5 > 7$
$3 + 10 > 5$	$3 + 10 > 7$	$3 + 7 > 5$
$5 + 10 > 3$	$7 + 10 > 3$	$5 + 7 > 3$

archaeological excavation of temple

➤ **Use the problem from the previous page to help you understand how to determine if a given set of side lengths can make a triangle.**

1 Could Imani be correct? Explain why or why not.

2 Look at the figure in **Picture It** with side lengths 3, 5, and 10. Look at **Analyze It**. Why is it impossible to draw a triangle with these lengths?

3 Look at the figure in **Picture It** with side lengths 3, 7, and 10. Look at **Analyze It**. Why is it impossible to draw a triangle with these lengths?

4 Look at the figure in **Picture It** with side lengths 3, 5, and 7. Look at **Analyze It**. Why is it possible to draw a triangle with these lengths?

5 Without drawing, how can you show if it is possible to form a triangle with side lengths 5, 7, and 10? Explain why your method works.

6 **Reflect** Think about all the models and strategies you have discussed today. Describe how one of them helped you better understand how to determine if three lengths can be used to form a triangle.

Apply It

➤ **Use what you learned to solve these problems.**

7 Lian builds model boats. He has three leftover pieces that are 2 in., 3 in., and 4 in. long. Can he use the pieces to form a unique triangle, more than one triangle, or no triangle with those side lengths? Show your work.

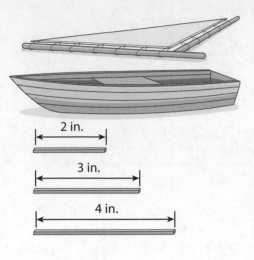

2 in.

3 in.

4 in.

SOLUTION _____

8 A triangle has sides with lengths 5 and 11. The length of the third side is an integer. What are the least and greatest possible lengths of the third side? Show your work.

SOLUTION _____

_____

9 Consider the four lengths 2, 5, 6, and 8. Which combinations of three of those lengths can form a triangle? Explain. Support your explanation with drawings.

Practice Drawing Triangles from Side Lengths

➤ **Study the Example showing how to draw a triangle from side lengths. Then solve problems 1–7.**

Example

Do the side lengths 3, 4, and 5 form a unique triangle or no triangle? Support your reasoning with drawings.

You can compare the sum of the two shorter side lengths to the longest side length.

Since **3 + 4 > 5**, these side lengths can form a triangle.

When you know all three side lengths of a triangle, there is only one possible triangle you can make.

So, the side lengths 3, 4, and 5 form a unique triangle.

---

1 Do the side lengths 6, 6, and 14 form a triangle? Explain. Support your explanation with drawings.

2 Are the two triangles below the same? Explain why or why not.

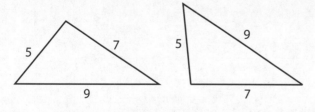

3 Students want to make some triangular banners. Which set of side lengths can be used to make a triangular banner?

A 5 in., 5 in., 15 in.

B 12 in., 12 in., 24 in.

C 9 in., 9 in., 18 in.

D 18 in., 23 in., 23 in.

4 Brett has pieces of steel that are 8 in. and 12 in. long. He wants to weld the pieces together with a third piece of steel to make a triangular frame. What is the range of lengths he can use for the third piece? Show your work.

SOLUTION _____

5 Juanita has three straws that are 5 in. long and three straws that are 10 in. long. Name one combination of three straw lengths she can use to form a triangle and one combination that cannot form a triangle. Explain your thinking.

6 Hannah has an eraser $1\frac{1}{2}$ in. long, a pencil $5\frac{7}{8}$ in. long, and a marker $7\frac{5}{8}$ in. long. Can she arrange these items into a triangle? Explain your thinking.

7 Patrick uses scrap metal to build sculptures. He wants to build a sculpture with triangles. He finds metal rods that are 20 in., 27 in., 47 in., and 67 in. long. Which **combinations of three of these lengths** can Patrick use to form a triangle? Justify your answer.

Develop Conditions for Drawing Triangles

➤ **Read and try to solve the problem below.**

Consider the following sets of conditions for a triangle.

Set A: a side length of 3 cm, a right angle, and a 30° angle

Set B: a side length of 3 cm between a right angle and a 30° angle

Set C: a side length of 3 cm and two right angles

Try to draw a triangle that meets each set of conditions. Does each set of conditions result in a unique triangle, more than one triangle, or no triangle? How do you know?

TRY IT

Math Toolkit grid paper, protractors, rulers, straws

DISCUSS IT

Ask: How did you get started using the conditions to draw triangles?

Share: I started by . . .

LESSON 29 Draw Plane Figures with Given Conditions   **641**

➤ **Explore different ways to decide if conditions result in a unique triangle, more than one triangle, or no triangle.**

Consider the following sets of conditions for a triangle.

Set A: a side length of 3 cm, a right angle, and a 30° angle

Set B: a side length of 3 cm between a right angle and a 30° angle

Set C: a side length of 3 cm and two right angles

Try to draw a triangle that meets each set of conditions. Does each set of conditions result in a unique triangle, more than one triangle, or no triangle? How do you know?

Solve It

You can draw figures for each set of conditions.

You can measure the sides of each triangle. Round each side length to the nearest tenth of a centimeter.

Set A: The conditions result in more than one triangle. You can place the 3-cm side across from the right angle, the 60° angle, or the 30° angle.

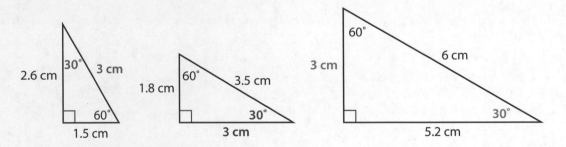

Set B: The conditions result in a unique triangle.

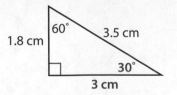

Set C: The conditions result in no triangle.

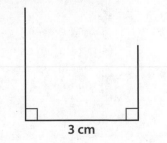

➤ **Use the problem from the previous page to help you understand how to decide if conditions result in a unique triangle, more than one triangle, or no triangle.**

1 Look at **Solve It**. How are the conditions in Set B different from those in Set A? How does that difference affect the number of triangles you can form?

2 Look at **Solve It**. How are the conditions in Set C different from those in Set B? How does that difference affect the number of triangles you can form?

3 You can form three unique triangles with a 4-cm side, a 45° angle, and a 60° angle. You can form just one unique triangle with a 4-cm side between a 45° angle and a 60° angle. Why does changing the conditions affect the number of unique triangles you can form?

4 **Reflect** Think about all the models and strategies you have discussed today. Describe how one of them helped you better understand how to solve the **Try It** problem.

Apply It

➤ **Use what you learned to solve these problems.**

5 Leon and Mariko each draw triangles with two 40° angles and a 3-cm side length. Is it possible that their triangles are different? Explain. Support your explanation with drawings.

6 The conditions for a triangle are a right angle between a side length of 3 and a side length of 4. Do the triangles at the right show that the conditions result in more than one triangle? Explain why or why not.

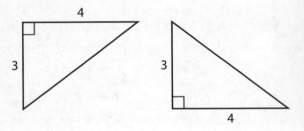

7 Jiro is helping an artist paint a mural. The artist asks him to paint a triangle with a 70° angle and sides that are 6 ft and 8 ft long. Do these conditions result in a unique triangle, more than one triangle, or no triangle? Explain. Support your explanation with drawings.

Practice Conditions for Drawing Triangles

➤ **Study the Example showing how to identify conditions that result in a unique triangle. Then solve problems 1–5.**

Example

Are the triangles below the same? Explain your reasoning.

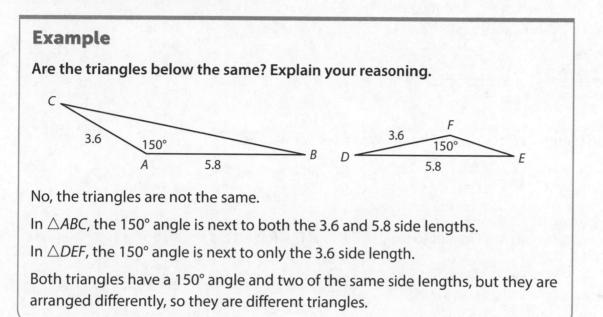

No, the triangles are not the same.

In △ABC, the 150° angle is next to both the 3.6 and 5.8 side lengths.

In △DEF, the 150° angle is next to only the 3.6 side length.

Both triangles have a 150° angle and two of the same side lengths, but they are arranged differently, so they are different triangles.

1 Consider the triangles at the right.

   a. Are the triangles the same? Explain your reasoning.

   b. How could you form a different triangle with a 30° angle, a 40° angle, and a 5-unit side length?

2 The equilateral triangle at the right has three 60° angles and a 3-unit side. Do the conditions result in a unique triangle? Explain your reasoning.

3 Ms. Lin has students build triangular frames with a 2-ft base and two 45° angles. Students build frames like the ones below.

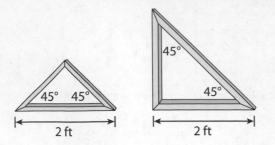

a. Do both frames meet the conditions? Explain why or why not.

b. What condition can Ms. Lin add to make sure all of the frames are the same?

4 Can you form a unique triangle, more than one triangle, or no triangle with angles that measure 50°, 90°, and 110°? Explain. Support your explanation with drawings.

5 Malik claims that a 120° angle and side lengths of 3 cm and 4 cm can form more than one unique triangle. He draws these triangles as proof. Is Malik correct? Explain why or why not.

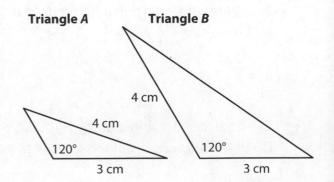

Develop Drawing Quadrilaterals

➤ **Read and try to solve the problem below.**

Do the side lengths 3 cm, 3 cm, 5 cm, and 5 cm form a unique quadrilateral? Use a drawing to show how you know.

TRY IT

 Math Toolkit grid paper, protractors, rulers, straws, tracing paper

DISCUSS IT

Ask: How is your solution similar to mine? How is it different?

Share: My solution is similar to yours because ... It is different because ...

➤ **Explore different ways to draw quadrilaterals.**

Do the side lengths 3 cm, 3 cm, 5 cm, and 5 cm form a unique quadrilateral?
Use a drawing to show how you know.

Solve It

You can form quadrilaterals with opposite sides that are the same length.

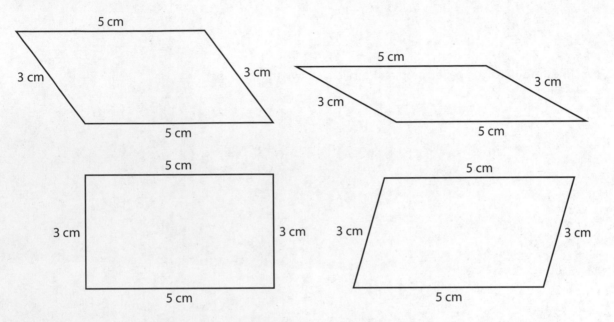

The side lengths 3 cm, 3 cm, 5 cm, and 5 cm form more than one unique quadrilateral.

Solve It

You can form quadrilaterals with opposite sides that are different lengths.

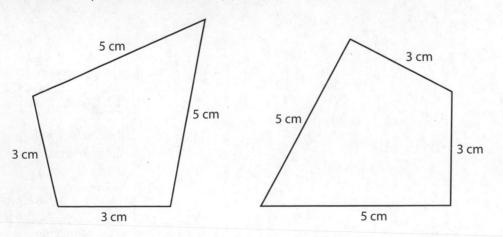

The side lengths 3 cm, 3 cm, 5 cm, and 5 cm form more than one unique quadrilateral.

➤ **Use the problem from the previous page to help you understand when conditions result in one, more than one, or no quadrilateral.**

1 Look at the quadrilaterals in the first **Solve It**. How are they different from each other?

2 Look at the quadrilaterals in the **Solve Its**. Why are they not the only quadrilaterals with sides that are 3 cm and 5 cm long?

3 Explain why there is only one unique rectangle with side lengths of 3 and 5 but more than one unique parallelogram with side lengths of 3 and 5.

4 When you know all the side lengths of a triangle, there is only one possible triangle you can make. When you know all the side lengths of a quadrilateral, there is more than one possible quadrilateral you can make. Why?

5 **Reflect** Think about all the models and strategies you have discussed today. Describe how one of them helped you better understand how to solve the **Try It** problem.

Apply It

➤ **Use what you learned to solve these problems.**

6 Can a quadrilateral with one obtuse angle and three right angles exist? Explain your thinking. Support your explanation with drawings.

7 A rectangle has side lengths of 2 units and 4 units. Can you form a different quadrilateral using the same four side lengths? Explain why or why not. Support your explanation with drawings.

8 A rhombus has side length 5 cm. Do those conditions result in a unique quadrilateral? Explain why or why not. Support your explanation with drawings.

Practice Drawing Quadrilaterals

➤ **Study the Example showing how to draw a quadrilateral that fits given conditions. Then solve problems 1–5.**

Example

A parallelogram has one pair of $\frac{3}{4}$-in. sides and one pair of $1\frac{1}{8}$-in. sides. Do those conditions result in a unique quadrilateral? Why or why not?

You can draw figures to find out.

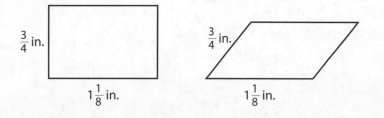

No, because you can draw more than one quadrilateral with those conditions.

1 Does each set of conditions result in a unique parallelogram, more than one parallelogram, or no parallelogram? Explain your thinking.

a. A parallelogram with side lengths $\frac{3}{4}$ in. and $1\frac{1}{8}$ in. is a rectangle.

b. A parallelogram with side lengths $\frac{3}{4}$ in. and $1\frac{1}{8}$ in. is a rhombus.

c. A parallelogram with side lengths $\frac{3}{4}$ in. and $1\frac{1}{8}$ in. has a right angle.

Vocabulary

parallelogram
a quadrilateral with opposite sides parallel and equal in length.

rectangle
a quadrilateral with 4 right angles. Opposite sides of a rectangle are the same length.

rhombus
a quadrilateral with all sides the same length.

2 Estela and Gavin make a poster together. Estela asks Gavin to draw a quadrilateral with a 45° angle between side lengths of 5 in. and 10 in. Do Estela's directions result in a unique quadrilateral? Explain. Support your explanation with drawings.

3 Can four 60° angles form a unique quadrilateral? Explain. Support your explanation with drawings.

4 Does a parallelogram with a right angle and side lengths of 3 cm and 4 cm exist? If so, is it unique? Explain. Support your explanation with drawings.

5 Cece draws these two figures to prove there is more than one parallelogram with a 40° angle between a 2-cm side and a 6-cm side. Is Cece correct? Explain.

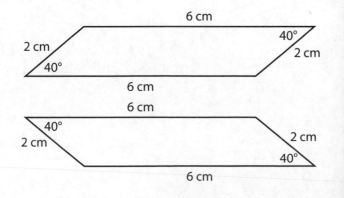

Refine Drawing Plane Figures with Given Conditions

➤ **Complete the Example below. Then solve problems 1–9.**

Example

In the diagram, $\overline{FD}$ intersects $\overline{EB}$ at point *A*. Which triangles in the diagram, if any, are the same?

Look at how you could show your work using angle relationships.

∠*FAB* and ∠*EAD* are vertical angles, so ∠*EAD* is a right angle.

$\overline{AB}$ and $\overline{EA}$ both have length 8.
$\overline{AD}$ and $\overline{FA}$ both have length 6.

You can flip △*FAB* to cover △*EAD* exactly.

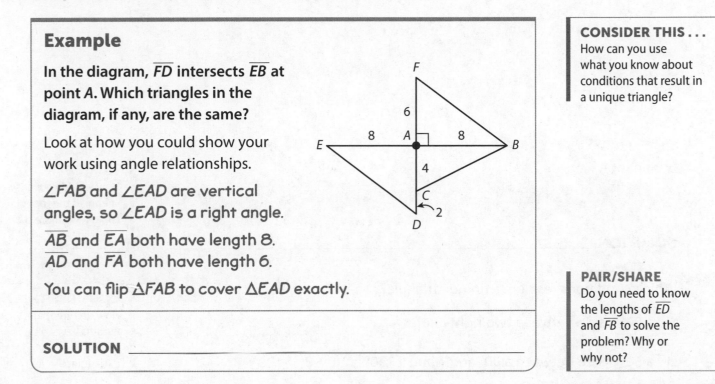

SOLUTION _____

Apply It

1 Can a quadrilateral with side lengths of 3 in., 4.5 in., and 6 in. and two right angles exist? If so, do those conditions make it unique? Show your work.

SOLUTION _____

2 Can an isosceles triangle have exactly one 9-in. side length and a 33-in. perimeter? If so, is the triangle unique? Show your work.

CONSIDER THIS...
What makes a triangle an isosceles triangle?

PAIR/SHARE
How would your answer change if the triangle could have more than one 9-in. side?

SOLUTION

3 Which conditions result in a unique triangle?

A a 5-cm side between two right angles

B a 5-cm side between a 90° angle and a 120° angle

C a 5-cm side between a 30° angle and a 60° angle

D a 30° angle, a 60° angle, and a 90° angle

Ramona chose D as the correct answer. How might she have gotten that answer?

CONSIDER THIS...
How do three side lengths have to be related in order to form a triangle?

PAIR/SHARE
How can you check your answer?

4 Zahara draws a rectangle with sides that are 5 cm and 9 cm long. Adrian draws a parallelogram with sides that are 5 cm and 9 cm long and one right angle. Raúl claims that both shapes are the same quadrilateral. Is Raúl correct? Explain why or why not. Support your explanation with drawings.

5 Bianca says she can draw an equilateral triangle with any positive number as a side length. Do you agree or disagree? Explain your thinking.

6 Tell whether each set of conditions results in *one triangle, more than one triangle,* or *no triangle.*

	One Triangle	More Than One Triangle	No Triangle
a. isosceles triangle with at least one 40° angle and one 4-ft side	○	○	○
b. isosceles triangle with exactly one 40° angle and two 4-ft sides	○	○	○
c. three 60° angles	○	○	○
d. equilateral triangle with side length 5.5 cm	○	○	○
e. two obtuse angles	○	○	○

7 Lamont wants to make a bookend in the shape of a triangle. He joins two pieces of wood that are 7 in. and 9 in. long at a right angle. Can a triangle with a right angle between a 7-in. and a 9-in. side exist? If so, is it unique? Explain.

8 Which conditions result in a unique quadrilateral? Select all that apply.

A a parallelogram with a right angle and one side with length 3 in.

B a rectangle with side lengths 2 ft and 3 ft

C a rhombus with a side 3 m long and a right angle

D a trapezoid with a right angle and side lengths 2 m and 6 m

E a square with a side that is 10 cm long

F a quadrilateral with side lengths 6 in., 7 in., 8 in., and 9 in.

9 **Math Journal** Choose three side lengths that can form a triangle and three side lengths that cannot form a triangle. Explain why the side lengths you chose can or cannot form a triangle.

✔ End of Lesson Checklist

☐ **INTERACTIVE GLOSSARY** Write a new entry for *condition*. Tell what it means for a triangle to satisfy a condition.

☐ **SELF CHECK** Go back to the Unit 6 Opener and see what you can check off.

Study an Example Problem and Solution

Math IN Action

SMP 1 Make sense of problems and persevere in solving them.

➤ **Read this problem involving volume. Then look at one student's solution to this problem on the following pages.**

Designing an Overpass

Anica is an engineer working on the plans for a highway overpass. She needs to finish the design of a concrete pier that will be constructed of right prisms and help support the overpass. Look at the requirements and notes for the concrete pier.

Finish the design by selecting values for a, b, and c that meet the requirements. How many pounds of concrete are needed to make the pier?

Pier Requirements

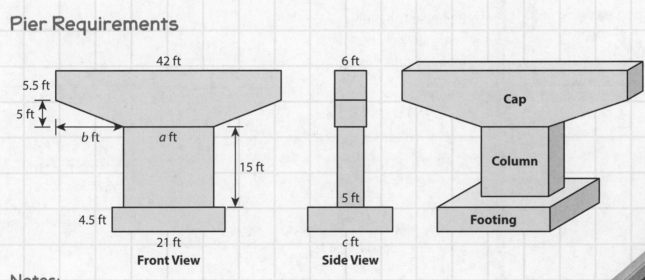

Front View   **Side View**

Notes:

- The length of the top piece, or cap, is 42 ft. a is 30% to 50% of the cap length.

- The length of the bottom piece, or footing, is 21 ft. c, the width of the footing, must be between 14 ft and 21 ft.

- The front and side views of the pier are each symmetric about a vertical line.

- The concrete used to make the pier weighs 150 pounds per cubic foot.

One Student's Solution

First, I have to select values for *a* and *c*.

I know that *a* needs to be 30% to 50% of the cap length of 42 ft. I will use 40% of the cap length.

40% of 42 = 0.40(42)

= 16.8

I will use 16.8 ft for *a*.

I know that *c* needs to be between 14 ft and 21 ft. I will use 16 ft for *c*.

Next, I need to calculate the value of *b*.

> **NOTICE THAT . . .**
> The value of *b* depends on the value you use for *a*.

Because the pier is symmetric, I know that *b* plus *a* plus *b* is equal to 42 ft.

$$b + a + b = 42$$

$$b + 16.8 + b = 42$$

$$2b + 16.8 = 42$$

$$2b = 25.2$$

$$b = 12.6$$

My value for *b* is 12.6 ft.

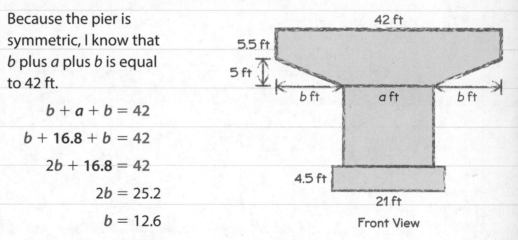

42 ft

5.5 ft

5 ft

b ft   *a* ft   *b* ft

4.5 ft

21 ft

Front View

Now, I will find the volume of each part of the pier. I will start with the footing.

The footing is a right rectangular prism.

$$V = Bh$$

$$= (21 \cdot 16)(4.5)$$

$$= 1,512$$

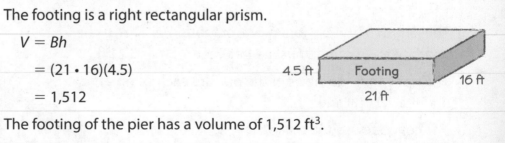

4.5 ft   Footing   16 ft

21 ft

The footing of the pier has a volume of 1,512 ft³.

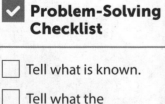

✓ Problem-Solving Checklist

☐ Tell what is known.

☐ Tell what the problem is asking.

☐ Show all your work.

☐ Show that the solution works.

Next, I will find the volume of the column.

The column is a right rectangular prism.

$V = Bh$

$= (16.8 \cdot 5)(15)$

$= 1,260$

The column of the pier has a volume of 1,260 ft³.

Column 15 ft

16.8 ft   5 ft

Then, I can find the volume of the cap.

The front face of the cap is a base of a right prism. Its area is the area of a rectangle minus the area of two identical right triangles.

Area of rectangle:

$(42)(5.5 + 5) = 441$

Area of triangle:

$\frac{1}{2}(12.6)(5) = 31.5$

6 ft   42 ft

5.5 ft   Cap

5 ft

12.6 ft   12.6 ft

Area of base of prism:

$441 - 2(31.5) = 378$

$V = Bh$

$= (378)(6)$

$= 2,268$

The cap of the pier has a volume of 2,268 ft³.

> **NOTICE THAT . . .**
> The cap is a right prism so the volume of the cap is the area of its base multiplied by its height. The bases of the prism are the front and back faces.

Finally, I can determine the weight of the concrete needed.

I can add the volumes of the footing, column, and cap to find the volume of the pier.

$1,512 + 1,260 + 2,268 = 5,040$

The pier has a volume of 5,040 ft³. The concrete for the pier weighs 150 pounds per cubic foot.

$(5,040)(150) = 756,000$

756,000 pounds of concrete are needed to make the pier.

> **NOTICE THAT . . .**
> To find the weight of the concrete needed, multiply the total volume of the pier by the weight of 1 cubic foot of concrete.

Try Another Approach

> ➤ **There are many ways to solve problems. Think about how you might solve the Designing an Overpass problem in a different way.**

Designing an Overpass

Anica is an engineer working on the plans for a highway overpass. She needs to finish the design of a concrete pier that will be constructed of right prisms and help support the overpass. Look at the requirements and notes for the concrete pier.

Finish the design by selecting values for a, b, and c that meet the requirements. How many pounds of concrete are needed to make the pier?

Pier Requirements

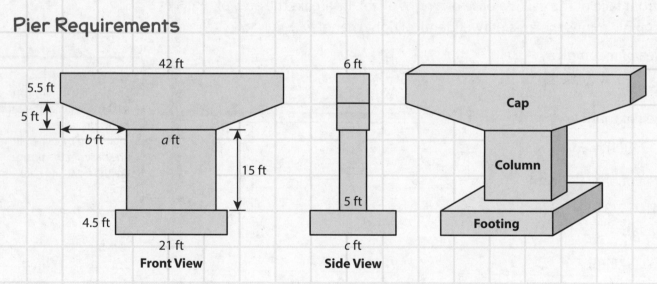

Front View   **Side View**

Notes:

- The length of the top piece, or cap, is 42 ft. a is 30% to 50% of the cap length.

- The length of the bottom piece, or footing, is 21 ft. c, the width of the footing, must be between 14 ft and 21 ft.

- The front and side views of the pier are each symmetric about a vertical line.

- The concrete used to make the pier weighs 150 pounds per cubic foot.

Plan It

➤ **Answer these questions to help you start thinking about a plan.**

a. What value will you choose for *a*? How can you show that this value meets the given requirements?

b. How can you use your value for *a* to determine the value of *b*?

Solve It

➤ **Find a different solution for the Designing an Overpass problem. Show all your work on a separate sheet of paper. You may want to use the Problem-Solving Tips to get started.**

PROBLEM-SOLVING TIPS

Math Toolkit geometric solids, grid paper, isometric dot paper

---

Key Terms

right prism	rectangular prism	volume
base	face	compose
decompose	right triangle	polygon

Models You may want to use . . .

• a drawing of the pier that includes your values for *a*, *b*, and *c*.

• area and volume formulas to find the total volume of the pier.

Reflect

Use Mathematical Practices As you work through the problem, discuss these questions with a partner.

• **Use Models** How can you use the front and side views of the pier to determine the dimensions of the footing, the column, and the cap?

• **Use Structure** How will you find the volume of the pier cap? How could you check your work by finding this volume in a different way?

Discuss Models and Strategies

➤ **Read the problem. Write a solution on a separate sheet of paper. Remember, there can be lots of ways to solve a problem.**

☐ Tell what is known.

☐ Tell what the problem is asking.

☐ Show all your work.

☐ Show that the solution works.

Determining Bridge Angles

A park trail will include a bridge that will go over a creek. Paulo and Jessica are engineers working on the bridge design. They have located three possible sites for the bridge, and need to create a more detailed design of the bridge that could be built at each site. Read this email from Jessica and help Paulo respond.

Delete   Archive | Reply   Reply All   Forward

To: Paulo
Subject: Bridge design

Hi Paulo,

Here is the design we selected for the creek bridge. I have enlarged the highlighted part of the bridge structure. All beams that appear to be horizontal or vertical are horizontal or vertical.

The length and angle measures of the bridge will change depending on the site. For each site, $m\angle 2 = m\angle 3$ and $m\angle 5 = m\angle 7$.

Site	Bridge Length (ft)	$m\angle 1$
A	40	43.8°
B	32	37.4°
C	27	32.9°

WHAT I NEED FROM YOU:
• Choose one site (I will do the other two sites).
• Calculate the measure of each numbered angle (1 to 8) for a bridge at that site.
• Explain or show how you determined the measure of each angle.

Thank you!

Jessica

Plan It and Solve It

➤ **Find a solution to the Determining Bridge Angles problem.**

Write a detailed plan and support your answer. Be sure to include:

- the site you chose (A, B, or C).
- the measure of each numbered angle (1 to 8) for the bridge site you selected.
- an explanation or work showing how you determined the measure of each angle.

PROBLEM-SOLVING TIPS

Math Toolkit grid paper, tracing paper

Key Terms

complementary angles	supplementary angles	vertical angles
straight angle	right angle	adjacent angles
acute angle	obtuse angle	vertex

Sentence Starters

- I know that ∠1 and ∠2 are ... angles because ...
- I know that ∠3 and ∠5 are ... angles because ...

Reflect

Use Mathematical Practices As you work through the problem, discuss these questions with a partner.

- **Use Structure** Why can you determine the measures of ∠3, ∠4, ∠5, and ∠6 if you are given the measure of any one of these angles?

- **Make an Argument** How do you know that ∠7 and ∠8 cannot both be acute angles?

Bridge designs often include triangles because triangles add strength and stability to a structure.

Persevere On Your Own

➤ **Read the problem. Write a solution on a separate sheet of paper.**

Planning a Park

Carolina is an environmental engineer working on the plans for a city park. The main features of the park include a swimming pool, a playground, and a picnic area. Read this email from Carolina's manager, Arturo, and help Carolina complete her assignment.

To: Carolina
Subject: Main park features

Good morning, Carolina,

The site for the swimming pool has been approved and is shown on the map. Next, we need to select the sites for the playground and the picnic area.

The three sites should form the vertices of a triangle. The playground should be between 100 m and 120 m from the pool. The picnic area should be between 60 m and 80 m from the pool. All three sites must be within the park boundary.

YOUR ASSIGNMENT:

- Decide how far the playground and picnic area will be from the pool.

- Based on your decision, determine the possible distances between the playground and the picnic area.

- Make scale drawings of two different plans showing possible locations of the playground and picnic area. For each drawing, label the actual distances between each of the main features.

Thanks!

Arturo

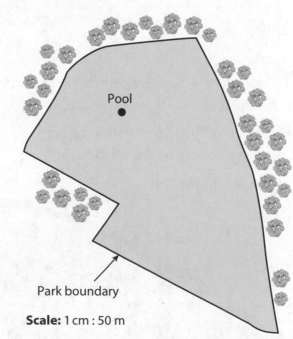

Park boundary

Scale: 1 cm : 50 m

✓ **Problem-Solving Checklist**

☐ Tell what is known.

☐ Tell what the problem is asking.

☐ Show all your work.

☐ Show that the solution works.

Solve It

➤ **Find a solution to the Planning a Park problem.**

- Decide how far the playground and picnic area will be from the pool. Your decision should be based on the requirements in the email.

- Determine the possible distances between the playground and the picnic area, based on their distances from the pool.

- Make scale drawings of two different plans showing possible locations of the playground and picnic area. For each drawing, label the actual distances between each of the main features (pool, playground, and picnic area).

Reflect

Use Mathematical Practices After you complete the problem, choose one of these questions to discuss with a partner.

- **Use Tools** What tools did you use to make your scale drawings? How were the tools helpful?

- **Critique Reasoning** Are your partner's scale drawings reasonably accurate? How do you know?

There are more than 2 million acres of parks in the 100 largest cities in the United States.

In this unit you learned to . . .

Skill	Lesson(s)
Solve problems involving area and surface area.	25
Solve problems involving volume.	26
Describe plane sections of prisms, pyramids, and cylinders.	27
Solve problems with angles.	28
Draw triangles and quadrilaterals to meet given conditions.	29
Listen carefully during discussion in order to understand and explain another person's ideas.	25–29

Think about what you have learned.

➤ **Use words, numbers, and drawings.**

1 Two important things I learned are . . .

 2 Something I know well is . . .

 3 I still need to work on . . .

Vocabulary Review

➤ **Review the unit vocabulary. Put a check mark by items you can use in speaking and writing. Look up the meaning of any terms you do not know.**

Math Vocabulary

☐ adjacent angles

☐ complementary angles

☐ cylinder

☐ plane section

☐ prism

☐ straight angle

☐ supplementary angles

☐ vertical angles

Academic Vocabulary

☐ composite

☐ result (verb)

☐ unique

➤ **Use the unit vocabulary to answer the questions.**

1 Identify at least three angles or sets of angles in this figure. Use at least one math or academic vocabulary term to describe each angle or angle relationship. Underline each term you use.

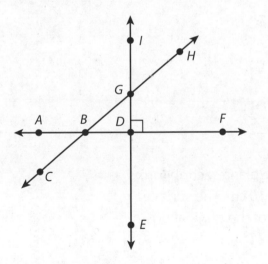

2 Name a three-dimensional shape that could be sliced to form each of these plane sections.

a. A circle, an oval, and a rectangle

b. A rectangle, a parallelogram, and a triangle

UNIT 6 • Vocabulary Review • Geometry: Solids, Triangles, and Angles   **667**

➤ **Use what you have learned to complete these problems.**

1 Which of the following conditions form a unique triangle?

   A a 6-in. side, a 7-in. side, and a 13-in. side

   B an 8-in. side between a right and an obtuse angle

   C a 4-in. side, a 9-in. side, and a 12-in. side

   D two 45° angles and a right angle

2 What percent of the rectangle is shaded? Show your work.

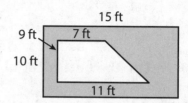

SOLUTION _____

3 Ali slices a right triangular prism parallel to its bases. The plane section forms a right triangle with sides that measure 6 cm, 8 cm, and 10 cm. The surface area of the original prism is 264 cm². What is the height of the original prism? Show your work.

SOLUTION _____

4 $\overleftrightarrow{EF}$ intersects $\overleftrightarrow{CD}$ at point W. What is the measure of $\angle DWF$?

A 17°

B 18°

C 33°

D 162°

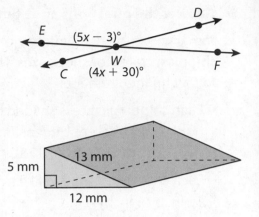

5 The volume of the right triangular prism is 540 mm³. What is the surface area of the prism? Show your work.

SOLUTION _____

6 A right triangular prism is sliced by a plane parallel to its bases. A right square pyramid is sliced the same way. Which statements about the plane sections that are formed are correct? Choose all the correct answers.

A Both plane sections have the same number of sides.

B Both plane sections are the same size and shape as the bases of the three-dimensional figures from which they were formed.

C The plane section of the prism has four angles, but the plane section of the pyramid does not.

D The plane section of the pyramid has four angles, but the plane section of the prism does not.

E The plane section of the prism is a triangle, but the plane section of the pyramid is a square.

Performance Task

➤ **Answer the questions and show all your work on separate paper.**

Jamal works for an online company that sells shoes. He designs shipping crates for shoeboxes. The shipping crates must meet the following requirements:

- Each shipping crate is shaped like a right rectangular prism and holds one shoebox. Dimensions of the crate must be in increments of 0.25 in. (0, 0.25, 0.50, 0.75).

- Each shoebox is shaped like a right rectangular prism that measures 11 in. by 6 in. by 4 in.

- Each shipping crate must contain 100 in.^{3} to 150 in.^{3} of packing peanuts in addition to the shoebox. There can be no extra space in the shipping crate. Packing peanuts cost $0.15 per 20 in.^{3}.

- The shipping crates are made of cardboard. Cardboard costs $0.13 per 25 in.^{2}.

- The total cost of packing peanuts and cardboard for each shipping crate must be $3.00 or less.

Help Jamal design a shipping crate. Find dimensions of a crate that will hold one shoebox and an amount of packing peanuts that is within the required range. Round your calculations to the nearest hundredth. Then prove that the total cost of packing peanuts and cardboard for your design is $3.00 or less.

Reflect

Use Mathematical Practices After you complete the task, choose one of the following questions to answer.

- **Make Sense of the Problem** How are dimensions of the shoebox related to dimensions of the shipping crate?

- **Be Precise** Why is cardboard priced per square inch while packing peanuts are priced per cubic inch?

Unit 7

Probability

Theoretical Probability, Experimental Probability, and Compound Events

 **Self Check**

Before starting this unit, check off the skills you know below.
As you complete each lesson, see how many more skills you can check off!

I can . . .	Before	After
Describe the probability of an event using words and numbers.	☐	☐
Find probabilities of single events.	☐	☐
Use the results of an experiment to find the experimental probability of an event.	☐	☐
Find the theoretical probability of an event.	☐	☐
Compare theoretical and experimental probabilities.	☐	☐
Find probabilities of compound events.	☐	☐
Use simulations to find probabilities of events.	☐	☐
Explain ideas about probability clearly by using models to show why the ideas make sense for the problem.	☐	☐

Prepare for Probability

➤ **You already know a lot about probability just from your everyday experiences. Sort the events by how likely they are to happen in your next math class. Then add at least two of your own events to each category.**

read poetry	discuss ratios	work in groups	take a test
need a pencil	ask questions	mix liquids	see classmates
go bowling	dance	think about math	have a substitute

Definitely	**Probably**	**Probably Not**	**Definitely Not**

Explain why you decided an event would probably happen. Then explain why you decided an event would probably not happen. Meet with a partner and compare your ideas.

Dear Family,

This week your student is exploring probability concepts.

Consider the **experiment** of rolling a number cube. Each of the numbers 1, 2, 3, 4, 5, and 6 is a possible **outcome** of the experiment. An **event** is a set of one or more outcomes. For example, rolling an even number is an event with the possible outcomes 2, 4, and 6. A **probability** describes the likelihood of an event occurring.

The probability that an event will happen can be described using both words and numbers.

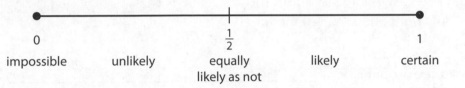

0		$\frac{1}{2}$		1
impossible	unlikely	equally likely as not	likely	certain

Your student will be modeling problems like the one below.

> There are 3 green marbles, 3 red marbles, and 6 blue marbles in a bag. Ravi reaches into the bag and selects 1 marble without looking. Describe some different events from this experiment and their probabilities.

➤ **ONE WAY** to describe probabilities is with words.

- Selecting a yellow marble is *impossible*. There are no yellow marbles in the bag.
- Selecting a green or a blue marble is *likely*. More than half of the marbles are green or blue.
- Selecting a red marble is *unlikely*. Less than half of the marbles are red.

➤ **ANOTHER WAY** is to use numbers between 0 and 1.

- The probability of selecting either a green, a red, or a blue marble is 1. All marbles are one of those colors.
- The probability of selecting a blue marble is $\frac{1}{2}$. Half of the marbles are blue.
- The probability of selecting a red marble is less than $\frac{1}{2}$. Less than half of the marbles are red.

▶ Use the next page to start a conversation about probability.

Activity Thinking About Probability Around You

➤ **Do this activity together to investigate probability in the real world.**

Have you ever wondered why the weather forecast for the weekend changes from Monday to Friday?

Meteorologists use computer models to help make forecasts, or predictions, about the chance of different types of weather, such as rain or sun. The predictions are based on data and that data can change on an hourly basis.

The closer to an actual day, the more data there will be. This is why a five-day forecast is much more likely to be accurate than a ten-day forecast. A forecast about the weather in ten days is only right about half of the time!

 Where else do you see probability in the world around you?

? **UNDERSTAND:** How can you describe the likelihood of an event?

Explore Probability

Model It

➤ **Complete the problems about outcomes of an event.**

1 A standard number cube has six sides labeled 1 through 6. Think about rolling a number cube one time.

   a. Is it more likely that the cube will show *a multiple of 2* or *a multiple of 3*?

   b. How likely is the cube to show a 3?

   c. Why is it just as likely that the cube will show an even number as an odd number?

2 Doing something where you cannot know the **outcome** is called an **experiment**. In problem 1, rolling the number cube is the experiment. The outcomes are the possible results of the experiment.

   a. What are the possible outcomes of rolling a standard number cube?

   b. An **event** is a set of one or more outcomes. What are the possible outcomes for the event of rolling a multiple of 2?

   c. What are the possible outcomes for the event of rolling a multiple of 3?

   d. What are the possible outcomes for the event of rolling an even number? An odd number?

DISCUSS IT

Ask: Why do some events have only one outcome and others have more than one outcome?

Share: An event will probably happen when . . .

◎ **Learning Target** SMP 2, SMP 3, SMP 7
Understand that the probability of a chance event is a number between 0 and 1 that expresses the likelihood of the event occurring. Larger numbers indicate greater likelihood. A probability near 0 indicates an unlikely event, a probability around $\frac{1}{2}$ indicates an event that is neither unlikely nor likely, and a probability near 1 indicates a likely event.

Model It

➤ **Complete the problems about describing the likelihood of an event happening.**

3 **Probability** describes how likely an event is to occur. One way to describe probabilities is to use words. *Certain* describes an event that will occur. *Impossible* describes an event that can never occur. *Likely* describes events that will probably, but not certainly, occur. Events that will probably not occur, but could, can be described as *unlikely*. And if an event is as likely to occur as not occur, it can be described as *equally likely as not*.

Suppose you roll a standard number cube. Give the possible outcomes, if any, for each event.

Event	Outcomes	Probability
rolling a 7		impossible
rolling a number less than 2		unlikely
rolling a prime number		equally likely as not
rolling a number greater than 1		likely
rolling an integer		certain

DISCUSS IT

Ask: Why is rolling a 7 impossible?

Share: I think an event is certain when . . .

4 **Reflect** Four cards are in a bag. Each card has a picture of a lion, a giraffe, a goat, or a leopard. One card is selected from the bag at random.

Name an event with the given probability.

a. Impossible

b. Certain

c. Equally likely as not

d. Unlikely

Name:

Prepare for Understanding Probability

1 Think about what you know about fractions and rational numbers. Fill in each box. Use words, numbers, and pictures. Show as many ideas as you can.

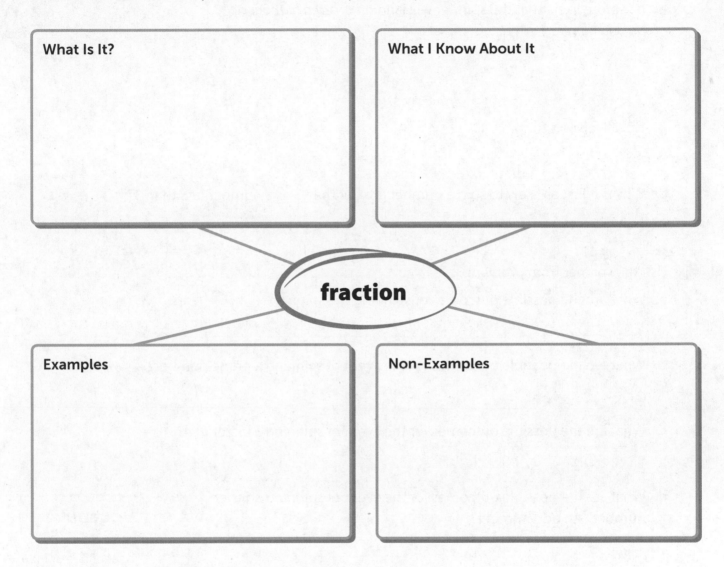

What Is It?

What I Know About It

fraction

Examples

Non-Examples

2 Wyatt says the fraction $\frac{6}{7}$ means 7 sixths. Is he correct? Explain.

➤ **Complete problems 3–5.**

3 A spinner has 5 equal-size sections numbered 1 through 5. The spinner is spun one time.

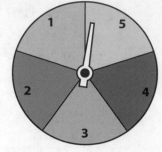

   a. Is it more likely that the spinner will land on *an even number* or *an odd number*? Why?

   b. How likely is it to spin a 1?

   c. Why is it just as likely to spin a number greater than 3 as a number less than 3?

4 Use the spinner from problem 3.

   a. What are the possible outcomes of spinning the spinner?

   b. What are the possible outcomes for the event of spinning a prime number?

   c. What are the possible outcomes for the event of spinning a factor of 4?

   d. What are the possible outcomes for the event of spinning an even number? An odd number?

5 Suppose you spin the spinner from problem 3 once. Give the possible outcomes, if any, for each event.

Event	Outcomes	Probability
spinning a number less than or equal to 2		unlikely
spinning a factor of 6		likely
spinning a 6		impossible

Vocabulary

event
a set of one or more outcomes of an experiment.

outcome
one of the possible results of a chance experiment.

probability
a number between 0 and 1 that expresses the likelihood of an event occurring.

Develop Understanding of Probability

Model It: Describe Probabilities with Words

➤ **Try these two problems involving representing probabilities.**

1 A bag contains 6 red marbles, 6 green marbles, and 12 blue marbles. Paloma reaches into the bag and selects a marble without looking.

a. What is the total number of marbles in the bag?

b. What is half the number of marbles in the bag?

c. Name an event that is impossible.

d. Name an event that is unlikely.

e. Name an event that is equally likely as not.

f. Name an event that is likely.

g. Name an event that is certain.

2 Consider the experiment from problem 1.

a. Draw a line from each event to show the probability of that event.

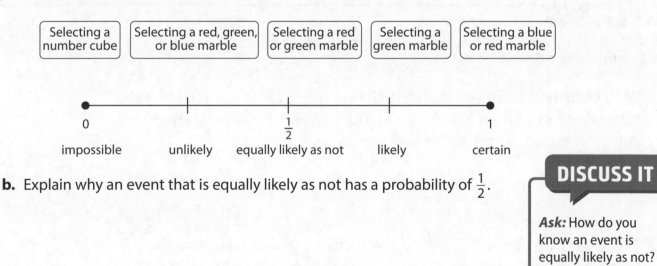

| Selecting a number cube | Selecting a red, green, or blue marble | Selecting a red or green marble | Selecting a green marble | Selecting a blue or red marble |

```
0              1/2                    1
●———————|———————|———————|———————●
impossible   unlikely  equally likely as not   likely   certain
```

b. Explain why an event that is equally likely as not has a probability of $\frac{1}{2}$.

> **DISCUSS IT**
>
> *Ask:* How do you know an event is equally likely as not?
>
> *Share:* *Equally likely as not* and *as likely as not* mean the same thing because . . .

Model It: Describe Probabilities with Numbers

➤ **Try this problem about describing probabilities with numbers.**

3 You can also use numbers to describe probabilities. Imagine that the cards shown are facedown and you select one card at random.

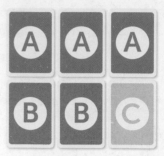

a. Name an event that has a probability of 0.

b. Name an event that has a probability of 1.

c. Name an event that has a probability of $\frac{1}{2}$.

d. Name an event that has a probability between 0 and $\frac{1}{2}$.

e. Name an event that has a probability between $\frac{1}{2}$ and 1.

DISCUSS IT

Ask: Which outcome is most likely?

Share: An event with a probability of $\frac{1}{2}$ is less likely to occur than an event with a probability of $\frac{3}{4}$ because . . .

CONNECT IT

➤ **Complete the problems below.**

4 What word describes the probability of rolling an integer on a standard number cube? How can you describe the same probability with a number? Explain why you can describe the probability both ways.

5 Each letter of the word EXPERIMENT is written on a separate slip of paper. One slip of paper is selected at random. Name two possible events that could occur. Describe their probabilities with both words and numbers.

Practice Probability

➤ **Study how the Example shows determining the probability for an event.
Then solve problems 1–5.**

Example

Andrew has a bag of apples, peaches, and oranges. There are 24 pieces of
fruit in all, 12 of which are oranges. Andrew selects a piece of fruit at
random. What is the probability that Andrew selects a peach?

There are 24 pieces of fruit in total.

Since 12 are oranges, the total number of apples and peaches is 12. There is at
least 1 apple in the bag. So, less than half of the pieces of fruit are peaches.

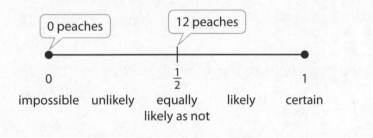

The probability that Andrew selects a peach is between 0 and $\frac{1}{2}$.

---

1. Consider the experiment in the Example.

   a. How likely is it that Andrew selects a pear?

   b. What is the probability that Andrew selects a piece of fruit that is not a peach?

2. There are 10 tiles numbered 1–10. What is the probability of selecting a
   tile at random with a number greater than 5? Explain.

Vocabulary

event
a set of one or more
outcomes of an
experiment.

probability
a number between 0
and 1 that expresses
the likelihood of an
event occurring.

3 Bruno has 8 coins. There are 3 dimes and 1 nickel. The rest are either pennies or quarters. Selecting a penny at random is unlikely, but not impossible. What is the greatest possible number of pennies in Bruno's collection? Explain.

4 Jasmine has a box with 3 green tennis balls, 2 red tennis balls, and 4 yellow tennis balls. She selects a tennis ball at random.

   a. Is it more likely that Jasmine selects a *red tennis ball* or a *green tennis ball*? Explain how you know.

   b. Is it more likely that Jasmine selects a *red tennis ball* or a *purple tennis ball*? Explain how you know.

   c. Is it more likely that Jasmine selects a tennis ball that is *not yellow* or *not green*? Explain how you know.

5 At a musical showcase, there are 10 performers playing an instrument and 5 performers singing. The showcase organizer will select the first performer at random. Describe the probability of each event in words. Explain your answers.

   a. The first performer is a singer.

plays instrument: 10
sings: 5

   b. The first performer plays an instrument.

Refine Ideas About Probability

Apply It

➤ **Complete problems 1–5.**

1 **Translate** Describe each probability in words.

a. $\frac{3}{4}$

b. $\frac{7}{8}$

c. $\frac{1}{3}$

d. $\frac{11}{20}$

e. $\frac{1}{20}$

2 **Compare** There is a 75% chance of rain in Seattle. There is a $\frac{3}{4}$ chance of rain in Tacoma. Is it more likely to rain in Seattle than in Tacoma? Explain.

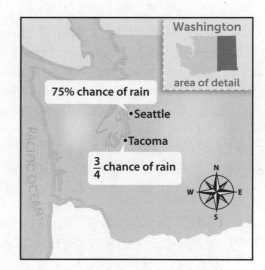

3 **Analyze** A bag contains 12 marbles. The probability of selecting a green, a yellow, or a blue marble from the bag is 1. The probability of selecting a yellow marble is $\frac{1}{2}$. Selecting a blue marble is more likely than selecting a green marble.

Charlotte says the greatest possible number of green marbles in the bag is 2.

Hai says the least possible number of green marbles is 0. Who is correct? Explain.

4 **PART A** Draw a spinner with the following characteristics:

• Landing on 1, 2, 3, or 4 is certain.

• It is more likely to land on 1 than not land on 1.

• It is equally likely to land on 2 or 3.

• It is twice as likely to land on 4 as on 2.

PART B Identify fractions that could describe the probability of landing on each number on your spinner. Justify your answers.

5 **Math Journal** A bag has 6 pink marbles, 4 purple marbles, and 2 orange marbles. You select a marble from the bag at random. Describe the likelihood of two events.

✓ **End of Lesson Checklist**

☐ **INTERACTIVE GLOSSARY** Find the entries for *event* and *probability*. Rewrite the definitions in your own words.

Dear Family,

This week your student is learning about experimental probability.

Experimental probability is the probability of an event happening, based on results from an experiment. When you find an experimental probability, you compare the number of times a certain event occurs (favorable outcomes) to the total number of **trials** in the experiment.

Experimental probability of an event = $\dfrac{\text{number of favorable outcomes}}{\text{number of trials}}$

Suppose you toss a coin 10 times and the coin lands heads up 4 times. You can use this data to find the experimental probability of tossing a coin and the coin landing heads up. There are **10 trials** and **4 favorable outcomes.**

Experimental probability of heads up = $\dfrac{4}{10}$ or 0.4 or 40%

You can use the results from an experiment to predict how often an event will occur in the future.

Your student will be solving problems like the one below.

> Kamal and Zara are playing a game that uses a spinner with three sections. One section shows a sun, one shows a moon, and one shows a star. After spinning the spinner 60 times, it has landed on the moon section 18 times. Based on these results, predict how many times the spinner will land on the moon section after 300 spins.

➤ **ONE WAY** to make a prediction is to use an equation.

$$\frac{18}{60} = \frac{\text{number of moons}}{300}$$

$$300\left(\frac{18}{60}\right) = 300\left(\frac{\text{number of moons}}{300}\right)$$

$$90 = \text{number of moons}$$

➤ **ANOTHER WAY** is to use a fraction.

The spinner lands on the moon $\frac{18}{60}$ of the time.

$$\frac{18}{60} \cdot 300 = 90$$

Using either method, you can predict that the spinner will land on the moon section about 90 times out of 300 spins.

 Use the next page to start a conversation about experimental probability.

Activity Thinking About Experimental Probability Around You

➤ **Do this activity together to investigate experimental probability in the real world.**

Have you ever celebrated Groundhog Day? It is a tradition celebrated on February 2 every year. The most-attended ceremony is held in Punxsutawney, in western Pennsylvania. According to folklore, if a groundhog sees its shadow, winter will last for another six weeks. If it does not see its shadow, then there will be an early spring.

Because there are records as far back as the 1800s, you could find how frequently the groundhog saw its shadow in the past. Then you could use this experimental probability to make a prediction about how often the groundhog will see its shadow in the future!

? When else might you use experimental probability to make a prediction?

Explore Experimental Probability

Previously, you learned how to describe the probability of a chance event. In this lesson, you will learn about experimental probability.

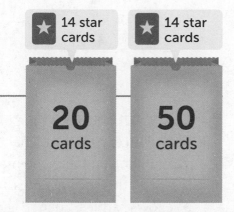

★ 14 star cards   ★ 14 star cards

20 cards   **50** cards

➤ **Use what you know to try to solve the problem below.**

A bag with 20 cards has 14 star cards. Another bag with 50 cards has 14 star cards. Chantel selects a card at random from each bag. From which bag is Chantel more likely to select a star card?

TRY IT

Math Toolkit bags, bowls, index cards, sticky notes, unit cubes

DISCUSS IT

Ask: How did you reach that conclusion?

Share: I saw that . . . so I . . .

◎ **Learning Targets**   SMP 1, SMP 2, SMP 3, SMP 4, SMP 5, SMP 6
- Approximate the probability of a chance event by collecting data on the chance process that produces it and observing its long-run relative frequency, and predict the approximate relative frequency given the probability.
- Develop a probability model by observing frequencies in data generated from a chance process.

CONNECT IT

1 **Look Back** From which bag is Chantel more likely to select a star card? Why?

2 **Look Ahead** Each time Chantel selects a card from a bag, she performs one **trial** of an experiment. Chantel uses a box of marbles to conduct a different experiment. She selects a marble, records its color, and puts it back in the box. She does this several times. In all, she selects 5 red marbles, 3 blue marbles, and 2 yellow marbles. Chantel can use **experimental probability** to describe the likelihood of getting a particular result in an experiment.

$$\text{Experimental probability of an event} = \frac{\text{number of favorable outcomes}}{\text{number of trials}}$$

a. How many trials were in Chantel's experiment?

b. Based on her results, what is the probability of selecting a blue marble?

c. A probability can be expressed as a fraction, decimal, or percent. What is the experimental probability of selecting a red marble, expressed as a fraction? A decimal? A percent?

d. You can think of all the marbles in the box as the population and the results of the experiment as a sample. Suppose Chantel repeats the experiment and this time gets 4 red marbles. Why would it be reasonable to predict that between 40% and 50% of the marbles in the box are red?

3 **Reflect** What does it mean if the experimental probability of an event is 1?

Prepare for Solving Problems Involving Experimental Probability

1 Think about what you know about probability. Fill in each box. Use words, numbers, and pictures. Show as many ideas as you can.

Word	In My Own Words	Example
event		
outcome		
probability		

2 Bridget says that when a standard number cube is rolled, getting an even number is an outcome. Uma says that getting an even number is an event. Who is correct? Explain.

3   One box has 80 raffle tickets, of which 35 are red.
    Another box has 50 raffle tickets, of which 35 are red.

35 red tickets   35 red tickets
TICKET   TICKET
80   50
raffle   raffle
tickets   tickets

a. Suppose Mia selects a raffle ticket at random from each
   box. From which box is she more likely to select a red raffle
   ticket? Show your work.

SOLUTION _____

_____

b. Check your answer to problem 3a. Show your work.

Develop Finding Experimental Probability

➤ **Read and try to solve the problem below.**

Erin rolls a standard number cube and records the results.

Number Rolled	1	2	3	4	5	6
Frequency	I	I	IIII		II	II

Based on these results, what is the probability of rolling each number?

TRY IT

 Math Toolkit grid paper, number cubes, number lines, sticky notes

DISCUSS IT

Ask: How do you know your answer is reasonable?

Share: I know my answer is reasonable because . . .

➤ **Explore different ways to find experimental probability.**

Erin rolls a standard number cube and records the results.

Number Rolled	1	2	3	4	5	6
Frequency	I	I	IIII		II	II

Based on these results, what is the probability of rolling each number?

Picture It

You can use a dot plot to display the results of an experiment.

Results of Rolling a Number Cube

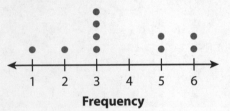

Frequency

Model It

You can write the experimental probability of each possible outcome in words.

Probability of rolling a 1 = $\dfrac{\text{number of 1s rolled}}{\text{number of trials}}$

Probability of rolling a 2 = $\dfrac{\text{number of 2s rolled}}{\text{number of trials}}$

Probability of rolling a 3 = $\dfrac{\text{number of 3s rolled}}{\text{number of trials}}$

Probability of rolling a 4 = $\dfrac{\text{number of 4s rolled}}{\text{number of trials}}$

Probability of rolling a 5 = $\dfrac{\text{number of 5s rolled}}{\text{number of trials}}$

Probability of rolling a 6 = $\dfrac{\text{number of 6s rolled}}{\text{number of trials}}$

➤ **Use the problem from the previous page to help you understand experimental probability.**

1 Look at **Model It**. What is the experimental probability of rolling each number?

Number Rolled	1	2	3	4	5	6
Frequency	|	|	||||		||	||
Experimental Probability						

2 How does the experimental probability of rolling a 3 compare to that of rolling a 6? Why?

3 Erin conducts the experiment again. Based on these results, what is the probability of rolling each number?

Number Rolled	1	2	3	4	5	6
Frequency	|||	|	||	||	|	|
Experimental Probability						

4 Erin rolled a number cube 10 times in both experiments. The experimental probability of rolling a 4 was different in Erin's two experiments. Why?

5 Suppose you conducted the same experiment as Erin. Should you expect your probabilities to be the same as those from either of Erin's experiments? Explain.

6 **Reflect** Think about all the models and strategies you have discussed today. Describe how one of them helped you better understand how to find experimental probability.

Apply It

➤ **Use what you learned to solve these problems.**

7 In a class, 18 students each toss a coin 10 times. They record how many times the result is heads. Based on these results, what is the probability of getting more than 5 heads? Show your work.

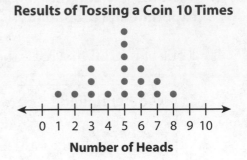

Results of Tossing a Coin 10 Times

Number of Heads

SOLUTION _____

8 A grocery store prints coupons on randomly selected receipts. A coupon was printed on 18 of the last 1,200 receipts. Based on these results, what is the probability that a coupon will be printed on the next receipt? Show your work.

1,200 receipts, **18** coupons printed

SOLUTION _____

9 Soledad has a spinner with a red, a blue, and a white section. She spins the spinner 20 times. Based on her results, what is the probability of the spinner landing on each color? Show your work.

Color	Red	Blue	White
Frequency	5	9	6

SOLUTION _____

Practice Finding Experimental Probability

➤ **Study the Example showing how to find experimental probability. Then solve problems 1–4.**

Example

Nicanor selects one diving ring from a bag without looking. He records the color and returns the diving ring to the bag. He repeats this several times. In all, he selects 3 red rings, 4 yellow rings, and 5 blue rings. Based on his results, what is the experimental probability of selecting each color?

Nicanor selects a diving ring from the bag $3 + 4 + 5$, or **12**, times.

Probability of red $= \dfrac{3}{12}$, or $\dfrac{1}{4}$

Probability of yellow $= \dfrac{4}{12}$, or $\dfrac{1}{3}$

Probability of blue $= \dfrac{5}{12}$

1 Look at the Example.

   a. Why is the denominator of each fraction 12?

   b. Mateo repeats Nicanor's experiment and has different results. Mateo selects 2 red rings, 3 yellow rings, and 7 blue rings. Based on Mateo's experiment, what is the experimental probability of selecting each color?

   c. Based on Nicanor and Mateo's results, would you predict there are more *red*, *yellow*, or *blue* diving rings in the bag? Explain.

Vocabulary

experiment
a repeatable procedure involving chance that results in one or more possible outcomes.

experimental probability
the probability of an event occurring based on the results from an experiment.

2 Carissa conducts an experiment by rolling two number cubes, both numbered 1–6. She records the number of times she rolls the same number on both cubes. In 50 trials, she rolls the same number on both cubes 13 times. Based on the results, what is the probability of rolling the same number on both cubes, expressed as a percent? Show your work.

SOLUTION _____

3 A spinner has five sections, labeled 1 through 5. The spinner is spun 24 times. The results are shown in the table. The last row of the table is missing. Based on the results of the experiment, what is the probability that the spinner stops on 5? Explain.

Outcome	Frequency
1	4
2	3
3	7
4	6

4 Cheryl runs an experiment. She selects a tile at random from a bag of lettered tiles, records the letter, and replaces the tile. Her results are shown below.

A, D, E, B, F, C, F, D, E, B, A, B

a. Based on the results, what is the probability of selecting a vowel? Show your work.

SOLUTION _____

b. Is it likely that there are the same number of vowels and consonants in the bag? Explain.

Develop Using Experimental Probability to Make Predictions

➤ **Read and try to solve the problem below.**

Luis sets his music app to play a certain playlist on shuffle. His app tracks the genre of each song played.

Luis plays the same playlist on shuffle again and this time plays 130 songs. Based on the previous results, predict the number of country songs that will play.

TRY IT

Math Toolkit grid paper, number lines, sticky notes

DISCUSS IT

Ask: What strategy did you use to make your prediction?

Share: The strategy I used was . . .

➤ **Explore different ways to use experimental probability to make predictions.**

Luis sets his music app to play a certain playlist on shuffle. His app tracks the genre of each song played.

Genre	Hip-Hop	Pop	Rock	Country
Number of Songs Played	5	9	12	14

Luis plays the same playlist on shuffle again and this time plays 130 songs. Based on the previous results, predict the number of country songs that will play.

Model It

You can use the data to find the experimental probability.

There were $5 + 9 + 12 + 14$, or **40**, songs played.

$$\text{Probability of a country song} = \frac{\text{number of country songs played}}{\text{number of trials}}$$
$$= \frac{14}{40}$$

Then use the experimental probability to predict future results.

About $\frac{14}{40}$ of the 130 songs should be country songs.

$$\frac{14}{40} \cdot 130$$

Model It

You can use an equation to make a prediction.

The experimental probability for 40 songs is $\frac{14}{40}$. You can use that to make a prediction for 130 songs.

c = number of country songs played in 130 trials

$$\frac{14}{40} = \frac{c}{130}$$

➤ **Use the problem from the previous page to help you understand how to use experimental probability to make predictions.**

1 Look at the **Model Its**. How is finding $\frac{14}{40} \cdot 130$ like solving $\frac{14}{40} = \frac{c}{130}$?

2 Why are both 45 and 46 reasonable predictions for the number of country songs played in 130 songs?

3 When 40 songs were played, 30% were rock songs. Why should you not expect exactly 30% of the 130 songs played to be rock songs?

4 How can you use data from an experiment to make a prediction about how often an event will happen in a future experiment with more or less trials?

5 Can you use Luis's results to predict how many times another person's playlist will play country songs? Explain.

6 **Reflect** Think about all the models and strategies you have discussed today. Describe how one of them helped you better understand how to make predictions using experimental probability.

Apply It

➤ **Use what you learned to solve these problems.**

7 A floor is covered with black tiles and green tiles that alternate. Daria rolls marbles on the floor. All of the marbles stop on a black tile, a green tile, or in a groove between the tiles. Daria finds that 30 stop on a black tile, 35 on a green tile, and 55 in a groove. Suppose Daria rolls 20 more marbles. Predict the number of those marbles that will stop in a groove. Show your work.

SOLUTION _____

8 Last season, Erik made 21 of the 35 free throws he attempted. Suppose he attempts 50 free throws this season. What is the most reasonable prediction of the number of free throws he will miss?

A 28

B 11

C 20

D 30

9 A taco stand lets the first customer every Monday select the type of taco that will be discounted Tuesday. The table shows the number of times each type of taco has been discounted so far. Based on these results, predict about how many times carne asada tacos will be discounted in the next 10 weeks. Show your work.

Type of Taco	Weeks Discounted
Carne Asada (Grilled Beef)	6
Carnitas (Pork)	10
Nopales (Cactus)	7
Pollo Asado (Grilled Chicken)	9

SOLUTION _____

Practice Using Experimental Probability to Make Predictions

➤ Study the Example showing how to use experimental probability to make a prediction. Then solve problems 1–4.

Example

A science class records the weather every day for 30 days. Based on their results, predict how many of the next 15 days will be rainy.

Weather	Sunny	Rainy	Cloudy Without Rain
Number of Days	13	9	8

Experimental probability of a rainy day: $\dfrac{\text{rainy days}}{\text{total days}} = \dfrac{9}{30}$

Probability of a rainy day · number of days = number of rainy days

$$\frac{9}{30} \cdot 15 = 4.5$$

You can predict that about 4 or 5 days in the next 15 days will be rainy.

---

1 A class rolls a number cube 100 times and records the results.

Number on Cube	1	2	3	4	5	6
Frequency	15	16	17	20	15	17

a. Use these results to predict about how many times the class will roll the number 4 in 1,000 trials. Show your work.

SOLUTION _____

b. Use these results to predict how many times an odd number will be rolled in 10,000 trials. Show your work.

SOLUTION _____

Vocabulary

experimental probability
the probability of an event occurring based on the results from an experiment.

trial
a single performance of an experiment.

2 Tiana spins a spinner several times. It stops on red 12 of those times. Based on this result, she predicts that if she spins the spinner 1,000 times, the spinner will stop on red 240 times. How many times did Tiana spin the spinner? Show your work.

SOLUTION _____

3 There is an upcoming election in Deyvi's town. Deyvi asks a random sample of voters whether they plan to vote for the current mayor, against the current mayor, or are undecided. His results are shown in the table. Use his results to predict how many people will be for, against, and undecided in a group of 2,000 voters. Show your work.

Vote	Number of Voters
For	25
Against	12
Undecided	3

SOLUTION _____

_____

Elizabeth's video game

4 A video game randomly generates in-game items for players. Elizabeth records the items she receives. Based on the items Elizabeth receives, she determines that the probability of receiving a speed boost is 0.21. She predicts that about 4 of her next 20 items will be speed boosts. Why is this a reasonable prediction?

Refine Solving Problems Involving Experimental Probability

➤ **Complete the Example below. Then solve problems 1–9.**

Example

Inés tosses a coin 50 times. It lands heads up 32 times.

Tomás tosses the same coin 50 times and it lands heads up 28 times.

Kendra tosses the same coin 50 times and it lands heads up 24 times.

Use their results to predict the number of times the coin will land heads up in 1,000 tosses.

Look at how you could show your work by combining the results.

Total number of heads: 32 + 28 + 24 = 84

Total number of trials: 50 + 50 + 50 = 150

Probability of heads: $\frac{84}{150}$

You can find $\frac{84}{150} \cdot 1{,}000$ to predict the number of heads in 1,000 tosses.

SOLUTION _____

CONSIDER THIS . . .
Inés, Tomás, and Kendra all perform the same experiment.

PAIR/SHARE
Why can you not add $\frac{32}{50}$, $\frac{28}{50}$, and $\frac{24}{50}$ to find the probability?

Apply It

1 Madison tosses a paper cup and records whether it lands on its side. In 20 trials, the cup lands on its side 19 times. In 90 trials, the cup lands on its side 81 times. Does the probability that the cup will land on its side increase or decrease when Madison runs more trials? Show your work.

CONSIDER THIS . . .
You cannot just compare the number of favorable outcomes.

PAIR/SHARE
Why does the experimental probability change when Madison runs more trials?

SOLUTION _____

2 There are 200 letter tiles in a bag. Ria selects a tile at random, writes down the letter, and puts the tile back. She does this 5 times. She selects the letters B, A, E, R, and S. Use Ria's results to predict about how many consonants she will select in the next 20 trials. Show your work.

CONSIDER THIS . . .
The letters A and E are not consonants.

PAIR/SHARE
What would not be a reasonable prediction?

SOLUTION _____

3 Ximena has a large bag of marbles. She selects a marble without looking, records the color, and returns the marble to the bag. In 25 trials, she selects a green marble 10 times. She selects a blue marble the other times. Which is the most reasonable prediction for how many times Ximena will select a blue marble in 100 trials?

A 35

B 40

C 50

D 60

Platon chose B as the correct answer. How might he have gotten that answer?

CONSIDER THIS . . .
Do you want to predict the number of times she selects a blue marble or a green marble?

PAIR/SHARE
What are other reasonable predictions you could make with Ximena's data? Why?

4 A kicker made 10 of his last 12 field goals. Predict about how many of his next 42 field goals the kicker will not make. Show your work.

Made 10 of last 12 field goals

SOLUTION _____

5 Students in a math class are divided into three groups. Each group is given a bag filled with an unknown number of marbles. The students in each group select a marble at random from their bag and then put it back. Each group does this 50 times. Which of the statements below are true? Select all that apply.

	Bag A	Bag B	Bag C
Red	39	10	3
White	2	15	15
Yellow	9	15	7
Purple	0	10	25

A There are definitely no purple marbles in Bag A.

B The probability of selecting a yellow marble from Bag C is approximately 7%.

C The probability of selecting a red marble from Bag B and the probability of selecting a purple marble from Bag B are the same.

D If the group selects 10 more marbles from Bag C, about 5 will be purple.

E Each bag definitely contains the same number of marbles.

F The probability of selecting a white marble from Bag B and the probability of selecting a white marble from Bag C are the same.

6 Diego selects a rubber ball from a bag at random, records the color, and replaces it. After 15 trials, the experimental probability of selecting a red ball is $\frac{7}{15}$, selecting a yellow ball is $\frac{1}{5}$, and selecting a green ball is $\frac{1}{3}$. On the 16th trial, Diego selects a purple ball. Now the experimental probability of selecting a yellow ball is _____.

7 Mr. Ramírez rolls a standard number cube one time and gets a 4. Mr. Ramírez says that means the probability of rolling a 4 is $\frac{1}{1}$. He says he can use that information to make a prediction about future rolls. Do you think Mr. Ramírez has enough information to make a useful prediction? Explain why or why not.

8 Aisha selects a pink, blue, or brown hair tie at random from her drawer every morning and puts it back every night. The table shows the colors of the hair ties she has worn over the last 14 days. Is it likely that there are equal numbers of pink, blue, and brown hair ties in the drawer? Explain.

Hair Tie Color	Frequency
Pink	4
Blue	6
Brown	4

9 **Math Journal** Two months ago, a car dealership sold 30 red cars and 120 cars that were not red. Last month the car dealership sold a total of 200 cars. Tarik predicts that the dealership sold 45 red cars last month. Do you think this is a reasonable prediction? Explain.

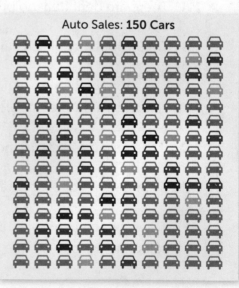

Auto Sales: **150 Cars**

✔ End of Lesson Checklist

☐ **INTERACTIVE GLOSSARY** Find the entry for *experimental probability*. Rewrite the definition in your own words.

☐ **SELF CHECK** Go back to the Unit 7 Opener and see what you can check off.

Dear Family,

This week your student is learning about theoretical probability.

The **theoretical probability** of an event occurring is what you would expect to happen in an experiment. For example, you expect a tossed coin to land heads up half the time. So, the theoretical probability of a coin landing heads up is 50%.

Your student has already learned about experimental probability, which lets you use the results from past experiments to predict the results of future experiments. The experimental probability of an event is not always the same as the theoretical probability. You might use experimental probability, theoretical probability, or both to make a prediction. Your student will be solving problems like the one below.

> There are cards labeled A, A, B, B, C, C, D, and D in a bag. Kenji selects a card at random, records the letter, and replaces it. He does this 10 times and gets cards labeled B, A, D, C, C, A, B, C, C, and A. What is the probability of selecting each letter?

➤ **ONE WAY** to find the probability is to find the theoretical probability of each outcome.

Outcome	A	B	C	D
Theoretical Probability	$\frac{2}{8}$	$\frac{2}{8}$	$\frac{2}{8}$	$\frac{2}{8}$

➤ **ANOTHER WAY** is to find the experimental probability of each outcome.

Outcome	A	B	C	D
Experimental Probability	$\frac{3}{10}$	$\frac{2}{10}$	$\frac{4}{10}$	$\frac{1}{10}$

You can use both theoretical probability and experimental probability to describe how likely it is that the next card Kenji draws is A, B, C, or D.

 Use the next page to start a conversation about theoretical probability.

Activity Thinking About Theoretical Probability Around You

➤ **Do this activity together to investigate theoretical probability in the real world.**

Have you ever played a game and gotten results that did not seem fair? Maybe you rolled a series of 1s on a number cube, or tossed a coin that landed tails up five times in a row.

Theoretical probability tells you about how often something should happen—over a long period of time. Each individual roll or toss is still random, and any outcome is possible.

So, when you roll a number cube or toss a coin just a few times, you can get results that seem unlikely.

? What are other situations where something unlikely happens?

Explore Theoretical Probability

Previously, you learned about experimental probability. In this lesson, you will learn about theoretical probability.

BIENVENIDO   **ADIOS**

➤ **Use what you know to try to solve the problem below.**

Each of the 10 letters in the word BIENVENIDO is written on a separate slip of paper and placed in a bag. Each of the 5 letters in the word ADIOS is written on a separate slip of paper and placed in another bag. Khadija plans to select a letter at random from each bag. She thinks she is equally likely to select a letter D from each bag. Show why you agree or disagree.

TRY IT   **Math Toolkit** bags, bowls, grid paper, index cards, sticky notes

DISCUSS IT

Ask: How would you explain what the problem is asking in your own words?

Share: The problem is asking . . .

◎ **Learning Targets**   SMP 1, SMP 2, SMP 3, SMP 4, SMP 5, SMP 6, SMP 7
Develop a probability model and use it to find probabilities of events. Compare probabilities from a model to observed frequencies; if the agreement is not good, explain possible sources of the discrepancy.
• Develop a uniform probability model by assigning equal probability to all outcomes, and use the model to determine probabilities of events.

CONNECT IT

1 Look Back Is Khadija equally likely to select a letter D from each bag? Explain.

2 Look Ahead When you find the probability of an event based on results from an experiment, you are finding the experimental probability of that event. The **theoretical probability** of an event is found by analyzing the possible outcomes, rather than by conducting an experiment. Consider the spinners below. The sections on Spinner 1 are all the same size. Sections B and C on Spinner 2 are the same size. All sections on Spinner 3 are the same size.

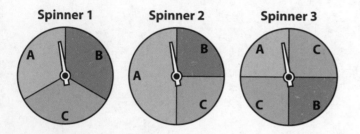

a. The **sample space** for an experiment is the set of all possible unique outcomes. For all of these spinners, the sample space is the same. What is the sample space for the spinners?

b. Sometimes all of the outcomes of an experiment are equally likely. Other times, all outcomes are not equally likely. Explain why the outcomes for Spinner 1 are equally likely but the outcomes for Spinner 2 are not.

c. When outcomes are equally likely, you can find the theoretical probability of an event using the fraction $\frac{\text{number of favorable outcomes}}{\text{total number of outcomes}}$. What is the probability of spinning an A on Spinner 1?

d. For Spinner 3, the outcomes are not equally likely. To find the probability of spinning a C, consider what fraction of the spinner consists of the favorable outcome C. What is the probability of spinning a C on Spinner 3?

3 Reflect Which spinner in problem 2 is most likely to land on B? Explain.

Prepare for Solving Problems Involving Probability Models

1. Think about what you know about events and probability. Fill in each box. Use words, numbers, and pictures. Show as many ideas as you can.

What Is It?	What I Know About It

event

Examples	Non-Examples

2. How is an event different from an outcome? Use an example to explain.

3 Each of the seven letters in the word WELCOME is written on a separate slip of paper and placed in Box 1. Each of the seven letters in the word GOODBYE is written on a separate slip of paper and placed in Box 2. Jayden plans to select a letter at random from each box. He thinks he is equally likely to select a letter O from each box.

Box 1 **Box 2**

a. Show why Jayden is correct or incorrect.

b. Check your answer to problem 3a. Show your work.

Develop Finding Theoretical Probabilities

➤ **Read and try to solve the problem below.**

Keith is playing a board game in which he spins a spinner to determine how many spaces to move his game piece. He is 3 spaces away from the finish and can only move forward if he spins a 1, 2, or 3 on his next turn. All sections of the spinner have the same size. What is the probability that Keith moves forward on his next turn?

Math Toolkit index cards, number cubes, spinners, sticky notes

➤ **Explore different ways to understand finding theoretical probabilities.**

Keith is playing a board game in which he spins a spinner to determine how many spaces to move his game piece. He is 3 spaces away from the finish and can only move forward if he spins a 1, 2, or 3 on his next turn. All sections of the spinner have the same size. What is the probability that Keith moves forward on his next turn?

Picture It

You can draw a picture to make sense of the problem.

There are 6 possible outcomes.

There are **4 favorable** outcomes.

There are **2 non-favorable** outcomes.

Model It

You can find the theoretical probability of each event.

Probability of 1, 2, or 3 = **Probability of 1 + Probability of 2 + Probability of 3**

The spinner has 6 sections of the same size. It is equally likely that the spinner will land in any of the sections.

There are 6 possible outcomes: 1, 1, 2, 3, 4, and 5.

Probability of 1: $\dfrac{\text{number of sections labeled 1}}{\text{total number of outcomes}} = \dfrac{2}{6}$

Probability of 2: $\dfrac{\text{number of sections labeled 2}}{\text{total number of outcomes}} = \dfrac{1}{6}$

Probability of 3: $\dfrac{\text{number of sections labeled 3}}{\text{total number of outcomes}} = \dfrac{1}{6}$

Probability of 4: $\dfrac{\text{number of sections labeled 4}}{\text{total number of outcomes}} = \dfrac{1}{6}$

Probability of 5: $\dfrac{\text{number of sections labeled 5}}{\text{total number of outcomes}} = \dfrac{1}{6}$

➤ **Use the problem from the previous page to help you understand how to find theoretical probabilities.**

1 Look at **Picture It**. Keith can move forward only if he spins a 1, 2, or 3. Why are there 4 favorable outcomes, not 3? Why are there 6 possible outcomes in total?

2 What is the probability that Keith gets to move forward?

3 Suppose Keith could use the spinner at the right instead. All sections of the spinner have the same size. Would Keith be more or less likely to move forward with this spinner? Explain.

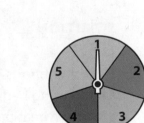

4 The probability that Keith will spin a 2 with the spinner in problem 3 is $\frac{1}{5}$.

The probability that he will spin a 2 with the spinner in **Try It** is $\frac{1}{6}$.

For both spinners, there is only one way to spin a 2. Why are the

probabilities for spinning a 2 not equal?

5 **Reflect** Think about all the models and strategies you have discussed today. Describe how one of them helped you better understand how to find theoretical probability.

Apply It

➤ **Use what you learned to solve these problems.**

6 A board game uses the spinner at the right. All sections of the spinner have the same size. In order to draw a bonus card, a player has to spin a prime number. Find the probability that a player will spin a prime number. Show your work.

SOLUTION _____

7 A teacher brings in bagels for his students. There are 4 everything bagels, 6 sesame seed bagels, and 8 whole wheat bagels in the bag. The first student selects a bagel at random from the bag. What is the probability that the bagel is whole wheat?

4
everything
bagels

6
sesame
bagels

8
whole wheat
bagels

A $\frac{1}{6}$

B $\frac{4}{9}$

C $\frac{1}{3}$

D $\frac{3}{8}$

8 Magdalena records the eye color of everyone on her soccer team. What is the probability that a randomly selected person on her soccer team has blue eyes? Green eyes? Brown eyes? Show your work.

Eye Color	Number of People
Blue	4
Green	1
Brown	15

SOLUTION _____

_____

Name:

Practice Finding Theoretical Probabilities

Tray A

➤ Study the Example showing how to find theoretical probabilities. Then solve problems 1–5.

Example

Ms. Aba has two paint trays with different sets of colors. She selects one color from each tray at random. What is the probability that she selects a blue from Tray A? From Tray B?

Tray B

	Reds	Yellows	Greens	Blues
Tray A	3	2	1	3
Tray B	2	2	2	2

The probability of selecting a blue from either tray is $\dfrac{\text{number of blues}}{\text{total number of colors}}$.

Tray A has 3 blues and 9 total colors. The probability of selecting a blue is $\dfrac{3}{9}$.

Tray B has 2 blues and 8 total colors. The probability of selecting a blue is $\dfrac{2}{8}$.

1 Consider the trays in the Example. Is the probability of selecting a yellow from Tray A the same as the probability of selecting a yellow from Tray B? Explain.

2 On the spinner shown, all sections have the same size. What is the probability of spinning a 5? Show your work.

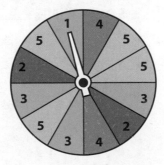

SOLUTION

3 Each player on a softball team will get a uniform with a randomly selected number between 1 and 30. No two players will have the same number. The first player to get a uniform thinks the probability that she will get a single-digit number is $\frac{9}{10}$. Is the player correct? Explain your reasoning.

4 A game is played with 33 cards. Some of the cards have letters, and the others have numbers. There are three possible colors for each card. Is there a greater probability of selecting a *yellow card* or a *letter card* at random? How much greater? Show your work.

	Red	Yellow	Blue
Number	8	8	8
Letter	3	3	3

SOLUTION _____

5 A supermarket has a bin of discount movies. There are 15 science fiction, 15 comedy, 15 horror, and 15 drama movies. Rodrigo selects a movie at random from the bin. What is the probability that he selects a science fiction movie? Show your work.

SOLUTION _____

Develop Comparing Theoretical and Experimental Probabilities

➤ **Read and try to solve the problem below.**

Katrina rolls a standard number cube and records the results.

Outcome	1	2	3	4	5	6
Frequency	3	6	2	5	4	4

Which numbers, if any, have been rolled exactly as often as you would expect?

Math Toolkit grid paper, number cubes, sticky notes

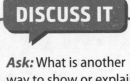

DISCUSS IT

Ask: What is another way to show or explain that?

Share: Another way is . . .

➤ **Explore different ways to compare theoretical and experimental probabilities.**

Katrina rolls a standard number cube and records the results.

Outcome	1	2	3	4	5	6
Frequency	3	6	2	5	4	4

Which numbers, if any, have been rolled exactly as often as you would expect?

Model It

You can use theoretical probability to make a prediction.

There are 6 faces on a standard number cube, so there are 6 possible outcomes.

All of the outcomes are equally likely. That means the theoretical probability of each outcome is $\frac{1}{6}$.

There are **24 trials**, and $\frac{1}{6} \cdot 24 = 4$. So, you would expect every number to be rolled 4 times.

Model It

You can compare theoretical and experimental probabilities.

The theoretical probability of each outcome is $\frac{1}{6}$.

The experimental probability of each outcome is $\frac{\text{favorable outcomes}}{\text{total number of trials}}$.

Outcome	1	2	3	4	5	6
Frequency	3	6	2	5	4	4
Experimental Probability	$\frac{3}{24} = \frac{1}{8}$	$\frac{6}{24} = \frac{1}{4}$	$\frac{2}{24} = \frac{1}{4}$	$\frac{5}{24}$	$\frac{4}{24} = \frac{1}{6}$	$\frac{4}{24} = \frac{1}{6}$

➤ **Use the problem from the previous page to help you understand how to compare theoretical and experimental probabilities.**

 Look at the **Model Its**. Why can you use both theoretical and experimental probability to make predictions? How are the two types of probability different?

2 Which numbers have been rolled exactly as often as you would expect?

3 Record the results of rolling a standard number cube 120 times. Repeat with 450 rolls. How do the experimental probabilities compare to $\frac{1}{6}$?

Outcome	1	2	3	4	5	6
Frequency in 120 rolls						
Frequency in 450 rolls						

4 The theoretical and experimental probabilities for the same outcome of an experiment will sometimes differ. Explain why this could happen.

5 **Reflect** Think about all the models and strategies you have discussed today. Describe how one of them helped you better understand how to solve the **Try It** problem.

Apply It

➤ **Use what you learned to solve these problems.**

6 The theoretical probability of tossing a coin and having it land heads up is $\frac{1}{2}$. Demi tosses a coin 50 times and her brother tosses a coin 120 times. Whose experimental probability of having the coin land heads up will likely be closer to $\frac{1}{2}$? Explain.

7 A bag contains several marbles. The theoretical probability of selecting a green marble at random is $\frac{1}{8}$. Eldora draws a marble from the bag without looking, records its color, and replaces it. She repeats this experiment 10 times and never draws a green marble. Eldora thinks this means there are no green marbles in the bag. Do you agree with Eldora? Why or why not?

8 Sophia has a green, an orange, a blue, and a purple pen in the bottom of her backpack. Every day, she selects a pen at random for writing in her journal. She selects the green pen 3 times, the orange pen 5 times, the blue pen 4 times, and the purple pen 8 times. Which pen does she select as often as you would expect? Show your work.

SOLUTION _____

Practice Comparing Theoretical and Experimental Probabilities

➤ **Study the Example showing how to compare theoretical and experimental probabilities. Then solve problems 1–5.**

Example

Shanika places 1 red, 1 blue, 1 black, and 1 green sock in a bag. She selects a sock without looking, records the color, and puts the sock back in the bag. Her results are shown. How does the experimental probability of Shanika selecting a black sock compare to the theoretical probability?

8 red   4 blue

5 green   7 black

The equally likely outcomes are red, blue, black, and green.

Theoretical probability of black sock: $\dfrac{\text{number of favorable outcomes}}{\text{number of possible outcomes}} = \dfrac{1}{4}$

Experimental probability of black sock: $\dfrac{\text{number of black socks selected}}{\text{number of trials}} = \dfrac{7}{24}$

Because $\dfrac{1}{4} = \dfrac{6}{24}$ and $\dfrac{6}{24} < \dfrac{7}{24}$, the theoretical probability is less than the experimental probability. However, the probabilities are relatively close.

1 Shanika's class works together to conduct 60 trials of the experiment described in the Example. Do you expect Shanika's or her class's experimental probability of selecting a black sock to be closer to the theoretical probability? Why?

2 A board game is played with a labeled cube. One face is labeled *Lose a Turn*, three faces are labeled *Move Ahead One Space*, and two faces are labeled *Move Back Two Spaces*. In 20 turns, the players roll *Lose a Turn* 8 times. Is this result what you would expect? Explain.

Vocabulary

experimental probability
the probability of an event occurring based on the results from an experiment.

theoretical probability
the probability of an event occurring based on what is expected to happen.

3 Agustin is playing a game in which he goes through a maze. At many points during the game, he needs to decide if he should take a path that goes to the right or one that goes to the left. Each time he tosses a coin to decide which way to go. When the coin lands heads up he goes to the right, and when it lands tails up he goes to the left. His results are shown.

Outcome	Frequency
Heads up (Right)	15
Tails up (Left)	11

a. What is the experimental probability of going to the right?

b. What is the theoretical probability of going to the right?

c. Why is the experimental probability of going to the right different from the theoretical probability?

d. Suppose Agustin tosses the coin 200 times. How should the experimental probability of going to the right change?

4 Describe an event involving a standard number cube for which the experimental probability and the theoretical probability are both equal to $\frac{1}{3}$.

5 The theoretical probability of selecting a blue tile from a bag of tiles is 0.4. Lola selects a tile at random from the bag and then replaces it. She does this 10 times. Which are a possible result of the experiment? Select all that apply.

A The experimental probability of selecting a blue tile is greater than 0.4.

B The experimental probability of selecting a blue tile is less than 0.4.

C The experimental probability of selecting a blue tile is exactly 0.4.

D The theoretical probability of selecting a tile is 0.5.

E The theoretical probability of selecting a tile that is not blue is 0.6.

Refine Solving Problems Involving Probability Models

➤ **Complete the Example below. Then solve problems 1–9.**

Example

On the spinner, the angle of the sun section is 60°, the moon section is 45°, and the star section is 135°. What is the probability that a spin lands on the comet section?

Look at how you could show your work using theoretical probability.

Angle of the comet section:
360° − 60° − 45° − 135° = 120°

The comet section takes up $\frac{120}{360}$ of the spinner.

SOLUTION _____

CONSIDER THIS ...
There are 360 degrees in a circle.

PAIR/SHARE
How can you find the probabilities for all the sections?

Apply It

1 The table below shows the cars and trucks a rental center has in stock. What is the probability that a randomly chosen vehicle is a truck? What is the probability that a randomly chosen car is red? Show your work.

	Blue	Black	Silver	Red	Other
Cars	14	16	17	9	11
Trucks	11	6	17	4	25

CONSIDER THIS ...
Cars and trucks are both types of vehicles.

PAIR/SHARE
In each case, how did you find the total number of possible outcomes?

SOLUTION _____

2 Elon rolls a standard number cube 20 times. Which numbers have an experimental probability of being rolled that is less than their theoretical probability? Show your work.

Outcome	1	2	3	4	5	6
Frequency	|||	|||||			̶|̶|̶|̶|̶	̶|̶|̶|̶|̶	||

SOLUTION _____

_____

3 Seth plays a game with a bag of letter tiles. There are 63 vowel tiles and 81 consonant tiles. Seth selects a tile at random, records whether it is a vowel or consonant, and puts it back in the bag. In 12 trials, he selects 6 vowels. Which statement about the probability of selecting a vowel is correct?

A The theoretical probability is less than 0.5 and the experimental probability is greater than 0.5.

B The theoretical probability is less than 0.5 and the experimental probability is equal to 0.5.

C The theoretical and the experimental probability are both equal to 0.5.

D The theoretical probability is greater than 0.5 and the experimental probability is equal to 0.5.

Dolores chose C as the correct answer. How might she have gotten that answer?

4 The spinner at the right is spun five times. The results are 14, 4, 7, 2, and 5. Compare the theoretical probability of spinning a number divisible by 3 to the experimental probability.

5 A restaurant has a spinner that customers can spin to win a free drink or meal. The theoretical probability of winning a drink is $\frac{4}{5}$. Suppose four customers in a row spin the spinner and win a drink. Does that mean the next customer who spins the spinner must win a meal? Explain.

6 Isaiah says that the spinner at the right has 4 sections, so the theoretical probability of landing on each section is $\frac{1}{4}$. Is Isaiah correct? Explain.

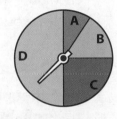

7 Spinner A and Spinner B are each divided into equal-size sections. Tell whether each statement is *True* or *False*.

Spinner A

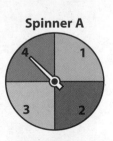

Spinner B

	True	False
a. The probability of spinning a 1 on both spinners is equal.	○	○
b. The probability of spinning a 4 on Spinner B is $\frac{1}{3}$.	○	○
c. The probability of spinning an even number on Spinner A is $\frac{1}{2}$.	○	○
d. The probability of spinning a 3 on Spinner B is greater than the probability of spinning a 3 on Spinner A.	○	○

8 Carlota has a bag filled with cell phone cases that have the school logo on them. There are blue, white, gray, and black cases in the bag. She selects a case at random and then returns it to the bag. She repeats this process four times. Which statements about Carlota's experiment could be true? Select all that apply.

A The theoretical probability of removing a blue case is 1.

B The experimental probability of removing a black case is 0.

C The experimental probability of removing a white case is exactly the same as the theoretical probability.

D If Carlota does not remove any black cases, then there must not be any black cases in the bag.

E All of the cell phone cases removed are the same color.

9 **Math Journal** Draw a spinner for which the theoretical probability of spinning each outcome is similar to the experimental probabilities in the table below. Explain your reasoning.

Shape	Heart	Diamond	Circle	Square
Experimental Probability	$\frac{9}{20}$	$\frac{4}{20}$	$\frac{2}{20}$	$\frac{5}{20}$

✓ End of Lesson Checklist

☐ **INTERACTIVE GLOSSARY** Find the entry for *theoretical probability*. Add two important things you learned about theoretical probability in this lesson.

☐ **SELF CHECK** Go back to the Unit 7 Opener and see what you can check off.

Solve Problems Involving Compound Events

Dear Family,

This week your student is learning about probability of compound events.

A **compound event** is an event that consists of two or more simple events. You can describe the probability of a compound event occurring just as you can describe the probability of one event occurring.

An example of a compound event is tossing a coin two times. Each toss is a simple event with two outcomes (heads or tails). There are four possible outcomes for the compound event. The possible outcomes are heads then heads, heads then tails, tails then heads, and tails then tails.

Your student will be solving problems like the one below.

A gift shop offers a choice of wrapping paper with dots or stripes and a choice of a red, blue, or purple bow. What is the probability that the next gift will be wrapped in striped paper with either a red or blue bow?

➤ **ONE WAY** to find the probability is to use a table to find the possible outcomes.

	Red	Blue	Purple
Dots	DR	DB	DP
Stripes	SR	SB	SP

There are 6 possible outcomes and **2 favorable outcomes**.

$\frac{2}{6} = \frac{1}{3}$

➤ **ANOTHER WAY** is to use a **tree diagram**.

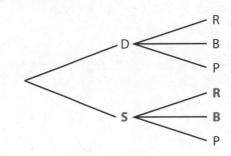

Out of the 6 total outcomes, 2 are striped paper with either a red or blue bow.

So, the probability is $\frac{2}{6}$, or $\frac{1}{3}$.

Using either method, the probability that the next gift will be wrapped in striped paper with either a red or blue bow is $\frac{2}{6}$, or $\frac{1}{3}$.

 Use the next page to start a conversation about compound events.

Activity Thinking About Compound Events Around You

➤ **Do this activity together to investigate compound events in the real world.**

Do you use passcodes (or numeric passwords) to access a phone, computer, key lock box, website, door, or anything else?

Even though shorter passcodes are easier to remember, they are also easier for someone else to guess. You can think of guessing someone's passcode as a compound event, where guessing each digit is an event. First you guess the first digit, then the second digit, and so on.

The probability of randomly guessing a four-digit passcode is one in ten thousand, but the probability of randomly guessing a six-digit passcode it is one in a million!

? Where else do you see compound events in the world around you?

Explore Compound Events

Previously, you learned how to find the probability for a single event. In this lesson, you will learn about finding the probability for a compound event.

➤ **Use what you know to try to solve the problem below.**

Laqueta tosses two different coins. What are the possible outcomes for the way the coins land?

TRY IT   **Math Toolkit** coins, two-color counters

◎ **Learning Targets** SMP 1, SMP 2, SMP 3, SMP 4, SMP 5, SMP 6, SMP 8
Find probabilities of compound events using organized lists, tables, tree diagrams, and simulation.
- Understand that the probability of a compound event is the fraction of outcomes in the sample space.
- Represent sample spaces for compound events. For an event described in everyday language, identify the outcomes that compose the event.
- Design and use a simulation to generate frequencies for compound events.

CONNECT IT

1 **Look Back** What are the possible outcomes for tossing two different coins? Why are there more than two possible outcomes?

2 **Look Ahead** Tossing two coins, or tossing a coin two times, are examples of a **compound event**. A compound event is made up of two or more simple events, such as tossing a coin one time. One way you can represent the sample space for a compound event is with a **tree diagram**.

a. Suppose you toss a coin three times. How many simple events are in this compound event? Explain.

b. Complete the tree diagram below to show all of the possible outcomes of tossing a coin three times. Use H to represent a coin landing heads up and T to represent a coin landing tails up.

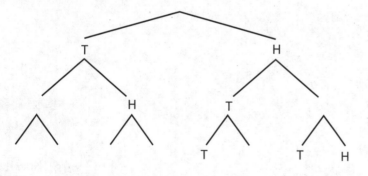

c. How many outcomes are in this compound event?

d. List the possible outcomes for this compound event.

3 **Reflect** When you toss a coin three times, why is the outcome HHT different from the outcome THH?

Prepare for Solving Problems Involving Compound Events

1   Think about what you know about outcomes of experiments. Fill in each box. Use words, numbers, and pictures. Show as many ideas as you can.

What Is It?	What I Know About It

sample space

Examples	Non-Examples

2   Allen says the sample space for rolling a standard number cube is an even number, an odd number, a prime number, or a composite number. Is Allen correct? Explain your reasoning.

3 Noah is spinning a spinner with two equal-size sections, one pink and the other blue. He spins the spinner two times in a row.

a. What are the possible outcomes for the two spins? Show your work.

SOLUTION _____

b. Check your answer to problem 3a. Show your work.

Develop Finding Probabilities of Compound Events with Two Events

TEAM DWARF

➤ **Read and try to solve the problem below.**

For a role-playing game, Nikia randomly selects a team card and a character card. The teams are *dwarf*, *elf*, *gnome*, and *human*. The characters are *fighter*, *spy*, and *thief*. Nikia's favorite team is *dwarf* and her favorite character is the *spy*. What is the probability that Nikia selects at least one of her favorites?

TRY IT   **Math Toolkit** grid paper, index cards, sticky notes

DISCUSS IT

Ask: How would you explain what the problem is asking in your own words?

Share: The problem is asking . . .

➤ **Explore different ways to represent the sample space for a compound event.**

For a role-playing game, Nikia randomly selects a team card and a character card. The teams are *dwarf*, *elf*, *gnome*, and *human*. The characters are *fighter*, *spy*, and *thief*. Nikia's favorite team is *dwarf* and her favorite character is the *spy*. What is the probability that Nikia selects at least one of her favorites?

Model It

You can use a table to find the sample space.

Character	Team			
	Dwarf (D)	Elf (E)	Gnome (G)	Human (H)
Fighter (F)	DF	EF	GF	HF
Spy (S)	DS	ES	GS	HS
Thief (T)	DT	ET	GT	HT

Model It

You can use a tree diagram to find the sample space.

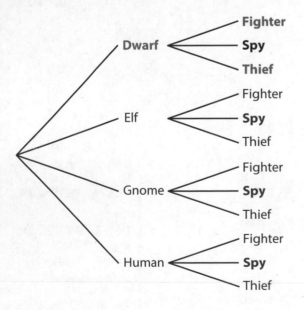

➤ **Use the problem from the previous page to help you understand how to find the probability of a compound event.**

1 How many outcomes are there? How many include *dwarf*? How many include *spy*?

2 There are 6 outcomes that include *dwarf* or *spy*. Why is that different from the sum of the number of outcomes that include *dwarf* and the number that include *spy*?

3 Look at the **Model Its**. How is using a table to find the number of favorable outcomes the same as using a tree diagram? How is it different?

4 What is the probability that Nikia selects at least one of her favorites? Exactly one of her favorites? Why are the probabilities different?

5 How is finding the probability of a compound event the same as finding the probability of a single event? How is it different?

6 **Reflect** Think about all the models and strategies you have discussed today. Describe how one of them helped you better understand how to represent the sample space for a compound event and find its probability.

Apply It

➤ **Use what you learned to solve these problems.**

7 A bag has 2 red marbles and 2 blue marbles. Jade randomly selects two marbles from the bag, one at a time. What is the probability that both marbles are the same color? Show your work.

SOLUTION _____

8 Akio spins Spinner A and then spins Spinner B. What is the probability that both spinners land on the same number? Show your work.

Spinner A

Spinner B

SOLUTION _____

9 Rachel plays a game where she tries to get her team to guess words. Each turn she spins a spinner with three equal-size sections to see if she will act, sing, or draw clues. What is the probability that Rachel does not draw clues in her next two turns? Show your work.

SOLUTION _____

Practice Finding Probabilities of Compound Events with Two Events

▶ **Study the Example showing how to find the probability of a compound event. Then solve problems 1–4.**

Example

Javier plays a game with two spinners. Each spinner has equal-size sections numbered 1–4. On each turn, Javier spins both spinners. To get to the next part of the game, he must spin two even numbers. What is the probability that Javier gets to the next part of the game on his next turn?

You can use a tree diagram to show the sample space.

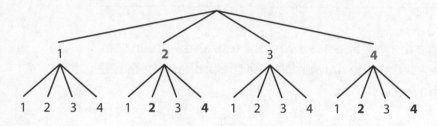

There are 16 outcomes and **4** are favorable. The probability that Javier gets to the next level on his next turn is $\frac{4}{16}$, or $\frac{1}{4}$.

1. Consider spinning the spinners in the Example.

   a. List all the outcomes with at least one 3.

   b. Is the probability of Javier spinning two odd numbers *the same as, greater than,* or *less than* the probability of Javier spinning two even numbers? Explain.

   c. Javier must spin two numbers with a sum of 5 or greater to win. What is the probability that Javier will win on his next turn? Explain.

LESSON 33 Solve Problems Involving Compound Events   **739**

2 Two people are playing the game *rock, paper, scissors*. In each round both players show rock, paper, or scissors at the same time. What is the probability that both players show rock in the first round? Show your work.

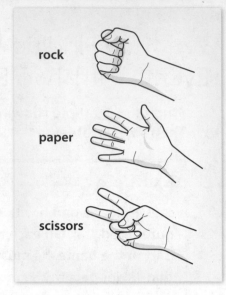

rock

paper

scissors

SOLUTION _____

3 Dawn has mismatched socks in a drawer. She has 3 white, 2 red, and 1 green sock. Dawn randomly selects two socks from the drawer. What is the probability that she selects a matching pair? Show your work.

SOLUTION _____

4 Ummi and Julio each have a bag that contains 2 blue marbles, 2 green marbles, and 2 purple marbles. Ummi selects a marble from her bag, replaces it, and then selects another. Julio selects a marble from his bag, does not replace it, and then selects another. Who has a greater probability of selecting two marbles of the same color from their bag? Explain.

Develop Finding Probabilities of Compound Events with More than Two Events

➤ **Read and try to solve the problem below.**

Lucía has a four-digit passcode on her phone. You know her code only uses the digits 0 and 1. What is the probability of guessing her passcode on the first try?

TRY IT

Math Toolkit coins, index cards, sticky notes, two-color counters

DISCUSS IT

Ask: How did you get started solving the problem?

Share: I started by . . .

➤ **Explore different ways to represent the sample space for a compound event with more than two events.**

Lucía has a four-digit passcode on her phone. You know her code only uses the digits 0 and 1. What is the probability of guessing her passcode on the first try?

Model It

You can use a tree diagram to model the sample space.

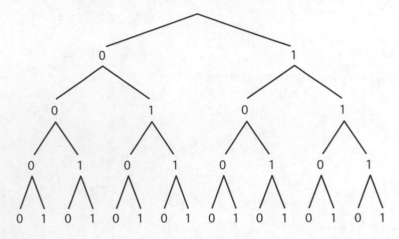

Model It

You can use an organized list to model the sample space.

Four 0s:	0000
Three 0s:	0001, 0010, 0100, 1000
Two 0s:	0011, 0101, 0110, 1010, 1100, 1001
One 0:	0111, 1011, 1101, 1110
Zero 0s:	1111

➤ **Use the problem from the previous page to help you understand how to find the probability of a compound event with more than two events.**

1 Look at the **Model Its**. Why are only the digits 0 and 1 in the models?

2 What is the probability of correctly guessing Lucía's passcode on the first try?

3 Look at the second **Model It**. Suppose Lucía uses a passcode with 6 digits that are all either 0 or 1. How would the list change?

4 Look at the tree diagram in the first **Model It**. Suppose Lucía changes her passcode so that she uses 0,1, or 2 for the first digit and 0 or 1 for the last three digits. How would the tree diagram change? What is the probability of guessing Lucía's new passcode?

5 How is finding the probability for more than two events the same as finding the probability for a single event or two events?

6 **Reflect** Think about all the models and strategies you have discussed today. Describe how one of them helped you better understand how to solve the **Try It** problem.

Apply It

➤ **Use what you learned to solve these problems.**

7 Vinh plays a game with the cards shown at the right. The cards are placed facedown and he selects three of the cards. What is the probability that he selects the two odd cards? Show your work.

SOLUTION _____

8 Maya lists all the possible outcomes of spinning the spinners below one time each.

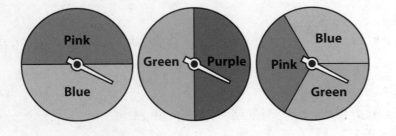

Pink, Purple, Pink   Pink, Purple, Green   Pink, Purple, Blue
Blue, Purple, Blue   Blue, Purple, Pink   Blue, Purple, Green

Is her list correct? Explain why or why not.

9 Kiara tosses four different coins. What is the probability that the coins land with two heads and two tails showing? Show your work.

SOLUTION _____

Practice Finding Probabilities of Compound Events with More than Two Events

➤ **Study the Example showing how to find the probability of a compound event with more than two events. Then solve problems 1–4.**

Example

A store has socks with different heights, patterns, and colors. The socks can be tall or short, have dots or be plain, and can be black, gray, or white. What is the probability that a random customer buys plain gray socks?

You can use an organized list to identify the possible combinations.

Let T represent tall socks and S short socks.

Let D represent socks with dots and P plain socks.

Let B represent black socks, G gray socks, and W white socks.

TDB	TDG	TDW	TPB	**TPG**	TPW
SDB	SDG	SDW	SPB	**SPG**	SPW

The probability a random customer buys plain gray socks is $\frac{2}{12}$, or $\frac{1}{6}$.

1 Refer to the situation in the Example.

a. Why do you not have to consider the height of the socks in the Example?

b. What is the probability that a random customer buys socks that are not plain gray socks? Explain.

c. What is the probability that a random customer buys tall socks with dots?

2 Yukio spins a spinner that is half yellow and half blue, then tosses a coin twice. What are the possible outcomes of this experiment? Show your work.

SOLUTION _____

3 You spin the spinner shown three times. What is the probability that the pointer stops in the section labeled A exactly two times? Explain.

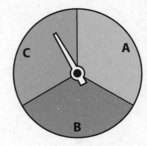

4 Geraldo sells sweatshirts in small, medium, and large sizes. The sweatshirts are sold both with and without hoods. They are available in gray, red, and black. Geraldo displays one sweatshirt in each size, color, and style combination.

a. How many sweatshirts does Geraldo display? Show your work.

SOLUTION _____

b. What is the probability that a sweatshirt randomly selected from the display has a hood?

c. Suppose you select a sweatshirt at random from the display. What are two different compound events that each have a probability of $\frac{1}{9}$?

Develop Using Simulations to Find Probabilities for Compound Events

➤ **Read and try to solve the problem below.**

The town swimming pool closes when it rains. The weather forecast says that there is a 50% chance that it will rain on each of the next five days. What is the probability that the pool will close for rain on exactly two of the next five days?

TRY IT

Math Toolkit coins, index cards, number cubes, sticky notes, two-color counters

DISCUSS IT

Ask: Why did you use that strategy to find the probability?

Share: I used that strategy because . . .

➤ **Explore different ways to use a simulation to find a probability.**

The town swimming pool closes when it rains. The weather forecast says that there is a 50% chance that it will rain on each of the next five days. What is the probability that the pool will close for rain on exactly two of the next five days?

Model It

You can use coins to run a simulation to model the outcomes.

A simulation can be used to model a situation.

Toss a coin and let heads (H) represent a day with rain and tails (T) a day without rain. Record the outcomes in groups of 5.

HTHTT	TTHHT	TTHTH	TTHHT
HHTHT	THTTH	HHTHH	THHTT
TTTHH	THTHT	TTHTH	HHTTH
TTHHH	THTHT	HTTHT	HHTTH

Model It

You can use number cubes to run a simulation to model the outcomes.

Roll a number cube and let odd numbers represent a day with rain and even numbers represent a day without rain. Record the outcomes in groups of 5.

46134	65244	13452	53141
34312	25413	42532	32145
61613	33452	66424	13232
11335	24624	55324	21324

➤ **Use the problem from the previous page to help you understand how to use a simulation to find a probability.**

1 Look at the **Model Its**. Why can you use a coin and a number cube to model the probability of a day with rain? Why are the outcomes recorded in groups of 5?

2 Look at the **Model Its**. Based on the coin simulation, what is the probability that the pool will close for rain exactly two of the next five days? What is the probability based on the number cube simulation?

3 The theoretical probability of the pool closing for rain exactly two of the next five days is $\frac{10}{32}$. Why are probabilities based on the two simulations different from the theoretical probability?

4 Suppose you run more trials of one of the simulations. Why will the probability you find likely be closer to the theoretical probability?

5 When might you want use a simulation to find the probability of an outcome instead of finding the theoretical probability?

6 **Reflect** Think about all the models and strategies you have discussed today. Describe how one of them helped you better understand how to use a simulation to find a probability.

Apply It

➤ **Use what you learned to solve these problems.**

7 There is a 33.$\overline{3}$% probability that it will snow on each of the next four days. Suppose you run a simulation by rolling four number cubes. Name an event you can use to represent a day with snow. Then find the probability that it snows at least one of the next four days based on the results below.

5653	6433	6214	6524	4111
4612	1154	6463	5526	5653
1524	4121	2261	3331	2216

8 Each day on a game show, the finalist chooses one of three doors. Behind one door is the grand prize. Describe a simulation to find the probability of the finalist winning the grand prize seven days in a row.

9 A cereal company puts coupons for a free movie ticket in 20% of their boxes, a free drink in 30% of their boxes, and a free popcorn in 40% of the boxes. Luke designs a simulation with the spinner. He lets the numbers 0–1 represent a movie ticket coupon, 2–4 represent a drink coupon, and 5–8 represent a popcorn coupon. He spins the spinner and records the results. His results are shown. Based on the simulation, what is the probability that Luke gets all three prizes in three boxes of cereal? Explain.

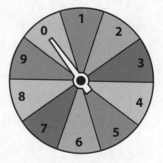

716	796	639	292	020	678	312
176	730	450	822	462	117	635
262	742	634	415	383	926	714

Practice Using Simulations to Find Probabilities for Compound Events

➤ **Study the Example showing how to use a simulation to find the probability of a compound event. Then solve problems 1–3.**

Example

Each text Morgan receives has an 80% probability of being from a friend. What is the probability that exactly two of the next three texts Morgan receives are from friends?

Use marbles to run a simulation. Let red marbles represent texts from friends and blue marbles represent texts not from friends. Place 4 red marbles and 1 blue marble in a bag. That means there is an 80% probability of selecting a red marble from the bag, because 80% of the marbles in the bag are red.

Select and replace a marble three times for each trial. Record the results.

RRR	BRR	RBR	RRR	BRR	RRR	RRR	RRR
RRR	RRR	RRR	RRR	RRR	BRR	BRB	RBR
RBR	RRB	RRB	RBR	RRR	BBB	RRB	RRR

Of the 24 trials, **10** have exactly two red marbles.

So, the experimental probability is $\frac{10}{24}$, or $\frac{5}{12}$.

---

1 Refer to the simulation in the Example.

a. Is it more likely that Morgan receives three texts or exactly two texts from her friends? Explain.

b. There is a 20% probability of snow on each of the next three days. Explain why you can use the simulation from the Example to find the probability of snow on exactly one of the next three days.

2 Quinn got 3 of 6 questions correct on a true or false quiz. He wonders if he could have done better by guessing at random. Quinn runs a simulation to model the results of guessing at random by tossing 6 coins for each trial. Quinn lets landing heads up (H) represent a correct answer.

HHTTHH	TTTHHT	HTTHHT	TTTTTH	HTTHHH	THTHTH	HTHHHT
HTHTHT	HTTTHH	THTHHH	TTHTTH	HHTHTH	HHTTHT	HTTTHH
HHHTHT	HTTHTT	HHTTTH	HHTHHT	THTTTT	THTHTT	TTTTTT

a. Based on the simulation, what is the probability of correctly guessing more than 50% of the answers? Explain how you know.

b. Suppose Quinn changes the simulation and lets landing tails up (T) represent a correct answer. Why does this simulation still model the situation?

3 Alec makes 75% of his free throws. He wants to know the probability that he makes at least four of his next six free throws. Alec runs a simulation. He spins a spinner with four equal sections and lets the numbers 1–3 represent making a free throw. Based on the simulation, what is the probability that Alec makes at least four of his next free throws? Explain.

232344	231342	121123	441432	311221
343133	341414	412312	141111	423131
432234	143132	423233	411332	143314

Refine Solving Problems Involving Compound Events

➤ **Complete the Example below. Then solve problems 1–9.**

Example

In a lake, 50% of the fish are brown trout. A researcher catches, tags, and releases five fish in the lake. What is the probability that at least three of the fish the researcher tags are brown trout?

Look at how you could use a simulation with number cubes.

Roll 5 number cubes, one to represent each fish.

Let the numbers 1–3 represent brown trout.

12454	14236	53261	63425	43215
42613	22143	21345	52312	43631
25413	25413	53416	25126	36114

SOLUTION _____

CONSIDER THIS . . .
Researchers catch an animal, attach a tag to it, and return it to the wild as a way to study wildlife.

PAIR/SHARE
What is another way you could use a number cube to run a simulation for this situation?

Apply It

1 In a game, you roll two standard number cubes each turn. You get an extra turn when you roll doubles. What is the probability of getting an extra turn? Show your work.

CONSIDER THIS . . .
When you roll doubles, you roll the same number on both number cubes.

PAIR/SHARE
How do you know you found all the favorable outcomes?

SOLUTION _____

2 A taco shop makes tacos with chicken, beef, or vegetable filling, a hard or soft shell, and red or green salsa. There is 1 taco of each combination in a box. Suppose you select the first taco from the box at random. What is the probability the taco has chicken filling but not red salsa? Show your work.

CONSIDER THIS . . .
Each option is an event in this compound event.

SOLUTION _____

_____

PAIR/SHARE
How would the probability change if the taco could not have chicken?

3 Pablo notices that the bus to school is late 30% of the time. He wants to know the probability that the bus will be late exactly 2 of the next 10 school days. Which simulation can Pablo use to find this probability?

CONSIDER THIS . . .
There are 10 single events in this compound event.

A Take 5 pieces of paper. Label 3 of them *late*. Put them in a bag. Draw and replace a piece of paper. Record the outcomes in groups of 10.

B Roll a standard number cube. Let multiples of 3 represent the bus being late to school. Record the outcomes in groups of 10.

C Place 3 blue marbles and 7 red marbles in a bag. Let blue marbles represent the bus being late to school. Draw and replace a marble. Record the outcomes in groups of 10.

D Make a spinner that is 30% red. Let red represent the bus being late to school. Spin the spinner. Record the outcomes in groups of 20.

Lilia chose B as the correct answer. How might she have gotten that answer?

PAIR/SHARE
How can you check your work on this kind of problem?

4 A café lunch special has two options for an appetizer, five options for a sandwich, and three options for a side dish.

There are _____ possible outcomes.

city cafe

Lunch Combo

APPETIZERS
(choose one)
Soup Of The Day
Corn Bread

SANDWICHES
(choose one)
Grilled Cheese
Roast Beef
Tuna Salad
Turkey
Vegetable

SIDE DISHES
(choose one)
Coleslaw
Garden Salad
Potato Salad

5 Malcolm takes a quiz with 5 multiple choice questions. Each question has 4 choices and 1 correct answer. Malcolm designs a simulation to find the probability of passing the quiz by guessing answers at random. He generates random numbers from 1 to 4 and lets 1 represent a correct answer. Each trial has 5 numbers. He runs 15 trials and records the results.

44342	24133	11242	41244	11233
22412	12144	42214	12342	43231
14332	43423	22413	11124	41343

To pass the quiz, you need at least 4 correct answers. Based on his results, Malcolm concludes that it is impossible to pass a quiz with random guessing. Is Malcolm correct? Explain why or why not.

6 The letters A, C, and T are each written on a separate card. The cards are selected in a random order. Based on the tree diagram, which is a valid conclusion? Select all that apply.

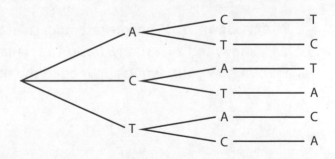

A The probability of the letters spelling CAT is $\frac{1}{6}$.

B The probability that T will be the first letter selected is $\frac{1}{3}$.

C The probability that A will be the first letter selected is $\frac{1}{15}$.

D The sample space consists of 6 outcomes.

E It is less likely to spell TAC than CAT.

7. When rolling two standard number cubes, what is the probability of rolling at least one 6?

A $\frac{12}{36}$

B $\frac{6}{36}$

C $\frac{11}{36}$

D $\frac{1}{36}$

8. Ellie has a playlist on shuffle. Her list is made of an equal number of country, hip-hop, and pop songs. When three pop songs play in a row, Ellie thinks her music player is broken. Do you agree or disagree? Explain.

9. **Math Journal** The forecast for each of the next three days is 50% rain, 25% snow, and 25% sunny. Design a simulation to model the situation. Explain how your simulation models the situation.

✓ End of Lesson Checklist

☐ **INTERACTIVE GLOSSARY** Find the entry for *compound event*. Rewrite the definition in your own words.

☐ **SELF CHECK** Go back to the Unit 7 Opener and see what you can check off.

Math IN Action

SMP 1 Make sense of problems and persevere in solving them.

Study an Example Problem and Solution

➤ **Read this problem involving probabilities of compound events. Then look at one student's solution to this problem on the following pages.**

Treasure Chests

Ryan and Enrique are designing a new video game. Read an email from Ryan about one part of the game, where players find different items by opening treasure chests. Then help Enrique respond to the email.

○ ○ ○

🗑 Delete   ▢ Archive | ✉ Reply   ✉ Reply All   ✉ Forward

To: Enrique
Subject: Probabilities of Finding Treasure

Hi Enrique,

Please help me finish a plan for the treasure chests in the player starting area. Here is what we have decided on so far:

• When a player opens one of these chests, they will get one item chosen at random from an *item collection*.

• The item collection needs to contain at least two different coins and at least two different jewels from the options shown.

• The item collection may contain more than one of the same item.

• Each chest should be as likely as not to contain a coin.

• If a player opens two chests in this area, they should be likely to find an emerald in at least one.

PLEASE PROVIDE:

• A description of the item collection you suggest using for the chests and the theoretical probability of finding each item in a chest.

Coins

Bronze   Silver   Gold

Jewels

Diamond   Ruby   Pearl   Emerald

• The theoretical probability of finding an emerald in at least one chest if a player opens two chests.

• The number of players you would expect to find at least one emerald if 1,000 players open two chests each.

Thanks!

Ryan

One of the most valuable treasures, known as the Bactrian gold, was found in the 1970s. It contained more than 20,000 gold ornaments.

One Student's Solution

> **NOTICE THAT . . .**
> Coins need to be equally likely as not to appear, so half of the items in the collection need to be coins and half need to be jewels.

First, I have to describe the item collection.

This is the player starting area, so I will not put gold coins in the chests. I will include two bronze coins and one silver coin in the item collection.

Players should be likely to find an emerald if they open two chests, so I will include more than one emerald. I will include two emeralds and one pearl in the item collection.

My item collection includes two different coins and two different jewels: bronze coin, bronze coin, silver coin, emerald, emerald, pearl.

Next, I need to calculate the theoretical probability of finding each item in a chest.

> **NOTICE THAT . . .**
> You can determine the theoretical probability of finding each coin or jewel using the fraction
> $$\frac{\text{number of coins or jewels}}{\text{total number of items}}.$$

There are six items in the collection. There are two bronze coins and two emeralds, so the probability of finding either of these items is $\frac{2}{6}$, or $\frac{1}{3}$.

There is one silver coin and one pearl in the collection, so the probability of finding either of these items is $\frac{1}{6}$.

There are no gold coins, diamonds, or rubies in the collection, so it is impossible to find these items. The probability of finding each of these items is 0.

Now, I can check that a coin will be equally likely as not to appear in a chest.

I need to find the sum of the probabilities for all three coins.

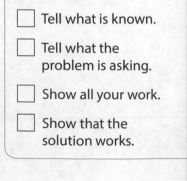

Probability of finding a bronze coin		Probability of finding a silver coin		Probability of finding a gold coin
$\frac{1}{3}$	+	$\frac{1}{6}$	+	0

Because $\frac{1}{3} + \frac{1}{6} + 0 = \frac{1}{2}$, a coin is equally likely as not to appear in a chest.

☑ **Problem-Solving Checklist**

☐ Tell what is known.

☐ Tell what the problem is asking.

☐ Show all your work.

☐ Show that the solution works.

Then, I can determine the probability of finding an emerald in at least one chest if a player opens two chests.

I can use a table to describe the sample space.

First Chest	Second Chest					
	Bronze Coin (B)	Bronze Coin (B)	Silver Coin (S)	Emerald (E)	Emerald (E)	Pearl (P)
Bronze Coin (B)	BB	BB	BS	BE	BE	BP
Bronze Coin (B)	BB	BB	BS	BE	BE	BP
Silver Coin (S)	SB	SB	SS	SE	SE	SP
Emerald (E)	EB	EB	ES	EE	EE	EP
Emerald (E)	EB	EB	ES	EE	EE	EP
Pearl (P)	PB	PB	PS	PE	PE	PP

> **NOTICE THAT . . .**
> Each outcome that includes an emerald is a favorable outcome.

There are 36 total outcomes and 20 favorable outcomes. The probability of finding an emerald in at least one chest is $\frac{20}{36}$, or $\frac{5}{9}$. Because $\frac{5}{9}$ is greater than $\frac{1}{2}$, it is likely for a player to find an emerald in at least one chest.

> **NOTICE THAT . . .**
> There are 16 outcomes where an emerald is not found in either chest, so the probability of not finding an emerald is $\frac{16}{36}$. The sum of all the probabilities should be 1, and $\frac{20}{36} + \frac{16}{36} = 1$.

Finally, I can determine how many players, p, I would expect to find an emerald if 1,000 players open two chests each.

I can use an equation to make a prediction.

$$\frac{20}{36} = \frac{p}{1,000}$$

$$1,000 \cdot \frac{20}{36} = \frac{p}{1,000} \cdot 1,000$$

$$\frac{20,000}{36} = p$$

$$556 \approx p$$

If 1,000 players each open two chests, about 556 players should find an emerald.

Try Another Approach

➤ **There are many ways to solve problems. Think about how you might solve the Treasure Chests problem in a different way.**

Treasure Chests

Ryan and Enrique are designing a new video game. Read an email from Ryan about one part of the game, where players find different items by opening treasure chests. Then help Enrique respond to the email.

🗑 Delete   🗄 Archive | ✉ Reply   ✉ Reply All   ✉ Forward

To: Enrique
Subject: Probabilities of Finding Treasure

Hi Enrique,

Please help me finish a plan for the treasure chests in the player starting area. Here is what we have decided on so far:

- When a player opens one of these chests, they will get one item chosen at random from an *item collection*.

- The item collection needs to contain at least two different coins and at least two different jewels from the options shown.

- The item collection may contain more than one of the same item.

- Each chest should be as likely as not to contain a coin.

- If a player opens two chests in this area, they should be likely to find an emerald in at least one.

Coins: Bronze Silver Gold

Jewels: Diamond Ruby Pearl Emerald

PLEASE PROVIDE:

- A description of the item collection you suggest using for the chests and the theoretical probability of finding each item in a chest.

- The theoretical probability of finding an emerald in at least one chest if a player opens two chests.

- The number of players you would expect to find at least one emerald if 1,000 players open two chests each.

Thanks!

Ryan

Plan It

➤ **Answer these questions to help you start thinking about a plan.**

a. How many total items will you include in your item collection? How many items will be coins?

b. What items do you want to include more than one of in your collection? Why?

Solve It

➤ **Find a different solution for the Treasure Chests problem. Show all your work on a separate sheet of paper. You may want to use the Problem-Solving Tips to get started.**

PROBLEM-SOLVING TIPS

Math Toolkit index cards, grid paper, sticky notes, unit cubes

Key Terms

experiment	outcome	event
impossible	likely	unlikely
equally likely as not	theoretical probability	sample space

Models You may want to use . . .

• a tree diagram or an organized list to model a sample space.

• words or numbers to describe a theoretical probability.

Reflect

Use Mathematical Practices As you work through the problem, discuss these questions with a partner.

• **Persevere** Why might you need to try multiple item collections before deciding on your final answer?

• **Use Models** How could you calculate the experimental probability of finding an emerald in at least one chest?

Diamonds are the hardest known substance. 80% of diamonds are used for purposes such as cutting, drilling, grinding, and polishing.

Discuss Models and Strategies

➤ **Read the problem. Write a solution on a separate sheet of paper. Remember, there can be lots of ways to solve a problem.**

Bonus Round

If players complete a level of the video game in a certain amount of time, they will get a bonus round where they have a chance to win a prize. Look at the mockup of the bonus round Enrique plans to share with Ryan. The sticky notes show important features of the round.

Describe a set of 16 cards that could be used for this bonus round. Then design a simulation to determine the experimental probability of getting a match using the set of cards you described. If 500 players complete this bonus round, how many do you expect to win a prize?

Plan It and Solve It

➤ **Find a solution to the Bonus Round problem.**

Write a detailed plan and support your answer. Be sure to include:

- a list of the 16 cards that will be displayed.

- a description of the simulation you will use to determine the experimental probability of getting a match.

- the results of the simulation and how you calculated the experimental probability.

- the number of players you expect to win a prize if 500 players complete the bonus round.

PROBLEM-SOLVING TIPS

Math Toolkit index cards, number cubes, spinners, two-color counters, unit cubes

Key Terms

experiment	outcome	compound event
simulation	trial	experimental probability
sample space	tree diagram	

Questions

- How many pairs of cards for each prize will you include in the set?

- How can you use experimental probability to predict the future results of the same experiment?

Reflect

Use Mathematical Practices As you work through the problem, discuss these questions with a partner.

- **Make Sense of Problems** How does your partner's simulation model choosing two cards? How does your partner's simulation model the four prizes?

- **Make an Argument** When you do your simulation, will you complete more or fewer than 15 trials? Why?

Persevere On Your Own

➤ **Read the problem. Write a solution on a separate sheet of paper.**

Mining Locations

Players tested part of the video game designed by Enrique and Ryan and gave feedback. Read the email from Enrique about the player concerns and help Ryan respond to the email.

Delete   Archive   Reply   Reply All   Forward

To: Ryan
Subject: Player Concerns About Mining Locations

Hi Ryan,

There are 30 mining locations in all. A material is randomly assigned to each location at the start of the game. Players visit locations to mine for materials they need. The table shows how many locations are currently assigned each material.

Players have reported that there seem to be some problems with how likely they are to find certain materials. Here are some of their concerns and how I think we should address them.

Player Concerns and How to Fix:

- Players are getting too much ore and not enough rock. Make it just as likely that a player will find rock as they will find ore.

- Players need coal frequently. Make sure players are twice as likely to find coal as marble.

- Sapphire is the most valuable item players can mine. Make sure players are least likely to find sapphire.

- Players report that it is impossible to find turquoise. Make sure every material is assigned to at least one location.

Material Type	Material	Number of Locations
Ore	Iron	5
Ore	Aluminum	6
Ore	Lead	5
Rock	Marble	5
Rock	Coal	4
Gem	Turquoise	0
Gem	Quartz	2
Gem	Sapphire	3

Please update the table to address the player concerns. Then let me know the new probabilities for finding ore, rock, coal, marble, and sapphire.

Thanks,

Enrique

Solve It

➤ **Find a solution to the Mining Locations problem.**

- Provide an updated table that addresses all of the player concerns.

- Calculate the theoretical probability of finding ore, rock, coal, marble, and sapphire.

- Explain how you know each of the concerns has been addressed.

Reflect

Use Mathematical Practices After you complete the problem, choose one of these questions to discuss with a partner.

- **Use Models** Would a tree diagram or organized list be helpful models in this problem? Explain how they could help, or why they would not.

- **Use Structure** If 75 players test your new version of the game, how many of them would you expect to find ore in the first mining location they visit? Would you expect the same result in your partner's new version of the game?

Electronic Delay Storage Automatic Calculator (EDSAC), which performed its first calculation in 1949, was the first electronic computer to run a computer game.

In this unit you learned to . . .

Skill	Lesson(s)
Describe the probability of an event using words and numbers.	**30, 31**
Find probabilities of single events.	**30, 31, 32**
Use the results of an experiment to find the experimental probability of an event.	**31**
Find the theoretical probability of an event.	**32**
Compare theoretical and experimental probabilities.	**32**
Find probabilities of compound events.	**33**
Use simulations to find probabilities of events.	**33**
Explain ideas about probability clearly by using models to show why the ideas make sense for the problem.	**30, 31, 32, 33**

Think about what you have learned.

➤ **Use words, numbers, and drawings.**

1 The most important math I learned was _____ because . . .

2 A mistake I made that helped me learn was . . .

3 One thing I am still confused about is . . .

Vocabulary Review

➤ **Review the unit vocabulary. Put a check mark by items you can use in speaking and writing. Look up the meaning of any terms you do not know.**

Math Vocabulary

☐ compound event

☐ event

☐ experiment

☐ experimental probability

☐ outcome

☐ probability

☐ sample space

☐ theoretical probability

☐ tree diagram

☐ trial

Academic Vocabulary

☐ at random

☐ conduct (verb)

☐ likelihood

☐ simulate

☐ simulation

➤ **Use the unit vocabulary to answer the questions.**

1 Explain what *probability* means. Use at least three math or academic vocabulary terms in your explanation. Underline each term you use.

2 What might you do when finding an experimental probability? Use at least three math or academic vocabulary terms in your answer. Underline each term you use.

3 What is the difference between a simple event and a compound event?

4 Why might you draw a tree diagram? What could it help you find? Use at least three math or academic vocabulary terms in your answer. Underline each term you use.

➤ **Use what you have learned to complete these problems.**

1 Harold has a jar of coins; 5 are quarters, 4 are dimes, 7 are pennies, and 8 are nickels. He selects a coin at random. Decide if each outcome is likely or unlikely. Choose *Likely* or *Unlikely* for each outcome.

	Likely	**Unlikely**
a. Selecting a dime	○	○
b. Selecting a penny or nickel	○	○
c. Selecting a quarter or dime	○	○
d. Selecting a nickel	○	○

2 Mrs. Jackson has a box of markers. She selects a marker at random, records the color, and returns the marker to the box. In 15 trials, she selects a blue marker 9 times and a red marker the other times. Which is the most reasonable prediction for how many times Mrs. Jackson will select a red marker in 60 trials?

A 24   **B** 36   **C** 45   **D** 51

3 Kasey and Vail both flip a coin. Each coin has a heads side and a tails side. What is the probability that both coins land on heads? Show your work.

SOLUTION _____

4 Dmitri has a deck of cards with 13 hearts, 13 diamonds, 13 spades, and 13 clubs. Dmitri selects a card at random, writes the suit, and returns the card to the deck. He does this 30 times. Which suits have an experimental probability of being selected that is greater than their theoretical probability? Show your work.

Suit	Hearts	Diamonds	Spades	Clubs
Frequency	9	8	10	3

SOLUTION _____

5 Hayley flips a quarter, rolls a standard number cube, and flips a nickel. What is the probability of Hayley rolling a number less than 5 and the coins landing on different sides? Show your work.

SOLUTION _____

_____

6 A game is played with 45 cards. Some cards have adjectives, some cards have verbs, and some cards have nouns. Each word is spelled using all capital letters or all lowercase letters. Which statement about the probability of choosing a card is true? Choose all the correct answers.

	Adjectives	Verbs	Nouns
Capital Letters	3	6	9
Lowercase Letters	12	10	5

A The probability of choosing a card with capital letters is $\frac{2}{5}$.

B The probability of choosing a card with a verb is $\frac{16}{29}$.

C The probability of choosing a card with a noun in capital letters is $\frac{1}{5}$.

D The probability of choosing a card with a verb in lowercase letters is $\frac{2}{9}$.

E The probability of choosing a card with lowercase letters is $\frac{1}{2}$.

Performance Task

➤ **Answer the questions and show all your work on separate paper.**

Delara's favorite online game is called *Downtown*. In *Downtown*, players click a button at the beginning of each turn to determine the action to take on the online game board. Delara notes the actions she takes for 350 turns. Find the experimental probability for each action in *Downtown* using the table below.

Action	Number of Turns
Go forward 1 space.	53
Go backward 2 spaces.	103
Lose a turn.	71
Take another turn.	123

Delara wants to create her own version of the game. For her version, she wants to determine the action for each turn by using either a spinner with 12 equal parts or a deck of 40 cards. She wants the theoretical probability for each action in her version to be similar to the experimental probability for each action in the online version.

Determine the number of spaces on the spinner and the number of cards for each action that Delara can use to make her version.

Use your data to describe whether Delara's version should use a spinner or a deck of cards to match the experimental probabilities of the online version as closely as possible. Explain your reasoning.

Checklist

Did you . . .

☐ find the experimental probabilities for each action in the online version of *Downtown*?

☐ make sure the number of spaces on the spinner and number of cards for each action have theoretical probabilities that are similar to the experimental probabilities of the online version?

☐ describe whether Delara's game should use a spinner or a deck of cards, and why?

Reflect

Use Mathematical Practices After you complete the task, choose one of the following questions to answer.

• **Be Precise** How can you describe the meanings of the quantities in the probabilities?

• **Model** How would it help to create a spinner and draw diagrams of cards to solve the task?

Data Sets

Unit 5

MATH IN ACTION | SESSION 1 ■ □

Analyzing Hawk Data

Female Hawks	
Mass (g)	**Wing Length (mm)**
1,522	433
1,015	390
1,331	422
1,271	422
1,436	432
1,327	418
1,346	428
1,063	394
1,109	397
1,065	391
1,147	404
1,400	431
1,271	416
1,350	423
1,217	415
1,242	412
1,209	410
1,366	430
1,207	402
1,426	430

Male Hawks	
Mass (g)	**Wing Length (mm)**
908	374
917	378
826	364
1,003	393
962	386
868	374
920	378
1,064	409
956	385
978	388
911	377
960	385
930	383
924	379
1,042	408
767	362
756	356
933	383
991	390
844	368

Data Sets

Unit 5

MATH IN ACTION | SESSION 2 ■ ■

Counting Bears

Data from Black Bear Study

First Year of Study			
Sample	Bears in Sample	Marked Bears in Sample	Marked Bears in Population
1	20	0	0
2	10	5	20
3	6	3	25
4	4	2	28
5	15	5	30

Second Year of Study			
Sample	Bears in Sample	Marked Bears in Sample	Marked Bears in Population
1	15	0	0
2	31	4	15
3	20	13	42
4	14	9	49
5	13	10	54

Data from Grizzly Bear Study

First Year of Study			
Sample	Bears in Sample	Marked Bears in Sample	Marked Bears in Population
1	8	0	0
2	8	2	8
3	11	2	14
4	10	3	23
5	6	2	30

Second Year of Study			
Sample	Bears in Sample	Marked Bears in Sample	Marked Bears in Population
1	6	0	0
2	8	1	6
3	19	4	13
4	10	6	28
5	20	14	32

Set 1 Equivalent Expressions

➤ **Solve the problems. Show your work.**

1 Write $3x - 7 + 2(2x - 7)$ as the product of 7 and another factor.

2 Are $3(x - 4) - 2(2.5x - 1)$ and $-2(x + 5)$ equivalent expressions?

Set 2 Rewrite Expressions

➤ **Solve the problems.**

1 You can represent the perimeter of a shape with the two expressions $6x - 8$ and $4(1.5x - 2)$. What does $4(1.5x - 2)$ tell you about the shape that $6x - 8$ does not?

2 Alyssa has a coupon to get $2.50 off of each movie ticket she buys. She writes the cost of m movie tickets as $10m - 2.50m$. Then she writes it as $7.50m$. What two pieces of information does the expression $10m - 2.50m$ tell you that $7.50m$ does not?

Set 3 Multi-Step Equations

➤ **Use reasoning to solve the equations. Show your work.**

1 $5x + 5 = 30$

2 $6x - 12 = 6$

3 $2(x + 2) = 10$

Set 4 Solve Multi-Step Problems

➤ **Solve the problems. Show your work.**

1 The product of a number, n, and 12, minus 4 is 14. What is the number, n?

2 The sum of 6 and 2 times a number, n, is 1. What is the number, n?

Set 5 Solve Multi-Step Real-World Problems

➤ **Solve the problems. Show your work.**

1 A group of friends go to a concert. They spend $12.50 each on concert tickets and $5 each on transportation to the concert. The group spends a total of $105. How many friends go to the concert?

2 Elise has a box of pencils. Each pencil weighs $\frac{3}{10}$ ounce. The empty box weighs 0.4 ounce. The total weight of the box of pencils is 4 ounces. How many pencils are in the box?

3 The perimeter of a triangle is 30 inches. The length of the shortest side is $\frac{1}{3}$ the length of the hypotenuse, and 0.5 times the length of the remaining side. What is the length of the shortest side?

Name:

Set 6 Solve Multi-Step Equations

➤ **Solve the equations. Show your work.**

1 $6s + 15 = 22.5$

2 $8(x - 4) = 30$

3 $\dfrac{3(m + 4)}{5} = 2$

Set 7 Write and Solve Inequalities

➤ **Write an inequality to represent and solve each problem. Show your work.**

1 The product of $x - 3$ and 6 is at least 15. What are all the possible values of x? Graph the solution.

2 Sam wants to have an average greater than 75% on his math tests. His grades so far are 78%, 63%, and 79%. What grades can he earn on his next test to reach his goal? Graph the solution.

Set 8 Add with Negative Numbers

➤ **Fill in the blanks with *negative* or *positive* for problems 1–3.**

1 The sum of two negative numbers is always _____ .

2 The sum of -9.6 and $3\frac{1}{2}$ is _____ .

3 The sum of 21 and -15.5 is _____ .

➤ **Fill in the blanks with *greater than* or *less than* for problems 4–6.**

4 The sum of a negative number and a positive number is always _____ the positive number.

5 The sum of a negative number and a positive number is always _____ the negative number.

6 The sum $-3 + a$ is _____ -3 if a is negative.

Set 9 Subtract with Negative Integers

➤ **Fill in the blanks with *negative* or *positive*.**

1 The difference $-9 - 3$ is _____ .

2 The difference $-3 - (-9)$ is _____ .

3 If a is positive and b is _____ , the difference $a - b$ is always positive.

4 If a is negative and b is _____ , the difference $a - b$ is always negative.

Set 10 Multiply with Negative Integers

➤ **Fill in the blanks with *negative* or *positive*.**

1 The product of a negative number and a _____ number is always a positive number.

2 The product of four negative numbers is always _____ .

3 The product of three negative numbers and two positive numbers is always _____ .

Set 1 Solve Problems with Percents

➤ **Solve the problems. Show your work.**

1 The regular price of a pair of shoes is $72. The shoes are on sale for 40% off. Camilo uses a coupon to get an additional discount of 5% off the sale price. How much does he pay for the shoes?

2 There are 24 members at the art club's first meeting. At the second meeting, there are 25% fewer members. At the third meeting, the number of members increases by 50% from the second meeting. How many members attend the third meeting?

Set 2 Solve Percent Change Problems

➤ **Solve the problems. Show your work.**

1 Last year, Carter's fastest time running a mile was 6 minutes. This year, he can run a mile in 5.5 minutes. To the nearest percent, what is the percent change?

2 The original price of a dress is $80. During a sale, it is marked down by 20%. Then, it is marked down by 50% of the sale price. What is the percent change from the original cost to the final sale price?

Set 3 Solve Percent Error Problems

➤ **Solve the problems. Show your work.**

1 Landon estimates it will take 4 hours to finish his essay. It actually takes 3 hours. To the nearest percent, what is the percent error?

2 Beth says the distance to school is 2.8 kilometers. The actual distance is 3.5 kilometers. What is the percent error?

3 A path is 2.5 kilometers long. Joseph's estimate of the length of the path has an 8% error. His estimate is greater than the actual length of the path. What is his estimate?

Set 4 Divide with Rational Numbers

➤ **Divide. Show your work.**

1 $-72 \div 6$

2 $3 \div -\frac{2}{3}$

3 $-28 \div (-3.5)$

4 $-9 \div 0.3$

5 $4\frac{1}{2} \div (-3)$

6 $-1.2 \div (-0.01)$

Set 5 Multiply and Divide with Negative Numbers

➤ **Multiply or divide. Show your work.**

1 $-\frac{1}{5}(-30)$

2 $-3\frac{1}{5} \div \frac{4}{7}$

3 $9\left(-6\frac{1}{4}\right)$

4 $11.7 \div (-6.5)$

5 $-4\frac{1}{3} \times (-6.2)$

6 $-1.2(-6) \div (-0.5)$

Set 6 Add Opposites

➤ **Write an addition equation to represent and solve each problem.**

1 The temperature increases by 6°F to 0°F. What was the original temperature?

2 Fajah has $8. She spends $8 on her lunch. How much money does she have after buying lunch?

3 A diver is swimming at an elevation of −12 meters relative to sea level. She swims up 12 meters. What is her elevation now?

4 A football team gains 5 yards on their first play. It loses 5 yards on the next play. How many yards did it gain in total over the two plays?

5 The temperature changes by −2°C to 0°C. What was the original temperature?

Set 7 Add with Negative Numbers

➤ **Add. Show your work.**

1 $-6 + (-29)$

2 $8 + (-31)$

3 $-5.5 + 3.6$

4 $3\frac{1}{2} + \left(-4\frac{1}{3}\right)$

5 $-1\frac{4}{5} + \left(-2\frac{1}{2}\right)$

6 $6.4 + (-8.6)$

Set 8 Solve Proportional Relationship Problems

➤ **Solve the problems. Show your work.**

1 A recipe for 12 carrot muffins calls for $\frac{3}{4}$ cup of carrots. Dean has $1\frac{2}{3}$ cups of carrots. Does he have enough carrots to make 30 carrot muffins? If not, how many more cups of carrots does he need?

2 Kea makes 9 gallons of orange paint. She uses 3 gallons of yellow paint for every 1 gallon of red paint. How many more gallons of yellow paint does she use than of red paint?

Set 1 Solve Problems with Percents

➤ **Solve the problems. Show your work.**

1 Ivan's family eats dinner at a restaurant. He wants to leave a 20% tip on a $45.26 check. How much money does Ivan pay for dinner, including the tip?

2 Ella deposits $800 in her account. The account earns yearly simple interest at a rate of 2.5%. In 4 years, how much does Ella earn in interest?

3 Owen pays $29.12 for a book. The sales tax on the book is 4%. The book is on sale for 20% off. What is the original price of the book?

Set 2 Solve Percent Change Problems

➤ **Find the percent change. Show your work.**

1 What is the percent change from 15 to 20?

2 On the first night, 250 people attend a play. On the second night, 205 people attend. What is the percent change in attendance?

3 Lecia's weekly salary changes from $840 to $966. What is the percent change in her salary?

Set 3 Solve Percent Error Problems

➤ **Solve the problems. Show your work.**

1 Dylan guesses that there are 200 pennies in a jar. The actual number of pennies is 320. What is Dylan's percent error?

2 Corey puts potatoes in bags that will weigh about 6 lb each. He wants the bags to have a percent error less than or equal to 5%. What weights are possible?

Set 4 Equivalent Linear Expressions

➤ **Solve the problems. Show your work.**

1 Are $-2(4 - 3x) + 3(x + 1) + 1$ and $4(2x - 1) + x$ equivalent expressions?

2 Write an expression equivalent to $5 - 3(2t - 3) + 4(t + 2)$ that is the difference of two terms.

Set 5 Write and Solve Multi-Step Equations

➤ **Write and solve an equation to solve each problem. Show your work.**

1 The perimeter of a rectangular garden is 360 ft. The garden is 3 times as long as it is wide. What is the length of the garden?

2 Claire has $88.50 in her bank account. She gets paid for 8 hours of work and deposits her entire paycheck. Now she has $180.50 in her account. How much does Claire earn per hour?

Set 6 Write and Solve Inequalities

➤ **Write and solve an inequality to solve each problem. Show your work.**

1 6 more than the product of $-\frac{1}{2}$ and x is less than 5. What are all the possible values of x? Graph the solution.

2 Ariana has $40 to spend buying books online. Each book costs $8.50. It costs $4.00 to ship a package of books. How many books can Ariana buy?

Set 7 Express Rational Numbers as Decimals

➤ **Express each fraction as a decimal. Show your work.**

1 $2\frac{3}{5}$

2 $\frac{5}{8}$

3 $\frac{12}{32}$

4 $7\frac{7}{9}$

5 $\frac{4}{15}$

6 $\frac{5}{12}$

Set 8 Use the Four Operations with Negative Numbers

➤ **Solve the problems. Show your work.**

1 The temperature of a freezer changes from $-15.5°C$ to $-18°C$ in $\frac{1}{3}$ hour. At what hourly rate does the temperature of the freezer change?

2 The five members of a math team each receive a score at a competition.

$-5, 8, 6, 0, -6$

What is the mean of their scores?

Interactive Glossary/Glosario interactivo

English/Español	Example/Ejemplo	Notes/Notas

Aa

acute angle an angle that measures more than 0° but less than 90°.

ángulo agudo ángulo que mide más de 0° pero menos de 90°.

acute triangle a triangle that has three acute angles.

triángulo acutángulo triángulo que tiene tres ángulos agudos.

additive inverses two numbers whose sum is zero. The additive inverse of a number is the opposite of that number, i.e., the additive inverse of a is $-a$.

-2 and 2

$\frac{1}{2}$ and $-\frac{1}{2}$

inverso aditivo dos números cuya suma es cero. El inverso aditivo de un número es el opuesto de ese número; por ejemplo, el inverso aditivo de a es $-a$.

adjacent angles two non-overlapping angles that share a vertex and a side.

ángulos adyacentes dos ángulos que no se superponen y que comparten un vértice y un lado.

$\angle ADB$ and $\angle BDC$ are adjacent angles.

algorithm a set of routine steps used to solve problems.

$$
\begin{array}{r}
17 \text{ R } 19 \\
31\overline{)546} \\
-31\downarrow \\
\hline
236 \\
-217 \\
\hline
19
\end{array}
$$

algoritmo conjunto de pasos rutinarios que se siguen para resolver problemas.

angle a geometric shape formed by two rays, lines, or line segments that meet at a common point.

ángulo figura geométrica formada por dos semirrectas, rectas o segmentos de recta que se encuentran en un punto común.

English/Español	Example/Ejemplo	Notes/Notas

area the amount of space inside a closed two-dimensional figure. Area is measured in square units such as square centimeters.

área cantidad de espacio dentro de una figura bidimensional cerrada. El área se mide en unidades cuadradas, como los centímetros cuadrados.

6 units

Area = 30 units² | 5 units

---

associative property of addition regrouping the terms does not change the value of the expression.

propiedad asociativa de la suma reagrupar los términos no cambia el valor de la expresión.

$(a + b) + c = a + (b + c)$

$(2 + 3) + 4 = 2 + (3 + 4)$

---

associative property of multiplication regrouping the terms does not change the value of the expression.

propiedad asociativa de la multiplicación reagrupar los términos no cambia el valor de la expresión.

$(a \cdot b) \cdot c = a \cdot (b \cdot c)$

$(2 \cdot 3) \cdot 4 = 2 \cdot (3 \cdot 4)$

---

axis a horizontal or vertical number line that determines a coordinate plane. The plural form is *axes*.

eje recta numérica horizontal o vertical que determina un plano de coordenadas.

y y-axis

x-axis

x

−2 O 2

−2

Bb

balance point the point that represents the center of a data set. In a two-variable data set, the coordinates of the balance point are the mean of each variable.

punto de equilibrio punto que representa el centro de un conjunto de datos. En un conjunto de datos de dos variables, las coordenadas del punto de equilibrio son la media de cada variable.

Data set: (1, 1), (3, 4), (5, 6), (7, 8)

$$\frac{1 + 3 + 5 + 7}{4} = 4$$

$$\frac{1 + 4 + 6 + 8}{4} = 4.75$$

Balance point: (4, 4.75)

---

base (of a parallelogram) a side of a parallelogram from which the height is measured.

base (de un paralelogramo) lado de un paralelogramo desde el que se mide la altura.

---

base (of a power) in a power, the number that is used as a repeated factor.

base (de una potencia) en una potencia, el número que se usa como factor que se repite.

8^2

base

---

base (of a three-dimensional figure) a face of a three-dimensional figure from which the height is measured.

base (de una figura tridimensional) cara de una figura tridimensional desde la que se mide la altura.

---

base (of a triangle) a side of a triangle from which the height is measured.

base (de un triángulo) lado de un triángulo desde el que se mide la altura.

Interactive Glossary/Glosario interactivo

box plot a visual display of a data set on a number line that shows the minimum, the lower quartile, the median, the upper quartile, and the maximum. The sides of the box show the lower and upper quartiles and the line inside the box shows the median. Lines connect the box to the minimum and maximum values.

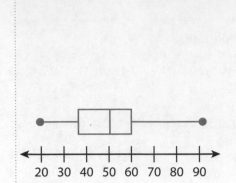

diagrama de caja representación visual de un conjunto de datos en una recta numérica que muestra el mínimo, el cuartil inferior, la mediana, el cuartil superior y el máximo. Los lados de la caja muestran los cuartiles inferior y superior y la recta del centro muestra la mediana. Las rectas conectan la caja con los valores mínimo y máximo.

Cc

center (of a circle) the point inside a circle that is the same distance from every point on the circle.

centro (de un círculo) punto dentro de un círculo que está a la misma distancia de todos los puntos del círculo.

center

---

circle a two-dimensional shape in which every point is the same distance from the center.

círculo figura bidimensional en que todos los puntos están a la misma distancia del centro.

---

circumference the distance around the outside of a circle. It can be thought of as the perimeter of the circle.

circunferencia distancia alrededor del exterior de un círculo. Se puede considerar como el perímetro del círculo.

circumference

---

closed figure a two-dimensional figure that begins and ends at the same point.

figura cerrada figura bidimensional que comienza y termina en el mismo punto.

Closed figure   Open figure

---

cluster a group of data points that are close to each other.

agrupación conjunto de datos que están cerca unos de otros.

cluster

0 1 2 3 4

---

coefficient a number that is multiplied by a variable.

coeficiente número que se multiplica por una variable.

$5x + 3$

coefficient

commission a fee paid for services, often a percent of the total cost. A salesperson who earns a commission often gets a percent of the total sale.	A 5% commission on $4,000 is 0.05($4,000), or $200.	
comisión tarifa que se paga por servicios, que suele ser un porcentaje del costo total. Un vendedor que gana una comisión por lo general recibe un porcentaje de la venta total.		
common denominator a number that is a common multiple of the denominators of two or more fractions.	A common denominator for $\frac{1}{2}$ and $\frac{3}{5}$ is 10 because $2 \cdot 5 = 10$.	
denominador común número que es múltiplo común de los denominadores de dos o más fracciones.		
commutative property of addition changing the order of the addends does not change the sum.	$a + b = b + a$ $4.1 + 7.5 = 7.5 + 4.1$	
propiedad conmutativa de la suma cambiar el orden de los sumandos no cambia el total.		
commutative property of multiplication changing the order of the factors does not change the product.	$ab = ba$ $4(7.5) = 7.5(4)$	
propiedad conmutativa de la multiplicación cambiar el orden de los factores no cambia el producto.		
compare to describe the relationship between the value or size of two numbers or quantities.	$-4 < 8.5$	
comparar describir la relación que hay entre el valor o el tamaño de dos números o cantidades.		

complementary angles two angles whose measures sum to 90°.

ángulos complementarios dos ángulos cuyas medidas suman 90°.

∠AEB and ∠BEC

complex fraction a fraction in which the numerator is a fraction, the denominator is a fraction, or both the numerator and the denominator are fractions.

fracción compleja fracción en la que el numerador es una fracción, el denominador es una fracción, o tanto el numerador como el denominador son fracciones.

$$\frac{\frac{1}{2}}{\frac{3}{4}}$$

compose to make by combining parts. You can put together numbers to make a greater number or put together shapes to make a new shape.

componer formar al combinar partes. Se pueden unir números para hacer un número mayor o unir figuras para formar una figura nueva.

composite number a number that has more than one pair of whole number factors.

número compuesto número que tiene más de un par de números enteros como factores.

16 is a composite number because 1 • 16, 2 • 8, and 4 • 4 all equal 16.

compound event an event that consists of two or more simple events.

evento compuesto evento que consiste en dos o más eventos simples.

Rolling a number cube twice

constant of proportionality the unit rate in a proportional relationship.

constante de proporcionalidad tasa unitaria en una relación proporcional.

Unit rate: $10 per hour
Constant of proportionality for dollars per hours: 10.

English/Español	Example/Ejemplo	Notes/Notas

convert to write an equivalent measurement using a different unit.

60 in. is the same as 5 ft.

convertir escribir una medida equivalente usando una unidad diferente.

---

coordinate plane a two-dimensional space formed by two perpendicular number lines called *axes*.

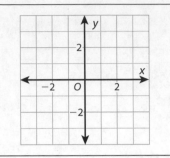

plano de coordenadas espacio bidimensional formado por dos rectas numéricas perpendiculares llamadas ejes.

---

corresponding terms terms that have the same position in two related patterns. For example, the second term in one pattern and the second term in a related pattern are corresponding terms.

Pattern A: 12, 18, 24, 30

Pattern B: 6, 9, 12, 15

términos correspondientes términos que tienen la misma posición en dos patrones relacionados. Por ejemplo, el segundo término en un patrón y el segundo término en un patrón relacionado son términos correspondientes.

---

cross-section a two-dimensional shape that is exposed by making a straight cut through a three-dimensional figure.

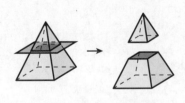

sección transversal figura bidimensional que se forma al hacer un corte recto a través de una figura tridimensional.

---

cube a rectangular prism in which each face of the prism is a square.

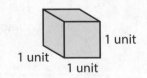

1 unit
1 unit
1 unit

cubo prisma rectangular en el que cada cara del prisma es un cuadrado.

English/Español	Example/Ejemplo	Notes/Notas
cylinder a three-dimensional figure with two parallel curved bases that are the same size. The bases are connected by a curved surface. **cilindro** figura tridimensional que tiene dos bases curvas paralelas que tienen el mismo tamaño. Las bases están conectadas por una superficie curva.		

Dd

English/Español	Example/Ejemplo	Notes/Notas
data a set of collected information. Often numerical information such as a list of measurements. **datos** conjunto de información reunida. Con frecuencia, información numérica como una lista de medidas.	Commute length (mi): 15, 22, 10.5, 21, 9.5	
decimal a number containing a decimal point that separates a whole from fractional place values (tenths, hundredths, thousandths, and so on). **decimal** número que tiene un punto decimal que separa un entero de los valores posicionales fraccionarios (décimas, centésimas, milésimas, etc.).	1.293	
decompose to break into parts. You can break apart numbers and shapes. **descomponer** separar en partes. Se puede separar en partes números y figuras.		

English/Español	Example/Ejemplo	Notes/Notas
degree (°) a unit used to measure angles.		
	There are 360° in a circle.	
grado (°) unidad que se usa para medir ángulos.		
denominator the number below the line in a fraction that tells the number of equal parts in the whole.		
	$\frac{3}{4}$	
denominador número debajo de la línea en una fracción que indica el número de partes iguales que hay en el entero.		
dependent variable a variable whose value depends on the value of a related independent variable.	$y = 5x$	
	The value of y depends on the value of x.	
variable dependiente variable cuyo valor depende del valor de una variable independiente relacionada.		
diameter a line segment that goes through the center of a circle and has endpoints on the circle. Also, the distance across a circle through the center.		
	diameter	
diámetro segmento de recta que pasa por el centro de un círculo y tiene extremos en el círculo. También, la distancia de un lado al otro del círculo a través del centro.		
difference the result of subtraction.	$\begin{array}{r} 16.75 \\ -\ 15.70 \\ \hline 1.05 \end{array}$	
diferencia resultado de la resta.		
digit a symbol used to write numbers.	The digits are 0, 1, 2, 3, 4, 5, 6, 7, 8, and 9.	
dígito símbolo que se usa para escribir números.		
dimension length in one direction. A figure may have one, two, or three dimensions.		
	5 in. 2 in. 3 in.	
dimensión longitud en una dirección. Una figura puede tener una, dos o tres dimensiones.		

English/**Español**	**Example**/Ejemplo	**Notes**/Notas

distribution a representation that shows how often values in a data set occur.

distribución representación que muestra la frecuencia con la que ocurren los valores en un conjunto de datos.

Pet	Frequency
Bird	7
Cat	12
Dog	8
Snake	3

distributive property multiplying each term in a sum or difference by a common factor does not change the value of the expression.

propiedad distributiva multiplicar cada término de una suma o diferencia por un factor común no cambia el valor de la expresión.

$$a(b + c) = ab + ac$$
$$5(4 + 2) = 5(4) + 5(2)$$

dividend the number that is divided by another number.

dividendo número que se divide por otro número.

$$22.5 \div 3 = 7.5$$

divisor the number by which another number is divided.

divisor número por el que se divide otro número.

$$22.5 \div 3 = 7.5$$

dot plot a data display that shows data as dots above a number line. A dot plot may also be called a *line plot*.

diagrama de puntos representación de datos que muestra datos como puntos sobre una *recta numérica*.

English/Español	Example/Ejemplo	Notes/Notas

Ee

edge a line segment where two faces meet in a three-dimensional shape.

arista segmento de recta en el que dos caras se unen en una figura tridimensional.

← edge

---

equal having the same value, same size, or same amount.

igual que tiene el mismo valor, el mismo tamaño o la misma cantidad.

$50 - 20 = 30$

$50 - 20$ is equal to 30.

---

equation a mathematical statement that uses an equal sign ($=$) to show that two expressions have the same value.

ecuación enunciado matemático que tiene un signo de igual ($=$) para mostrar que dos expresiones tienen el mismo valor.

$x + 4 = 15$

---

equilateral triangle a triangle that has all three sides the same length.

triángulo equilátero triángulo que tiene los tres lados de la misma longitud.

---

equivalent having the same value.

equivalente que tiene el mismo valor.

4 is equivalent to $\frac{8}{2}$.

---

equivalent expressions two or more expressions in different forms that always name the same value.

expresiones equivalentes dos o más expresiones en diferentes formas que siempre nombran el mismo valor.

$2(x + 4)$ is equivalent to $2x + 2(4)$ and $2x + 8$.

---

equivalent fractions two or more different fractions that name the same part of a whole or the same point on the number line.

fracciones equivalentes dos o más fracciones diferentes que nombran la misma parte de un entero o el mismo punto en la recta numérica.

$-\frac{5}{10}$ $\frac{4}{8}$

$-\frac{1}{2}$ $\frac{1}{2}$

-1 0 1

English/Español	Example/Ejemplo	Notes/Notas
equivalent ratios two ratios that express the same comparison. Multiplying both numbers in the ratio $a : b$ by a nonzero number n results in the equivalent ratio $na : nb$. **razones equivalentes** dos razones que expresan la misma comparación. Multiplicar ambos números en la razón $a : b$ por un número distinto de cero n da como resultado la razón equivalente $na : nb$.	$6 : 8$ is equivalent to $3 : 4$	
estimate (noun) a close guess made using mathematical thinking. **estimación** suposición aproximada que se hace por medio del razonamiento matemático.	$28 + 21 = ?$ $30 + 20 = 50$ 50 is an estimate of $28 + 21$.	
estimate (verb) to give an approximate number or answer based on mathematical thinking. **estimar** dar un número o respuesta aproximada basados en el razonamiento matemático.	$28 + 21$ is about 50.	
evaluate to find the value of an expression. **evaluar** hallar el valor de una expresión.	The expression $4.5 \div (1 + 8)$ has a value of 0.5.	
event a set of one or more outcomes of an experiment. **evento** conjunto de uno o más resultados de un experimento.	Experiment: rolling a number cube once Possible events: rolling an even number, rolling a 1	
experiment a repeatable procedure involving chance that results in one or more possible outcomes. **experimento** procedimiento repetible en el que se hacen pruebas y da uno o más resultados posibles.	Experiment: rolling a number cube once	

experimental probability the probability of an event occurring based on the results from an experiment.

A coin is flipped **30** times and lands heads up **17** times.

The experimental probability of the coin landing heads up is $\frac{17}{30}$.

probabilidad experimental probabilidad de que un evento ocurra con base en los resultados de un experimento.

---

exponent in a power, the number that shows how many times the base is used as a factor.

8^2

exponent

exponente en una potencia, el número que muestra cuántas veces se usa la base como factor.

---

exponential expression an expression that includes an exponent.

$3x^3$

expresión exponencial expresión que tiene un exponente.

---

expression a group of numbers, variables, and/or operation symbols that represents a mathematical relationship. An expression without variables, such as $3 + 4$, is called a *numerical expression*. An expression with variables, such as $5b^2$, is called an *algebraic expression*.

$\frac{32 - 4}{7}$

$3x + y - 9$

expresión grupo de números, variables y/o símbolos de operaciones que representa una relación matemática. Una expresión sin variables, como $3 + 4$, se llama *expresión numérica*. Una expresión con variables, como $5b^2$, se llama *expresión algebraica*.

Ff

face a flat surface of a solid shape.

cara superficie plana de una figura sólida.

face

factor (noun) a number, or expression with parentheses, that is multiplied.

factor número, o expresión entre paréntesis, que se multiplica.

$$4 \times 5 = 20$$

factors

factor (verb) to rewrite an expression as a product of factors.

descomponer volver a escribir una expresión como producto de factores.

$$12x + 42 = 6(2x + 7)$$

factor pair two numbers that are multiplied together to give a product.

par de factores dos números que se multiplican para dar un producto.

$$4 \times 5 = 20$$

factor pair

factors of a number whole numbers that multiply together to get the given number.

factores de un número números enteros que se multiplican para obtener el número dado.

$$4 \times 5 = 20$$

4 and 5 are factors of 20.

formula a mathematical relationship that is expressed in the form of an equation.

fórmula relación matemática que se expresa en forma de ecuación.

$$A = \ell w$$

fraction a number that names equal parts of a whole. A fraction names a point on the number line and can also represent the division of two numbers.

fracción número que nombra partes iguales de un entero. Una fracción nombra un punto en la recta numérica y también puede representar la división de dos números.

$$-\frac{1}{2} \qquad \frac{4}{8}$$

$$-1 \qquad 0 \qquad 1$$

English/Español	Example/Ejemplo	Notes/Notas

frequency a numerical count of how many times a data value occurs in a data set.

frecuencia conteo numérico de cuántas veces ocurre un valor en un conjunto de datos.

Data set: 12, 13, 12, 15, 12, 13, 15, 14, 12, 12

Data Value	Frequency
12	5
13	2
14	1
15	2

Gg

gap an interval of the number line for which a distribution has no data values.

espacio intervalo de la recta numérica para el que una distribución no tiene valores.

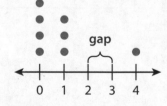

gratuity an amount added on to the cost of a service, often a percent of the total cost. Gratuity is often referred to as a *tip*.

propina cantidad que se suma al costo de un servicio; suele ser un porcentaje del costo total.

A gratuity of 18% on a $20 bill is 0.18($20), or $3.60.

English/Español	Example/Ejemplo	Notes/Notas
greatest common factor (GCF) the greatest factor two or more numbers have in common.	GCF of 20 and 30: $2 \cdot 5$, or 10 $20 = 2 \cdot 2 \cdot 5$ $30 = 2 \cdot 3 \cdot 5$	
máximo común divisor (M.C.D.) el mayor factor que dos o más números tienen en común.		
grouping symbol a symbol, such as braces {}, brackets [], or parentheses (), used to group parts of an expression that should be evaluated before others.	$3 \div (7 - 2) = 3 \div 5$ $\dfrac{3}{7 - 2} = \dfrac{3}{5}$	
símbolo de agrupación símbolo, como las llaves {}, los corchetes [] o los paréntesis (), que se usa para agrupar partes de una expresión que deben evaluarse antes que otras.		

Hh

height (of a parallelogram) the perpendicular distance from a base to the opposite side.		
altura (de un paralelogramo) distancia perpendicular desde una base hasta el lado opuesto.		
height (of a prism) the perpendicular distance from a base to the opposite base.		
altura (de un prisma) distancia perpendicular desde una base hasta la base opuesta.		

English/Español	Example/Ejemplo	Notes/Notas

height (of a triangle) the perpendicular distance from a base to the opposite vertex.

altura (de un triángulo) distancia perpendicular desde una base hasta el vértice opuesto.

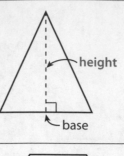

hexagon a polygon with exactly 6 sides and 6 angles.

hexágono polígono que tiene exactamente 6 lados y 6 ángulos.

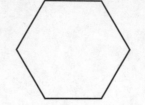

histogram a data display similar to a bar graph. A histogram groups the data into equal-size intervals. The height of each bar represents the number of data points in that group.

histograma presentación de datos parecida a una gráfica de barras. Un histograma agrupa los datos en intervalos de igual tamaño. La altura de cada barra representa el número de datos que hay en ese grupo.

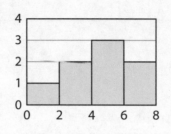

Ii

identity property of multiplication any number multiplied by 1 is itself.

$$3 \cdot 1 = 3$$

propiedad de identidad de la multiplicación cualquier número multiplicado por 1 es el mismo número.

---

independent variable a variable whose value is used to find the value of another variable. An independent variable determines the value of a dependent variable.

$y = 5x$

The value of x is used to find the value of y.

variable independiente variable cuyo valor se usa para hallar el valor de otra variable. Una variable independiente determina el valor de una variable dependiente.

---

inequality a mathematical statement that uses an inequality symbol ($<, >, \leq, \geq$) to show the relationship between values of expressions.

$4,384 > 3,448$

$x \geq -2$

desigualdad enunciado matemático que muestra con un signo de desigualdad ($<, >, \leq, \geq$) la relación que existe entre los valores de las expresiones.

---

integers the set of whole numbers and their opposites.

$-3, -1, 0, 2, 3$

enteros (positivos y negativos) conjunto de números enteros y sus opuestos.

---

interquartile range (IQR) the difference between the upper quartile and lower quartile.

interquartile range

20 30 40 50 60 70 80 90

rango entre cuartiles (REC) diferencia entre el cuartil superior y el cuartil inferior.

IQR: $60 - 35 = 25$

English/Español	Example/Ejemplo	Notes/Notas
inverse operations operations that undo each other. For example, addition and subtraction are inverse operations, and multiplication and division are inverse operations.		
	$300 \div 10 = 30$ $30 \times 10 = 300$	
operaciones inversas operaciones que se cancelan entre sí. Por ejemplo, la suma y la resta son operaciones inversas, y la multiplicación y la división son operaciones inversas.		
isosceles triangle a triangle that has at least two sides the same length.		
	8 in. 8 in. 6 in.	
triángulo isósceles triángulo que tiene al menos dos lados de la misma longitud.		

Ll

English/Español	Example/Ejemplo	Notes/Notas
least common multiple (LCM) the least multiple shared by two or more numbers.	LCM of 20 and 30: $2 \cdot 2 \cdot 3 \cdot 5$, or **60** $20 = 2 \cdot 2 \cdot 5$ $30 = 2 \cdot 3 \cdot 5$	
mínimo común múltiplo (m.c.m.) el menor múltiplo que comparten dos o más números.		

English/Español	Example/Ejemplo	Notes/Notas
like terms two or more terms that have the same variable factors.	$2x^2$ and $4x^2$	
términos semejantes dos o más términos que tienen los mismos factores variables.	1.2 and 5.1 $6xy$ and xy	
line a straight row of points that goes on forever in both directions.		
recta línea recta de puntos que continúa infinitamente en ambas direcciones.		
line of symmetry a line that divides a shape into two mirror images.		
eje de simetría línea que divide a una figura en dos imágenes reflejadas.		
line segment a straight row of points between two end points.		
segmento de recta fila recta de puntos entre dos extremos.	A ●———————● B	
lower quartile the middle number between the minimum and the median in an ordered set of numbers. The lower quartile is also called the 1st quartile or Q1.	lower quartile	
cuartil inferior el número del medio entre el mínimo y la mediana en un conjunto ordenado de números. El cuartil inferior también se llama primer cuartil, o Q1.	20 30 40 50 60 70 80 90	

Mm

markdown an amount subtracted from the cost of an item to determine the final price. The amount subtracted is often a percent of the cost.	A discount of $20 is the same as a markdown of $20.	
reducción de precio cantidad que se resta al costo de un artículo para determinar el precio final. La cantidad que se resta suele ser un porcentaje del costo.		
markup an amount added to the cost of an item to determine the final price. The amount added is often a percent of the cost.	A price increase of $25 is the same as a markup of $25.	
margen de ganancia cantidad que se suma al costo de un artículo para determinar el precio final. La cantidad que se suma suele ser un porcentaje del costo.		
maximum (of a data set) the greatest value in a data set.	Data set: 9, 10, 8, 9, 7	
máximo (de un conjunto de datos) mayor valor en un conjunto de datos.		
mean the sum of a set of values divided by the number of values. This is often called the *average*.	Data set: 9, 10, 8, 9, 7 Mean: $\dfrac{9 + 10 + 8 + 9 + 7}{5} = 8.6$	
media suma de un conjunto de valores dividida por el número de valores. Suele llamarse *promedio*.		
mean absolute deviation (MAD) the sum of the distances of each data point from the mean of the data set divided by the number of data points. It is always positive.	Data set: 9, 10, 8, 9, 7 Mean: 8.6 MAD: $\dfrac{0.4 + 1.4 + 0.6 + 0.4 + 1.7}{5} = 0.9$	
desviación media absoluta (DMA) suma de las distancias de cada dato desde la media del conjunto de datos dividido por el número de datos. Siempre es positiva.		

English/Español	Example/Ejemplo	Notes/Notas
measure of center a single number that summarizes what is typical for all the values in a data set. Mean and median are measures of center.	Data set: 9, 10, 8, 9, 7 Mean: 8.6 Median: 9	
medida de tendencia central único número que resume qué es típico para todos los valores en un conjunto de datos. La media y la mediana son medidas de tendecia central.		
measure of variability a single number that summarizes how much the values in a data set vary. Mean absolute deviation and interquartile range are measures of variability.	Data set: 9, 10, 8, 9, 7 MAD: 0.9 IQR: 1	
medida de variabilidad único número que resume cuánto varían los valores en un conjunto de datos. La desviación media absoluta y el rango entre cuartiles son medidas de variabilidad.		
median the middle number, or the halfway point between the two middle numbers, in an ordered set of values.	Data set: 9, 10, 8, 9, 7 7, 8, 9, 9, 10	
mediana el número del medio, o punto intermedio entre los dos números del medio, de un conjunto ordenado de valores.		
minimum (of a data set) the least value in a data set.	Data set: 9, 10, 8, 9, 7	
mínimo (de un conjunto de datos) valor mínimo en un conjunto de datos.		
multiple the product of a given number and any other whole number.	4, 8, 12, 16 are multiples of 4.	
múltiplo producto de un número dado y cualquier otro número entero.		

English/Español	Example/Ejemplo	Notes/Notas
multiplicative comparison a comparison that tells how many times as many.	$\frac{1}{2} \times 6 = 3$ tells that 3 is $\frac{1}{2}$ times as many as 6 and that 3 is 6 times as many as $\frac{1}{2}$.	
comparación multiplicativa comparación que indica cuántas veces más.		
multiplicative inverse a number is the multiplicative inverse of another number if the product of the two numbers is 1.	3 and $\frac{1}{3}$	
inverso multiplicativo un número es el inverso multiplicativo de otro número si el producto de los dos números es 1.		

Nn

negative numbers numbers that are less than 0. They are located to the left of 0 on a horizontal number line and below 0 on a vertical number line.

números negativos números que son menores que 0. Se ubican a la izquierda del 0 en una recta numérica horizontal y debajo del 0 en una recta numérica vertical.

net a flat, "unfolded" representation of a three-dimensional shape.

modelo plano representación plana "desplegada" de una figura tridimensional.

numerator the number above the line in a fraction that tells the number of equal parts that are being described.

$$\frac{3}{4}$$

numerador número que está sobre la línea en una fracción y que indica el número de partes iguales que se describen.

English/Español	Example/Ejemplo	Notes/Notas

Oo

obtuse angle an angle that measures more than 90° but less than 180°.

ángulo obtuso ángulo que mide más de 90° pero menos de 180°.

obtuse triangle a triangle that has one obtuse angle.

triángulo obtusángulo triángulo que tiene un ángulo obtuso.

opposite numbers numbers that are the same distance from 0 on the number line but in opposite directions. Opposite numbers have the same numeral, but opposite signs. The opposite of a number is also called the *additive inverse* of that number.

números opuestos números que están a la misma distancia del 0 en la recta numérica pero en direcciones opuestas. Los números opuestos son el mismo número, pero con el signo opuesto. El opuesto de un número también se llama *inverso de suma* de ese número.

-3 and 3

$-\frac{8}{15}$ and $\frac{8}{15}$

Order of Operations a set of rules that state the order in which operations should be performed to evaluate an expression.

orden de las operaciones conjunto de reglas que establecen el orden en el que deben hacerse las operaciones para evaluar una expresión.

Working from left to right:
1. Grouping symbols
2. Exponents
3. Multiplication/Division
4. Addition/Subtraction

ordered pair a pair of numbers, (x, y), that describes the location of a point in the coordinate plane. The x-coordinate gives the point's horizontal distance from the y-axis, and the y-coordinate gives the point's vertical distance from the x-axis.

par ordenado par de números, (x, y), que describen la ubicación de un punto en el plano de coordenadas. La coordenada x da la distancia horizontal del punto desde el eje y, y la coordenada y da la distancia vertical del punto desde el eje x.

(x, y)

x-coordinate y-coordinate

GL26 Interactive Glossary/Glosario interactivo ©Curriculum Associates, LLC Copying is not permitted.

origin the point (0, 0) on the coordinate plane where the *x*-axis and *y*-axis intersect.

origen el punto (0, 0) en el plano de coordenadas donde el eje *x* y el eje *y* se intersecan.

outcome one of the possible results of a chance experiment.

resultado uno de los efectos posibles de un experimento aleatorio.

Experiment: Rolling a number cube once

All possible outcomes: 1, 2, 3, 4, 5, 6

outlier a data value that is much greater or much less than most of the other values in the data set. An outlier seems to not quite fit with the rest of the data points.

valor atípico dato que es mucho mayor o mucho menor que la mayoría de los otros valores del conjunto de datos. Un valor atípico parece no ajustarse al resto de los datos.

Pp

| **parallel (∥)** always the same distance apart and never meeting.<br><br>**paralelos (∥)** que están siempre a la misma distancia y nunca se encuentran. | ```
A ▢          ▢ B



D ▢          ▢ C
```<br>$\overline{AB} \parallel \overline{CD}$ and $\overline{AD} \parallel \overline{BC}$ |
parallel lines lines that are always the same distance apart and never intersect. **rectas paralelas** rectas que siempre están a la misma distancia y nunca se intersecan.	
parallelogram a quadrilateral with opposite sides parallel and equal in length. **paralelogramo** cuadrilátero que tiene lados opuestos paralelos y de la misma longitud.	
partial products the products you get in each step of the partial-products strategy. You use place value to find partial products. **productos parciales** productos que se obtienen en cada paso de la estrategia de productos parciales. Se usa el valor posicional para hallar productos parciales.	218×6 Partial products: 6×200, or 1,200, 6×10, or 60, and 6×8, or 48
partial quotients the quotients you get in each step of the partial-quotient strategy. You use place value to find partial quotients. **cocientes parciales** cocientes que se obtienen en cada paso de la estrategia de cocientes parciales. Se usa el valor posicional para hallar cocientes parciales.	$2,124 \div 4$ Partial quotients: $2,000 \div 4$, or 500, $100 \div 4$, or 25, and $24 \div 4$, or 6
```

English/Español	Example/Ejemplo	Notes/Notas
partial sums the sums you get in each step of the partial-sums strategy. You use place value to find partial sums.	$124 + 234$ Partial sums: $100 + 200$, or 300, $20 + 30$, or 50, and $4 + 4$, or 8	
sumas parciales totales que se obtienen en cada paso de la estrategia de sumas parciales. Se usa el valor posicional para hallar sumas parciales.		

partial-products strategy a strategy used to multiply multi-digit numbers.	218 $\times \quad 6$ 48 (6 × 8 ones) 60 (6 × 1 ten) $+ 1,200$ (6 × 2 hundreds) 1,308	
estrategia de productos parciales estrategia que se usa para multiplicar números de varios dígitos.		

partial-quotients strategy a strategy used to divide multi-digit numbers.	6 25 500 4)2,125 $- 2,000$ 125 $- 100$ 25 $- 24$ 1	
estrategia de cocientes parciales estrategia que se usa para dividir números de varios dígitos.	The quotient 531 is the sum of partial quotients (6, 25, and 500) and the remainder (1).	

partial-sums strategy a strategy used to add multi-digit numbers.	312 $+ 235$ **Add the hundreds.** 500 **Add the tens.** 40 **Add the ones.** $+ \quad 7$ 547	
estrategia de sumas parciales estrategia que se usa para sumar números de varios dígitos.		

peak in a distribution, the shape formed when many data points are at one value or group of values.		
pico en una distribución, la figura que se forma cuando los puntos de muchos datos están en un valor o grupo de valores.		

English/Español	Example/Ejemplo	Notes/Notas
pentagon a polygon with exactly 5 sides and 5 angles.		
pentágono polígono que tiene exactamente 5 lados y 5 ángulos.		
per *for each* or *for every*. The word *per* can be used to express a rate, such as $2 per pound.	A price of $2 per pound means for every pound, you pay $2.	
por *por cada*. La palabra *por* se puede usar para expresar una tasa, como $2 por libra.		
percent per 100. A percent is a rate per 100. A percent can be written using the percent symbol (%) and represented as a fraction or decimal.	15% can be represented as $\frac{15}{100}$ or 0.15.	
porcentaje por cada 100. Un porcentaje es una tasa por cada 100. Un porcentaje se puede escribir usando el símbolo de porcentaje (%) y se representa como fracción o decimal.		
percent change the amount of change compared to the original (or starting) amount, expressed as a percent. Percent change = $\frac{\text{amount of change}}{\text{original amount}} \times 100$	Saturday: 250 people Sunday: 300 people Change from Saturday to Sunday: $300 - 250 = 50$ Percent change: $\frac{50}{250} \times 100 = 20\%$	
cambio porcentual cantidad de cambio en comparación con la cantidad original (o inicial) que se expresa como porcentaje. Cambio porcentual = $\frac{\text{cantidad de cambio}}{\text{cantidad original}} \times 100$		

English/Español	Example/Ejemplo	Notes/Notas

percent decrease the percent change when a quantity decreases from its original amount.

Percent decrease =

$$\frac{\text{amount of decrease}}{\text{original amount}} \times 100$$

Saturday: 250 people

Sunday: 200 people

Change from Saturday to Sunday: $250 - 200 = 50$

Percent change:

$$\frac{50}{250} \times 100 = 20\%$$

There is a 20% decrease from Saturday to Sunday.

disminución porcentual cambio porcentual cuando una cantidad disminuye desde su cantidad original. Disminución porcentual =

$$\frac{\text{cantidad de disminución}}{\text{cantidad original}} \times 100$$

---

percent error the difference between the correct value and the incorrect value compared to the correct value, expressed as a percent.

Percent error = $\frac{\text{amount of error}}{\text{correct value}} \times 100$

A bag of flour weighs 4.5 lb. It should weigh 5 lb.

Percent error:

$$\frac{5 - 4.5}{5} \times 100 = 10\%$$

error porcentual diferencia que hay entre el valor correcto y el valor incorrecto en comparación con el valor correcto, expresada como porcentaje.

Error porcentual = $\frac{\text{cantidad de error}}{\text{valor correcto}} \times 100$

---

percent increase the percent change when a quantity increases from its original amount.

Percent increase =

$$\frac{\text{amount of increase}}{\text{original amount}} \times 100$$

Saturday: 250 people

Sunday: 300 people

Change from Saturday to Sunday: $300 - 250 = 50$

Percent change:

$$\frac{50}{250} \times 100 = 20\%$$

There is a 20% increase from Saturday to Sunday.

incremento porcentual cambio porcentual cuando una cantidad se incrementa desde su cantidad original.

Aumento porcentual =

$$\frac{\text{cantidad de incremento}}{\text{cantidad original}} \times 100$$

perimeter the distance around a two-dimensional shape. The perimeter is equal to the sum of the lengths of the sides.

perímetro distancia alrededor de una figura bidimensional. El perímetro es igual a la suma de las longitudes de los lados.

60 yd

40 yd   40 yd

60 yd

Perimeter: 200 yd
(60 yd + 40 yd + 60 yd + 40 yd)

---

perpendicular (⊥) meeting to form right angles.

perpendicular (⊥) unión donde se forman ángulos rectos.

A   B

D   C

$\overline{AD} \perp \overline{CD}$

---

perpendicular lines two lines that meet to form a right angle, or a 90° angle.

rectas perpendiculares dos rectas que se encuentran y forman un ángulo recto, o ángulo de 90°.

---

pi (π) in a circle, the quotient $\frac{circumference}{diameter}$. Common approximations are 3.14 and $\frac{22}{7}$.

pi (π) en un círculo, el cociente de $\frac{circumferencia}{diámetro}$. Las aproximaciones communes son 3.14 y $\frac{22}{7}$.

$$\pi \approx 3.14 \text{ or } \frac{22}{7}$$

---

place value the value of a digit based on its position in a number.

valor posicional valor de un dígito que se basa en su posición en un número. Por ejemplo, el 2 en 3.52 está en la posición de las centésimas y tiene un valor de 2 centésimas, o 0.02.

The **2** in 3.**52** is in the hundredths place and has a value of **2 hundredths** or **0.02**.

English/Español	Example/Ejemplo	Notes/Notas
plane figure a two-dimensional figure, such as a circle, triangle, or rectangle.		
figura plana figura bidimensional, como un círculo, un triángulo o un rectángulo.		
plane section a two-dimensional shape that is exposed by making a straight cut through a three-dimensional figure.	plane section	
sección plana figura bidimensional que se expone al hacer un corte recto a través de una figura tridimensional.		
point a single location in space.	*A*	
punto ubicación única en el espacio.		
polygon a two-dimensional closed figure made with three or more straight line segments that meet only at their endpoints.		
polígono figura bidimensional cerrada formada por tres o más segmentos de recta que se encuentran solo en sus extremos.		
population the entire group of interest. Samples are drawn from populations.	Sample: 10 students from each Grade 8 homeroom in a school	
población grupo entero de interés. Las muestras se obtienen de las poblaciones.	Population: All Grade 8 students in the school	
positive numbers numbers that are greater than 0. They are located to the right of 0 on a horizontal number line and above 0 on a vertical number line.		
números positivos números que son mayores que 0. Se ubican a la derecha del 0 en una recta numérica horizontal y sobre el 0 en una recta numérica vertical.	−3 −2 −1 0 1 2 3	

English/Español	Example/Ejemplo	Notes/Notas
power an expression with a base and an exponent. **potencia** expresión que tiene una base y un exponente.	8^2	
power of 10 a number that can be written as a product of 10s. **potencia de 10** número que se puede escribir como el producto de 10.	100 and 1,000 are powers of 10 because $100 = 10 \times 10$ and $1,000 = 10 \times 10 \times 10$.	
prime number a whole number greater than 1 whose only factors are 1 and itself. **número primo** número entero mayor que 1 cuyos únicos factores son 1 y sí mismo.	2, 3, 5, 7, 11, 13	
prism a three-dimensional figure with two parallel bases that are the same size and shape. The other faces are parallelograms. A prism is named by the shape of the base. **prisma** figura tridimensional que tiene dos bases paralelas que tienen el mismo tamaño y la misma forma. Las otras caras son paralelogramos. La base determina el nombre del prisma.		
probability a number between 0 and 1 that expresses the likelihood of an event occurring. **probabilidad** número entre 0 y 1 que expresa la posibilidad de que ocurra un evento.	unlikely likely 0 $\frac{1}{2}$ 1 impossible equally likely as not certain	

product the result of multiplication.

$3 \cdot 5 = 15$

producto resultado de la multiplicación.

proportional relationship the relationship between two quantities where one quantity is a constant multiple of the other quantity. If the quantities x and y are in a proportional relationship, you can represent that relationship with the equation $y = kx$, where the value of k is constant (unchanging).

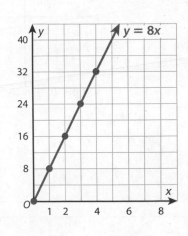

relación proporcional relación que existe entre dos cantidades en la que una cantidad es un múltiplo constante de la otra. Si las cantidades x y y están en una relación proporcional, esa relación se puede representar con la ecuación $y = kx$, en la que el valor de k es constante (no cambia).

Qq

quadrants the four regions of the coordinate plane that are formed when the *x*-axis and *y*-axis intersect at the origin.

cuadrantes las cuatro regiones del plano de coordenadas que se forman cuando los ejes *x* y *y* se intersecan en el origen.

Quadrant II | Quadrant I | Quadrant III | Quadrant IV

quadrilateral a polygon with exactly 4 sides and 4 angles.

cuadrilátero polígono que tiene exactamente 4 lados y 4 ángulos.

quotient the result of division.

cociente resultado de la división.

$$22.5 \div 3 = 7.5$$

Rr

radius (of a circle) a line segment from the center of a circle to any point on the circle. Also, the distance from the center to any point on a circle.

radio (de un círculo) segmento de recta desde el centro de un círculo hasta cualquier punto en el círculo. Además, la distancia desde el centro hasta cualquier punto en un círculo.

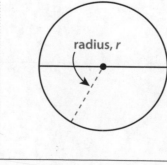

radius, *r*

English/**Español**	**Example**/Ejemplo	**Notes**/Notas
random sample a sample in which every element in the population has an equal chance of being selected.	The names of all of the students in the school are placed in a hat. Without looking, 30 names are selected. The 30 students are a random sample of the population.	
muestra aleatoria muestra en la que todos los elementos de la población tienen la misma probabilidad de ser elegidos.		
range the difference between the greatest value (maximum) and the least value (minimum) in a data set.	Data set: 9, 10, 8, 9, 7 Range: $10 - 7 = 3$	
rango diferencia entre el mayor valor (máximo) y el menor valor (mínimo) en un conjunto de datos.		
rate a ratio tells the number of units of one quantity for 1 unit of another quantity. Rates are often expressed using the word *per*.	5 miles per hour 2 cups for every 1 serving	
tasa razón que indica el número de unidades de una cantidad para 1 unidad de otra cantidad. Las razones suelen expresarse usando la palabra *por*.		
ratio a way to compare two quantities when there are *a* units of one quantity for every *b* units of the other quantity. You can write the ratio in symbols as *a* : *b* and in words as *a to b*.	 4 circles : 2 triangles	
razón manera de comparar dos cantidades cuando hay *a* unidades de una cantidad por cada *b* unidades de la otra cantidad. Se puede escribir la razón en símbolos como *a* : *b* y en palabras como *a a b*.		
rational number a number that can be expressed as the fraction $\frac{a}{b}$ where *a* and *b* are integers and $b \neq 0$. Rational numbers include integers, fractions, repeating decimals, and terminating decimals.	$\frac{3}{4}, -\frac{1}{8}, -3, 0, 1.2$	
número racional número que se puede expresar como la fracción $\frac{a}{b}$ en la que *a* y *b* son enteros y $b \neq 0$. Los números racionales incluyen los enteros, las fracciones, los decimales periódicos y los decimales finitos.		

ray a part of a line that has one end point and goes on forever in one direction.

semirrecta parte de una recta que tiene un extremo y continúa infinitamente en una dirección.

A   B

reciprocal for any nonzero number a, the reciprocal is $\frac{1}{a}$. The reciprocal of any fraction $\frac{a}{b}$ is $\frac{b}{a}$. Zero does not have a reciprocal. The reciprocal of a number is also called the *multiplicative inverse* of that number.

recíproco para cualquier número a distinto de cero, el recíproco es $\frac{1}{a}$. El recíproco de cualquier fracción $\frac{a}{b}$ es $\frac{b}{a}$. El cero no tiene recíproco. El recíproco de un número también se llama *inverso multiplicativo* de ese número.

The reciprocal of $\frac{5}{4}$ is $\frac{5}{4}$.

The reciprocal of $\frac{1}{6}$ is 6.

The reciprocal of -8 is $-\frac{1}{8}$.

rectangle a quadrilateral with 4 right angles. Opposite sides of a rectangle are the same length.

rectángulo cuadrilátero que tiene 4 ángulos rectos. Los lados opuestos de un rectángulo tienen la misma longitud.

rectangular prism a prism where the bases are rectangles.

prisma rectangular prisma en el que las bases son rectángulos.

reflection a transformation that flips (reflects) a figure across a line to form a mirror image.

reflexión transformación que gira (refleja) una figura del otro lado de una línea para formar una imagen reflejada.

A   B

English/**Español**	**Example**/Ejemplo	**Notes**/Notas
remainder the amount left over when one number does not divide another number a whole number of times.	$7 \div 2 = 3 \text{ R } 1$	
residuo cantidad que queda cuando un número no divide a otro un número entero de veces.	remainder	
repeating decimals decimals that repeat the same digit or sequence of digits forever. A repeating decimal can be written with a bar over the repeating digits.		
decimal periódico decimales que repiten el mismo dígito o secuencia de dígitos infinitamente. Un decimal periódico se puede escribir con una barra sobre los dígitos que se repiten.	$0.\overline{3}$ $2.\overline{51}$	
rhombus a quadrilateral with all sides the same length.		
rombo cuadrilátero que tiene todos los lados de la misma longitud.		
right angle an angle that measures 90°.		
ángulo recto ángulo que mide 90°.		
right prism a prism where each base is perpendicular to the other faces. In a right prism, the faces that are not bases are rectangles.		
prisma recto prisma en el que cada base es perpendicular a las otras caras. En un prisma recto, las caras que no son bases son rectángulos.		

English/Español	Example/Ejemplo	Notes/Notas
right rectangular prism a right prism where the bases and other faces are all rectangles.		
prisma rectangular recto prisma recto en el que las bases y las otras caras son rectángulos.		
right triangle a triangle with one right angle.		
triángulo rectángulo triángulo que tiene un ángulo recto.		
right triangular prism a right prism where the bases are triangles and the other faces are rectangles.		
prisma triangular recto prisma recto en el que las bases son triángulos y las otras caras son rectángulos.		
round to approximate the value of a number by finding the nearest ten, hundred, or other place value.		
redondear aproximar el valor de un número hallando la decena, la centena u otro valor posicional más cercano.	48 rounded to the nearest ten is 50.	

Ss

English/Español	Example/Ejemplo	Notes/Notas
sample a part of a population.	Population: All students in the school	
muestra parte de una población.	Sample: Three students in each homeroom	
sample space the set of all possible unique outcomes for an experiment.	Experiment: Rolling a number cube	
espacio muestral conjunto de todos los resultados posibles de un experimento.	Sample space: 1, 2, 3, 4, 5, 6	
scale tells the relationship between a length in a drawing, map, or model to the actual length.	Scale from a map to actual distances in a town:	
escala indica la relación que hay entre una longitud en un dibujo, un mapa o un modelo y la longitud real.	1 in. to 20 mi	
scale (on a graph) the value represented by the distance between one tick mark and the next on a number line.		
escala (en una gráfica) valor representado por la distancia que hay entre una marca y la siguiente en una recta numérica.	−10 −5 0 5 10 15 20 scale = 5	
scale drawing a drawing in which the measurements correspond to the measurements of the actual object by the same scale.	3 in. A 2 in. 6 in. B 4 in.	
dibujo a escala dibujo en el que las medidas se corresponden con las medidas del objeto real según la misma escala.	△A : △B is 1 : 2.	
scale factor the factor you multiply all the side lengths in a figure by to make a scale copy.	Scale from a map to the actual distance: 1 in. to 20 mi	
factor de escala factor por el que se multiplican todas las longitudes laterales en una figura para hacer una copia a escala.	Scale factor from distances on the map to the actual distances: 20	

scalene triangle a triangle that has no sides the same length.

triángulo escaleno triángulo que no tiene lados de la misma longitud.

side a line segment that forms part of a two-dimensional shape.

lado segmento de recta que forma parte de una figura bidimensional

side

simple interest a percent of an amount that is borrowed or invested.

interés simple porcentaje de una cantidad que se toma prestada o se invierte.

$I = Prt$

I = interest

P = principal (amount borrowed or invested)

r = interest rate

t = time

skewed left when most of the data points of a distribution are clustered near the greater values.

asimétrica a la izquierda cuando la mayoría de los datos de una distribución se agrupan cerca de los valores más altos.

Skewed Left

skewed right when most of the data points of a distribution are clustered near the lesser values.

asimétrica a la derecha cuando la mayoría de los datos de una distribución se agrupan cerca de los valores más bajos.

Skewed Right

solution of an equation a value that can be substituted for a variable to make an equation true.

solución de una ecuación valor que puede sustituir a una variable para hacer que una ecuación sea verdadera.

The solution to $19 = 4x - 1$ is $x = 5$.

English/Español	Example/Ejemplo	Notes/Notas
solution of an inequality a value that can be substituted for a variable to make an inequality true. **solución de una desigualdad** valor que puede sustituir a una variable para hacer que una desigualdad sea verdadera.	All values of x less than 5 ($x < 5$) are solutions to the inequality $5x < 25$.	
square a quadrilateral with 4 right angles and 4 sides of equal length. **cuadrado** cuadrilátero que tiene 4 ángulos rectos y 4 lados de la misma longitud.		
statistical question a question that can be answered by collecting data that are expected to vary. **pregunta estadística** pregunta que se puede responder reuniendo datos que se espera que varíen.	What is the typical amount of rain in April?	
straight angle an angle that measures 180°. The sides of a straight angle form a straight line. **ángulo llano** ángulo que mide 180°. Los lados de un ángulo llano forman una línea recta.	A B C $\angle ABC$ is a straight angle.	
sum the result of addition. **total** resultado de la suma.	$24 + 35 = 59$	
supplementary angles two angles whose measures sum to 180°. **ángulos suplementarios** dos ángulos cuyas medidas suman 180°.	$\angle WXZ$ and $\angle ZXY$ are supplementary angles.	

surface area the sum of the areas of all the faces of a three-dimensional figure.

área total suma de las áreas de todas las caras de una figura tridimensional.

5 units

4 units

5 units

Surface Area: $2(4)(5) + 2(4)(5) + 2(5)(5) = 130$ unit^2

---

symmetric when a distribution has the same shape on both sides of a middle point.

simétrico cuando una distribución tiene la misma forma en ambos lados de un punto que está en el medio.

Symmetric

Tt

tax a percent of income or of the cost of goods or services paid to the government.

impuesto porcentaje del ingreso o del costo de bienes o servicios que se paga al gobierno.

A 7% sales tax on a purchase of $40 is $2.80

---

term a number, a variable, or a product of numbers, variables, and/or expressions. A term may include an exponent.

término número, variable o el producto de números, variables y/o expresiones. Un término puede tener un exponente.

$4x + 9 + y^2$

term

English/Español	Example/Ejemplo	Notes/Notas
terminating decimals decimals that end, or end in repeated zeros.	0.25 5.6 −7.125	
decimal finito decimal en el que termina un número, o que termina en ceros repetidos.		
theoretical probability the probability of an event occurring based on what is expected to happen.	There are two equally likely outcomes to flipping a coin: heads up or tails up. The theoretical probability of the outcome heads up is $\frac{1}{2}$, or 50%.	
probabilidad teórica probabilidad de que ocurra un evento según lo que se espera que suceda.		
three-dimensional solid, or having length, width, and height. For example, a cube is three-dimensional.	height, width, length	
tridimensional sólido, o que tiene longitud, ancho y altura. Por ejemplo, un cubo es tridimensional.		
trapezoid (exclusive) a quadrilateral with exactly one pair of parallel sides.		
trapecio (exclusivo) cuadrilátero que tiene exactamente un par de lados paralelos.		
trapezoid (inclusive) a quadrilateral with at least one pair of parallel sides.		
trapecio (inclusivo) cuadrilátero que tiene al menos un par de lados paralelos.		
tree diagram a visual that shows all possible outcomes of an experiment.	There are 8 possible outcomes from flipping a coin 3 times.	
diagrama de árbol representación visual que muestra todos los resultados posibles de un experimento.		

English/Español	Example/Ejemplo	Notes/Notas
trial a single performance of an experiment.	Rolling a number cube once	
ensayo ejecución única de un experimento.		
triangle a polygon with exactly 3 sides and 3 angles.		
triángulo polígono que tiene exactamente 3 lados y 3 ángulos.		
triangular prism a prism where the bases are triangles.		
prisma triangular prisma en el que las bases son triángulos.		
two-dimensional flat, or having measurement in two directions, like length and width. For example, a rectangle is two-dimensional.	width length	
bidimensional plano, o que tiene medidas en dos direcciones, como longitud y ancho. Por ejemplo, un rectángulo es bidimensional.		

English/Español	Example/Ejemplo	Notes/Notas

Uu

unit fraction a fraction with a numerator of 1. Other fractions are built from unit fractions.

fracción unitaria fracción que tiene un numerador de 1. Otras fracciones se construyen a partir de fracciones unitarias.

$$\frac{1}{5}$$

unit rate the numerical part of a rate. For the ratio $a : b$, the unit rate is the quotient $\frac{a}{b}$.

tasa por unidad parte numérica de una tasa. Para la razón $a : b$, la tasa por unidad es el cociente $\frac{a}{b}$.

Rate: 3 miles per hour

Unit rate: 3

unknown the value you need to find to solve a problem.

incógnita valor que hay que hallar para resolver un problema.

$$20.5 + x = 30$$

upper quartile the middle number between the median and the maximum in an ordered set of numbers. The upper quartile is also called the 3rd quartile or Q3.

cuartil superior número del medio entre la mediana y el máximo en un conjunto ordenado de números. El cuartil superior también se llama tercer cuartil, o Q3.

upper quartile

20 30 40 50 60 70 80 90

Vv

variability how spread out or close together values in a data set are.

variabilidad la dispersión o cercanía de los valores en un conjunto de datos.

Gavin's Handstand Times

Time (s)

There is high variability in Gavin's handstand times.

---

variable a letter that represents an unknown number. In some cases, a variable may represent more than one number.

variable letra que representa un número desconocido. En algunos casos, una variable puede representar más de un número.

$$3x + 9 = 90$$

---

vertex the point where two rays, lines, or line segments meet to form an angle.

vértice punto en el que dos semirrectas, rectas o segmentos de recta se encuentran y forman un ángulo.

vertex

---

vertical angles opposite angles formed when two lines intersect. Vertical angles how the same measure.

ángulos opuestos por el vértice ángulos opuestos que se forman cuando se intersecan dos rectas. Los ángulos opuestos por el vértice tienen la misma medida.

$\angle$5 and $\angle$7

$\angle$2 and $\angle$4

---

volume the amount of space inside a solid figure. Volume is measured in cubic units such as cubic inches.

volumen cantidad de espacio dentro de una figura sólida. El volumen se mide en unidades cúbicas como las pulgadas cúbicas.

volume: 24 unit^3

English/Español	Example/Ejemplo	Notes/Notas

Ww

whole numbers the numbers 0, 1, 2, 3, 4, . . . Whole numbers are nonnegative and have no fractional part.

0, 8, 187

números enteros los números 0, 1, 2, 3, 4, . . . Los números enteros no son negativos y no tienen partes fraccionarias.

Xx

x-axis the horizontal number line in the coordinate plane.

eje x recta numérica horizontal en el plano de coordenadas.

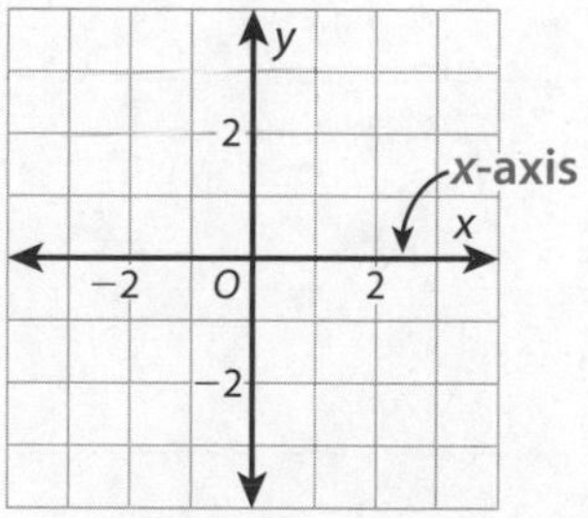

x-coordinate the first number in an ordered pair. It tells the point's horizontal distance from the y-axis.

(x, y)

x-coordinate

coordenada x primer número en un par ordenado. Indica la distancia horizontal del punto al eje y.

Yy

y-axis the vertical number line in the coordinate plane.

eje y recta numérica vertical en el plano de coordenadas.

---

y-coordinate the second number in an ordered pair. It tells the point's vertical distance from the *x*-axis.

coordenada y el segundo número en un par ordenado. Indica la distancia vertical del punto al eje *x*.

(x, y)

y-coordinate

Zz

zero pair two numbers whose sum is zero. Opposite numbers form a zero pair.

par cero dos números cuya suma es cero. Los números opuestos forman un par cero.

−3 and 3 form a zero pair.

1.2 and −1.2 form a zero pair.

Credits

Acknowledgment

Common Core State Standards © 2010. National Governors Association Center for Best Practices and Council of Chief State School Officers. All rights reserved.

Photography Credits

Cover: Bo1982/Shutterstock, Lorri Kajenna/Shutterstock, Exotic vector/Shutterstock, Jorge Salcedo/Shutterstock
Back Cover: 493 Eivaisla/Shutterstock, Jiri Hera/Shutterstock, Trygve Funjelsen/Shutterstock; 589 loskutnikov/Shutterstock, Beata Becla/Shutterstock; 717 Yuriy Redkin/Shutterstock
Text: ii, 58, 125, 359 New Africa/Shutterstock; ii, 95 Enrique Ramos/Shutterstock, Alena Brozova/Shutterstock; iii, 186 pictoplay/Shutterstock, 3DMI/Shutterstock; iv, 252 Danita Delmont/Shutterstock, Le Do/Shutterstock; v, 312 YamabikaY/Shutterstock; v, 335 visivastudio/Shutterstock, Gino Santa Maria/Shutterstock; v, 403 Chutima Chaochaiya/Shutterstock; vi, 420 jaroslava/Shutterstock; vi, 452 RemarkEliza/Shutterstock; vii, 593 nour eddine salhi/Shutterstock; viii, 695 design56/Shutterstock; viii, 705 iStock.com/Dmytro Aksonov; 1, 97 DimiSotirov/Shutterstock; 3 Romolo Tavani/Shutterstock; 4 Danita Delmont/Alamy Stock Photo; 8 The Metropolitan Museum of Art, New York, Rogers Fund, 1907, stevemart/Shutterstock; 12 alslutsky/Shutterstock; 14 Double-Matt/Shutterstock, Kamira/Shutterstock; 16 Witold Skrypczak/Alamy Stock Photo; 20 sergeykot/Shutterstock; 22 paul prescott/Shutterstock; 30 NaughtyNut/Shutterstock; 31 Oleksandra Naumenko/Shutterstock; 32 Courtesy of the Library of Congress, LC-USF33-030783-M2, dimitris_k/Shutterstock; 36 DWI YULIANTO/Shutterstock; 37 Fourleaflover/Shutterstock; 38 Dzmitrock/Shutterstock; 40 Fredy Thuerig/Shutterstock; 42 terekhov igor/Shutterstock; 45 Serg Salivon/Shutterstock, Kriengsuk Prasroetsung/Shutterstock; 47 Sandra Cunningham/Shutterstock, Yarygin/Shutterstock; 48 Nata-Lia/Shutterstock; 49 Melissa Sue/Shutterstock; 50 Susan Schmitz/Shutterstock; 55 onairda/Shutterstock; 59 Antonio V. Oquias/Shutterstock; 61 My Good Images/Shutterstock; 64 Production Perig/Shutterstock, Petr Nad/Shutterstock; 65 Binh Thanh Bui/Shutterstock; 66 Gabriela ZZ/Shutterstock.com; 71 Rawpixel.com/Shutterstock; 81 Baloncici/Shutterstock; 83 Tiger Images/Shutterstock, Vasileios Karafillidis/Shutterstock, NIPAPORN PANYACHAROEN/Shutterstock, marekuliasz/Shutterstock; 86 Alchie/Shutterstock, Leigh Lather/Shutterstock, Steve Cukrov/Shutterstock; 87 iStock.com/skynesher; 88 Kamenetskiy Konstantin/Shutterstock; 99 rjmiguel/Shutterstock; 102 B Brown/Shutterstock; 106 Andrey Eremin/Shutterstock; 108 iStock.com/4x6, Ververidis Vasilis/Shutterstock; 112 elnavegante/Shutterstock; 114 Fat Jackey/Shutterstock.com; 118 NazaBasirun/Shutterstock, Joe MoJo/Shutterstock, MookSmile/Shutterstock, donatas1205/Shutterstock; 119, 122 bazzier/Shutterstock, Kittichai/Shutterstock; 119 Lisa F. Young/Shutterstock; 124 stuar/Shutterstock, Steve Cukrov/Shutterstock; 126 Pixel-Shot/Shutterstock; 127 pflueglerphoto/Shutterstock, Sasin Paraksa/Shutterstock; 133, 181 Stocktrek Images, Inc./Alamy Stock Photo; 135 Paulo Miguel Costa/Shutterstock; 137 delcarmat/Shutterstock; 142 Eugene Onischenko/Shutterstock; 144 curiosity/Shutterstock; 146 Mike Price/Shutterstock, kubais/Shutterstock; 147 Darren J. Bradley/Shutterstock, VIS Fine Art/Shutterstock; 149 Josef Hanus/Shutterstock; 152 glenda/Shutterstock, Marian Weyo/Shutterstock, Branko Jovanovic/Shutterstock; 153 photoschmidt/Shutterstock; 154 iStock.com/Willowpix; 156 Paulo Oliveira/Alamy Stock Photo; 158 Michelle Holihan/Shutterstock; 160 idreamphoto/Shutterstock; 162 Moonlightphoto/Shutterstock, M. Unal Ozmen/Shutterstock; 164 danilo ducak/Shutterstock, scubadesign/Shutterstock; 168 D Stevenson/Shutterstock; 169 BERNATSKAIA OKSANA/Shutterstock, GalapagosPhoto/Shutterstock; 171 Daboost/Shutterstock, Lec Neo/Shutterstock; 174 Somchai Som/Shutterstock; 175 Rynio Productions/Shutterstock, George Fairbairn/Shutterstock; 182 Sergey Novikov/Shutterstock; 187 nolie/Shutterstock; 188 Tomas Ragina/Shutterstock; 191 benchart/Shutterstock; 194 kopbs2/Shutterstock; 196 Valentyna Chukhlyebova/Shutterstock, Checubus/Shutterstock; 197 Ty Hartlipp/Shutterstock; 198 iStock.com/MATJAZ SLANIC; 201 S.Bachstroem/Shutterstock; 203 Hal Brindley/Shutterstock, Steinar/Shutterstock; 207 Shaun Jeffers/Shutterstock; 208 Macrovector/Shutterstock, Vectorpocket/Shutterstock; 209 salajean/Shutterstock; 211 Anna Om/Shutterstock, reisegraf.ch/Shutterstock, Filip Fuxa/Shutterstock; 217, 275 Tamakhin Mykhailo/Shutterstock; 219 tsuneomp/Shutterstock; 231 Sky Cinema/Shutterstock; 233 FrameAngel/Shutterstock; 236 Steve Bower/Shutterstock, Volodymyr Goinyk/Shutterstock; 238 Johnny Adolphson/Shutterstock; 240 GoProPk/Shutterstock; 243 IrinaK/Shutterstock; 244 Michael J. Munster/Shutterstock.com; 246 Polushkina Svetlana/Shutterstock; 248 Subphoto/Shutterstock; 253 grynold/Shutterstock, tishomir/Shutterstock; 254 Matee Nuserm/Shutterstock, Vadarshop/Shutterstock; 260 ONiONA_studio/Shutterstock; 262 Izf/Shutterstock, Kenneth Sponsler/Shutterstock; 265 bonchan/Shutterstock, almaje/Shutterstock, gowithstock/Shutterstock, greisei/Shutterstock, givaga/Shutterstock;

Data Sets